The World's Tallest Midget

Other Books by Frank Deford

FICTION

The Spy in the Deuce Court
Everybody's All-American
The Owner
Cut 'n' Run

NONFICTION

Alex, the Life of a Child
Big Bill Tilden: The Triumphs and the Tragedy
There She Is
Five Strides on the Banked Track

The World's Tallest Midget

The Best of FRANK DEFORD

A *Sports Illustrated* Book

LITTLE, BROWN AND COMPANY
BOSTON   TORONTO

FIRST EDITION

Library of Congress Cataloging-in-Publication Data

Deford, Frank.
    The world's tallest midget.

    "A Sports illustrated book."
    1. Sports. I. Title.
GV707.D44 1987   796   86-27530
ISBN 0-316-17944-2

Excerpt from "Who's on First?" reprinted by permission of
Abbott and Costello Enterprises, Inc. All rights reserved.

Sports Illustrated books
are published by
Little, Brown and Company
in association with
Sports Illustrated magazine

RRD-VA

*Published simultaneously in Canada
by Little, Brown & Company (Canada) Limited*

PRINTED IN THE UNITED STATES OF AMERICA

For (of all people)
four editors:
      Jerry Tax
      Pat Ryan
      Gil Rogin
      Mark Mulvoy

Contents

The World's
Tallest Midget

Introduction

As nearly as I can tell, sportswriting has always been disparaged. It is, surely, the only form of literature wherein the worst of the genre is accepted as representative of the whole. Any well-written article or book about sports is invariably praised by serious, patronizing critics as "not really about sports" or "different from sportswriting" — stuff like that. Sportswriting is assumed to be second-rate, and, therefore, if any sportswriting is not second-rate, then, ergo, it must not be sportswriting.

Nonetheless, while the bias against sportswriting remains large, and any good sportswriter is usually dismissed as the world's tallest midget, I'll be the first to admit that there surely are an awful lot of perfectly dreadful sportswriters around and about. The profession yet attracts an inordinate number of men who are primarily sports fans, rather than journalists, men who want to do *something* to get them into the world of sports. We still get a lot of jock sniffers as sportswriters. But it is also even more apparent to me that nowadays, at the other extreme, a much better assortment of writers enter the field, unashamed, than ever did before. Some of these fellows are, too, women, which of course was all but unheard-of until very recently. To my mind, without a doubt, sportswriting is better now than ever it's been — so good, in fact, that (rest assured) a great deal of it isn't really sportswriting.

The simple advantages of writing about sports are manifest. The structure is heaven-sent. Every day, every game, every substitution, there is instant, well-formed drama: a beginning, plot development, and climax. The characters are, for the most part, colorful and fairly open and ingenuous. Some of the athletes are absolute dummies, and almost all of them are immature, but a fair share of the kids are extroverted, and an inordinate number of the coaches and train- ers and hangers-on and what we in the business always refer to as the *front*-office personnel are lively characters inclined to self- revelation. At least until quite recently, too, sports figures have been most accessible. Baseball players may still actually be interviewed in the odd moments while they are in the very midst of practice, and almost all male athletes casually discuss the state of the art while standing stark naked before groups of reporters. By contrast, show business stars, the folks most analogous to athletes, are hid- den behind hordes of PR minions and bodyguards, and are allowed to be observed only cosmetically, under controlled circumstances, like animals in a zoo. Sports people are certainly more accurately described and understood than anyone else in the public eye. If writing is what you want to do, the material is there in sports.

Sports is also, by and large, a very pleasant environment in which to work — *the toy shop,* Jimmy Cannon called the newspaper sports department — and no matter how much everyone bemoans the loss of the good old days (when the best players were merely drunks, rather than drug addicts), everyday sports is still a great deal more innocent and optimistic than most of the grim world that surrounds it. In other words, for a lot of reasons, we ought to *expect* sportswriting to be very good, as often, in fact, it is. It is just that the elitist bias against sportswriting continues, sustaining a gross negative misrepresentation.

There is also the assumption (which, I'll admit, still dogs me some) that sportswriting should be like sports playing, something you should do when you're young, before you move on to the se- rious things in life. I'm sure men like Cannon and Red Smith and Grantland Rice were being badgered on their deathbeds about what they were going to do when they grew up. And there is, too, a certain amount of evidence that supports this attitude, because, especially in years past, all sorts of talented sportswriters did go into other areas — political columnists like Ralph McGill and James Reston, a novelist like Paul Gallico, and humorists like Ring Lardner and my contemporary Roy Blount, Jr.

Indeed, I would suggest that any young journalist would be wise to break in at sports. Because the subject matter is so obvious, the construction so neat, it is the perfect place to develop as a writer, even if you haven't the slightest notion of staying long in the neighborhood.

But the inverse of that also obtains: No young writer should ever devote himself entirely to sportswriting when he is in high school or college or journalism school. Knowing more earned run averages than the next fellow has nothing whatsoever to do with sportswriting. As a general rule, in fact, the worst sportswriters are the experts, and more sportswriters have been done in by becoming pseudo-coaches than were ever ruined by booze, women, or jet lag. In sportswriting, a lot of knowledge is a dangerous thing.

Virtually without exception, I can say that the best sportswriters I've met were the men with the widest breadth of interest, men familiar with the whole world and able to apply its lessons and ironies to their sportswriting. This very much contradicts the accepted public image, though, for I recognize that most people think of us as idiots savants. At parties, people invariably confine their remarks to me to sports, expecting me to know the relative merits of all linebackers and power forwards in captivity, and if other topics do manage to come up despite themselves, I am usually talked down to, as you would to a child or someone unfamiliar with the language. People are perfectly astonished should I actually indicate that I know who the Chief Justice of the Supreme Court is or what country Brussels is in. When I show off this broad range of my knowledge, people stare wide-eyed at me, and I feel rather like those girls in the old B-movie comedies who have had their spectacles removed and are suddenly revealed as secret sexpots. Curiously, though, even when I am shown to be a Renaissance man, and while everyone assumes that I know everything about sports, no one ever imagines that I also might have some opinions about the second part of my title, about writing.

To be sure, as the foregoing suggests, sportswriters can be defensive. I can't imagine that any of us worth a dime doesn't go through a phase in which we question whether it is a fulfilled life in the toy shop. When it began to occur to me, seven or eight years into the profession, that I was beginning to look like a lifer, I did spend agonizing hours at the bar, staring into another disappearing bourbon or talking over the quandary with other sportswriters of like conflict. I could visualize grandchildren coming up to me in my dotage and saying, "Big Daddy, what did you do during Vietnam?"

And I would reply that I had been at the NBA playoffs. Or, "Poppy, where were you during the Civil Rights movement?" And I would explain that I missed that because of the Stanley Cup. But, finally, I resolved the issue with myself: that I am a writer, and that incidentally I write mostly about sports, and what is important is to write well, the topic be damned.

Yet I also know that that answer to myself is a bit too glib, even, perhaps, smug. For I'm pretty sure that if I had come to the business in 1932 or 1942 (and possibly even 1952) instead of 1962, I probably wouldn't have stayed the course as a sportswriter. But fortuitously, when I did settle in, several events were in motion that made sportswriting more appealing to me, and encourage still, I believe, more talented people to choose and to remain in the field.

Most important, virtually up to the moment when I stepped into sportswriting, both the focus for the reader and the ultimate for the writer was the newspaper column — a set piece of a few hundred words. Well, as I would imagine you can tell by reading the articles chosen for this collection, a column just wouldn't have been the best fit for me. I always marveled at Red Smith that, as fine as his work was, he could go on turning out the same-length piece, day in and day out, for bloody decades. It must be a real art, for him or for all the best columnists — Dutch miniaturists. Most of the best sports columnists today do, at least occasionally, venture into other territory, writing books or, anyway, articles. But Smith was the purest columnist. I was always very envious of him, imagining that he must have been the happiest of writers, the happiest of men.

I never knew anything about that, though, because I never met Red. This astonishes people who assume everybody in sportswriting must pal around with everybody else, but, in fact, there are a lot of very good writers I've never met. It's just the case, as it was with Red Smith, that nobody ever introduced us, and I was too shy to approach him.

Of course, people are always surprised when they hear that a journalist of any stripe is bashful, but, in reality, that's why most of us become journalists — because we're shy, but we're also curious, and if you have a press card, then you have a professional excuse to ask questions of strangers, which you don't have the nerve to do in life at large. It's like some guys become actors, because if you go out for a play, you meet girls. I tried that briefly, too.

Anyway, *Sports Illustrated,* with its longer articles and the time granted to create them, was not only ideal for me personally, but it also had a major effect upon American sportswriting. While the magazine article certainly didn't usurp the column as the model in the field, it did provide an alternative to it. After a while, some of the evening newspapers began to assay features in the *Sports Illustrated* fashion, and now even many of the morning papers run long sports articles — what are known as "takeouts" in newspaper terminology. Today, I think, as much good sportswriting can be found in takeouts as in columns.

The one single individual who should receive credit for this improvement of the breed is also the man who had the most influence upon me. His name was Andre Laguerre. *Sports Illustrated* was begun in 1954, but it was losing millions of dollars and still struggling to survive in 1960, when Laguerre took over as the managing editor, the boss. When he was finally replaced fourteen years later, *Sports Illustrated* was an utter success, and the pervasive influence of its quality writing had long since begun to be evident across the face of American sports journalism.

Laguerre was of French citizenship, but his mother was English, and he had spent several years of his youth in San Francisco, where his father was with the French consulate. Andre was pathologically shy, but he became de Gaulle's press secretary during the war because, although he was only a corporal at the time, Laguerre boldly wrote the general a note, telling him his press relations were awful.

Henry Luce hired Laguerre after the war, but even as Andre rose in power, he became more enigmatic a figure. One time, the plane Andre was flying back to France from London crashed just short of the Paris airport. "What did you do then, sir?" I asked breathlessly.

"I caught a cab, Frankie," he said, and then he took another drag on his cigar and a pull on his Scotch.

As intimidating as Andre was to most people, he would welcome company at the bars where he held court. Despite my salad years, I was permitted this social access because I came from Baltimore and was conversant about horses and gambling, Andre's favorite pursuits. Also, I could hold my liquor. Those were the days when sportswriters (and editors) were two-fisted drinkers. I came in right on the cusp. Today's sportswriters allow themselves an occasional white wine, and most of them jog in their spare time. They jog on road trips. Almost never any longer will you find a sportswriter who smokes a big, black cigar. It's not the same at all.

Laguerre was never without an expensive cigar, and he drank

prodigiously, usually at Chinese restaurants, because the custom there then was to give you every fourth drink free — I mean, if you drank the first three yourself. Andre had eight or twelve Scotches for lunch and another couple rounds of four after work. He told me once that the biggest decision a man had to make in his life was whether he was going to spend his spare time (I think that's what's known as *quality time* now) standing at the bar with his buddies, drinking and gambling and talking sports, or whether he was going to chase women.

That's how I know the past really was a simpler time.

Andre, who could barely manage to look a woman in the face, finally married in his forties, and he had two daughters, so, at least for a time, I became a surrogate son for him. He wanted me to become an editor, but I didn't have the stomach for it, and, besides, I usually felt like a traitor manhandling somebody else's words.

Still, even if Andre was an editor, he made me care for writing all the more. He wouldn't say it, but I know he liked it when he heard that, right out of the box, wet behind the ears, I would raise hell with his subordinate editors the minute they touched a word of my copy. Andre himself couldn't write a lick. As a writer, the best he'd ever done was to make race selections in Paris under the name of Eddie Snow. But he assembled a terrific staff of writers at *Sports Illustrated* in the sixties, he pampered us and humored us, and when his magazine started showing up in mailboxes all around the country, for the first time a lot of people understood that sports-writing could be a craft of quality and substance.

Very few people could imagine that before Laguerre put *Sports Illustrated* together. For example, I grew up in Baltimore, which was hardly a literary or journalistic backwater. The *Baltimore Sunpapers*, morning and afternoon, the journals of Mencken himself, were routinely celebrated as among the best dailies in the land, and the rival *News-Post* was a lively Hearst tiger. But all the sports columnists were uniformly abysmal. The *Morning Sun* editor turned out a column of little items, with standard headlines like "Do You Know That?" Trivia ahead of its time. Beyond that, two things consumed him: the Notre Dame football team and anguished complaints that baseball managers didn't order the bunt enough anymore. The *Evening Sun* columnist also held the job of commissioner of officials for the local high school conference, and so (as I discovered later when I worked there as a copy boy), he would come in early in the morning, dash off a vacuous rewrite of yester-day's news, and then spend the rest of the day on the phone, dis-patching this referee to the JV basketball game at Paterson Park, that umpire to the frosh-soph baseball game at Calvert Hall. At the *News-Post,* the sports columnist was also an ardent antivivisection-ist, and so his daily sports columns were filled with pictures of cuddly puppy dogs and cute kitty cats that were about to be gassed down at the pound if we didn't stir ourselves and stop this outrage. These three men were, if you will, my role models. And Baltimore was probably typical. Boston today boasts the best sports section in the country in the *Globe,* but even into the sixties, when I was regularly there covering the Celtics, Boston sportswriting was one step up from illiteracy, one decibel down from shouting.

I didn't know it when I was growing up, either, but in many cit-ies, sportswriters were on the take from whatever promoter had an arena to fill. Sportswriters were generally paid subsistence wages, and it was more or less expected that they would have to supple-ment their income with money under the table. Too often, sports-writers with integrity and/or bill collectors at the door would fi-nally just give up and go into public relations.

Neil Simon got Oscar Madison right.

Luckily for me as an impressionable youth, my father developed a reverence for President Eisenhower. After being a Democrat all his life, Daddy took to Ike, so much so that he began subscribing to the *New York Herald Tribune,* which was (as the *Sporting News* was "the bible of baseball" and *Variety* "the bible of show busi-ness") the bible of Eisenhower Republicanism. Coincidentally, it also boasted the best sports section that ever existed, with Mr. Smith doing the star turn most days.

Curiously, perhaps, I don't recall that this made me want to be-come a *sports* journalist, but it did encourage me to think more about becoming a journalist, for what impressed me about the *Trib*'s fine sportswriters was that they were writing on a news-paper. It was the quality, rather than the subject matter, that was a revelation to me in Baltimore.

So it was that when I was a sophomore at Princeton and ad-mitted to a big-deal creative writing course, and the professor asked us to name three writers who were our favorites or who had most influenced us or something like that, I wrote down Red Smith's name along with William Shakespeare and J. D. Salinger. It was an honest answer, but it was not the answer the professor was looking for.

He was Kingsley Amis, then celebrated as one of the Angry Young Men of Britain. He was at Princeton for this one year as writer-in-residence. When Amis found out who this Red Smith was who was being linked with Shakespeare (I think everybody wrote down J. D. Salinger, so that didn't count), he was titillated, and when he wrote a wry story for a British paper about his quaint experiences in New Jersey, prominent amongst the anecdotes was this one knee-slapper about how an especially rustic, provincial student had actually listed a sports hack as his favorite writer.

In any event, despite my appreciation for Smith and the fact that I became a sportswriter, Red's style never had any effect on me. It is common for writers to be asked whom they patterned themselves after, but I've never felt that anyone was a strong model for me, that I was in anybody's school. I don't even think I have a distinct style, but if, in fact, I do, I would still believe that constructing and pacing a story are my strongest assets. Those qualities are usually lacking with most American sportswriters, too. Our stories tend to be more comprehensive than well formed, and we put too much emphasis upon compiling facts, rather than on how we choose to dole the facts out.

It would no doubt please Kingsley Amis to learn that by far the single most important influence upon me was the British sports press — no one journalist in particular, but the whole genre. When I first traveled abroad, in my twenties, and came in touch with London newspapers, I was happily astonished at the style, and found it much more compatible with my own effort and ideas. For a long time I subscribed to the *London Sunday Times.*

Basically, the American game story is beholden to formula, starting with the canon that the score of the contest must be in the first sentence, even though the score has already been printed ten times larger in a headline right above the first sentence. The usual American sports piece is turned out in a very linear fashion, in the unadorned manner (at its worst) of a manual of some sort. I find entirely too much emphasis on the obvious play-by-play, with a surfeit of technical jargon and a glut of quotations from the principals. For some reason, American writers cannot just note that a hitter blasted a 450-foot home run and describe the scene in their own words. Instead, they have to rush down to the locker room and get the slugger to certify the fact by saying something superfluous like "I really got hold of that one."

The technology of sports, the bane of sportswriting, is pretty much on account of football, especially professional football. To my mind, without a doubt, the worst sportswriting in the United States is devoted to pro football. I suspect that the seminal problem is that there are simply too many people involved in a football game. It's like the House of Representatives. Nobody writes very well about that either. It's so difficult to personalize pro football, what with offensive teams, defensive teams, suicide squads, taxi squads, and even great numbers of coaches. As a consequence, writers are obliged to write about strategy and statistics, to the exclusion of the human element. Generally speaking, the smaller the number of people involved in a competition, the better it lends itself to writing. I imagine that is why so many otherwise compassionate and intelligent men of letters have been attracted to boxing. Tennis is a bloodless boxing, I think, which is why I have always been particularly fond of that sport. It's often boring to watch — whereas, by contrast, football is a very exciting spectator entertainment — but tennis is terrific to write about and football is a struggle.

Having said that, though, it is also true that I have written two novels about football, and that this collection probably contains more about football than any other sport. But of the four football pieces, three are about coaches and one about the hero-as-symbol. Unlike football action, which is something for television, the question of what football means to our society is a bountiful subject for any writer. Just stay away from the games.

The British style, which has always enchanted me, approaches a sport, a game, a tournament, whatever, as less a competition and more a presentation (which, come to think of it, is the way the British approach much of their life and work). British writers tend to *review* games rather than describe them. The devotion to minutiae of American sports journalism is studiously avoided by the British press, which seeks more to critique a performance as a whole, citing only one or two key or instructive moments in the detail American writers lavish on the quotidian. Just as football has so adversely affected American sportswriting, I suspect that soccer has greatly benefited British sportswriting, for soccer is so tedious to watch, so much the same, with barely a minute or two of consequential action out of ninety, that the writer is given almost a clean tablet on which to express himself. I would much prefer to read a British journalist writing about a soccer game (or even a cricket match) than I would want to drag through most American accounts of a football game, no matter how thrilling the action may have been.

Straightforward game accounts can only become more redundant, too. How can I possibly improve on the description of a jump shot when readers saw the jump shot with their own eyes on TV, then saw it replayed in slow motion, then saw it from different angles, and then saw it again and again on the sports news? *USA Today* has responded to this dilemma in, I believe, the most sensible way. *USA Today* makes no pretense at writing, but simply lists the way people scored in agate type, like stock quotations:

> Lynn doubled to right. Murray singled him home. Ripken homered over the left-field wall.

> $7\frac{7}{8}$ $7\frac{5}{8}$ $7\frac{3}{4}$ $-\frac{1}{8}$

Same thing.

The situation grows even worse because by now almost all important games are televised, and sports editors, stuck in their offices, see the games on TV and want their writers at the game to write in a way that conforms to what they saw on television.

This is a counter-development, though, because a quarter century ago, as I was entering the profession, television was a great boon to sportswriters and was most responsible for my staying on in sports journalism. At first, you see, television seemed to free writers from doing too much standard play-by-play. The thinking was: Look, television does something much better than we can do, so we, as writers, must go beyond television, write more background, write more about issues and personalities. Television also served sportswriters well because it made more people aware of sports, and of sports personalities. Only recently, as younger editors, who grew up in the thrall of television, have assumed authority, has there been a regression, and there is a perceived danger now that sportswriting will not complement television, but be its handmaiden. For most sports pages and sports journals now, if a sport isn't on television, it doesn't exist — and there goes the potential for a lot of good stories.

I was encouraged to stay in sportswriting because, certainly at
that time, the universe was expanding. A few years after he gave up
his column, someone asked Paul Gallico why he'd left sportswriting. "February," Gallico sighed. There'd been great gaps in the
sports calendar then, but largely because television wouldn't tolerate it, the vacuum was filled. Moreover, first in *Sports Illustrated*
and then in the sports sections of the best papers, the definition of
what constituted sports subject matter was greatly liberalized.
F. Scott Fitzgerald once bemoaned Ring Lardner's fate as a sportswriter, saying that "no matter how deeply Ring might cut into it,
his cake always has the diameter no larger than Frank Chance's
diamond" (Chance being a premier baseball player of the time).
But in my tenure as a sportswriter, I have written at length about
the following subjects: death, race, religion, politics, nationality,
sex, sexism, homosexuality, business, art, growing up, growing old,
sickness, insanity, history. I have been on assignment in all states
save North Dakota, on all continents save Antarctica — more than
thirty countries (and more than fifty airlines). Whatever sports has
been to me, it has not been parochial — which is, of course, what
most people assume it is.

The stories that I — and Bill Phillips, my editor at Little,
Brown — have selected for this collection should reflect some of
this diversity, for, obviously, while I chose many of the stories that
I simply liked the best, we also sought balance and variety. I passed
over several stories that I was fond of but that just seemed to have
been overwhelmed by events. I also made a few changes or dele-
tions in the copy where references once timely now seem to con-
fuse rather than to clarify.

Westport, Connecticut
August 28, 1986

PLAYING THE GAME

The Boxer and the Blonde

1985

THE boxer and the blonde are together, downstairs in the club cellar. At some point, club cellars went out, and they became family rooms instead. This is, however, very definitely a club cellar. Why, the grandchildren of the boxer and the blonde could sleep soundly upstairs, clear through the big Christmas party they gave when everybody came and stayed late and loud down here. The boxer and the blonde are sitting next to each other, laughing about the old times, about when they fell hopelessly in love almost half a century ago in New Jersey, at the beach. *Down the shore* is the way everyone in Pennsylvania says it. This club cellar is in Pittsburgh.

The boxer is going on 67, except in *The Ring* record book, where he is going on 68. But he has all his marbles; and he has his looks (except for the fighter's mashed nose); and he has the blonde; and they have the same house, the one with the club cellar, that they bought in the summer of 1941. A great deal of this is about that bright ripe summer, the last one before the forlorn simplicity of a Depression was buried in the thick-braided rubble of blood and Spam. What a fight the boxer had that June! It might have been the best in the history of the ring. Certainly, it was the most dramatic, all-time, any way you look at it. The boxer lost, though. Probably he would have won, except for the blonde — whom he loved so much, and wanted so much to make proud of him. And later, it was the blonde's old man, the boxer's father-in-law (if you can believe this), who cost him a rematch for the heavyweight championship of the world. Those were some kind of times.

The boxer and the blonde laugh again, together, remembering how they fell in love. "Actually, you sort of forced me into it," she says.

"I did you a favor," he snaps back, smirking at his comeback. After a couple of belts, he has been known to confess that although he fought twenty-one times against world champions, he has never yet won a decision over the blonde — never yet, as they say in boxing, *outpointed* her. But you can sure see why he keeps on trying. He still has his looks? Hey, you should see her. The blonde is past 60 now, and she's still cute as a button. Not merely beautiful, you understand, but schoolgirl cute, just like she was when the boxer first flirted with her down the shore in Jersey. There is a picture of them on the wall. Pictures cover the walls of the club cellar. This particular picture was featured in a magazine, the boxer and the blonde running, hand in hand, out of the surf. Never in your life did you see two better-looking kids. She was Miss Ocean City, and Alfred Lunt called him "a Celtic god," and Hollywood had a part for him that Errol Flynn himself wound up with after the boxer said no thanks and went back to Pittsburgh.

The other pictures on the walls of the club cellar are mostly of fighters. Posed. Weighing in. Toe to toe. Bandaged. And ex-fighters. Mostly in Las Vegas, it seems, the poor bastards. And celebrities. Sinatra, Hope, Bishop Sheen. Politicians. Various Kennedys. Mayor Daley. President Reagan. Vice-President Bush. More fighters. Joe Louis, whom the boxer loved so much, is in a lot of the pictures, but the largest single photograph belongs to Harry Greb, the Pittsburgh Windmill, the middleweight champeen, the only man ever to beat Gene Tunney. When the boxer's mother died that summer of '41, one of the things that mattered most then was to get her the closest possible plot in Calvary Cemetery to where Harry Greb already lay in peace.

But then, down on the far wall, around the corner from Greb, behind the bar, there's another big photograph, and it's altogether different from the others, because this one is a horizontal. Boxing pictures are either square, like the ring itself, or vertical, the fighter standing tall, fists cocked high. If you see a horizontal, it's almost surely not a boxing photograph. More than likely it's from another sport; it's a team picture, all the players spread out in rows. And sure enough, the photograph on the far wall is of the 1917 New York Giants, winners of the National League pennant, and there in the middle of the back row, with a cocky grin hung on his face, is Greenfield Jimmy Smith. The story really starts with him. He was the one who introduced the boxer and the blonde down the shore.

The book on Greenfield Jimmy Smith as a ballplayer was good mouth, no hit (.219 lifetime). His major talent earned him another nickname up in the bigs, Serpent Tongue. Muggsy McGraw, the Giants' manager, kept Smith around pretty much as a bench jockey. But after the Giants lost to the White Sox in the '17 Series, four games to two, McGraw traded him. That broke Smith's heart. He loved McGraw. They were both tough cookies.

"Ah, rub it with a brick," Greenfield Jimmy would say whenever anybody complained of an injury. He was just a little guy, maybe 5'9", a banty rooster, but one time he went over to the Dodger dugout and yelled, "All right, you so-and-sos, I'll fight you one at a time or in groups of five." Not a single Dodger took up the offer.

Greenfield Jimmy's grandchildren remember a day in Jimmy's sixties when he took them out for a drive. A truck got behind him coming up Forbes Avenue and sat on his tail, and Greenfield Jimmy slowed down. The truck driver rested on his horn until finally the grandfather pulled his car over and got out. Livid, the big truck driver came over and started hollering down at the little old guy. Softly, Greenfield Jimmy cut in, "Oh, I'm so sorry, but my neighbor over there saw the whole thing."

"What neighbor?" the big truck driver asked, twisting his head to catch a glimpse of this witness. That was his mistake. As soon as he turned to the side, Greenfield Jimmy reared back and popped him flush on the chin. The old man wasn't anything but a banjo hitter on the diamond, but he could sure slug off it.

Greenfield Jimmy played in the bigs as late as '22, but by then the Eighteenth Amendment was the law of the land, and he was discovering that his playing baseball was getting in the way of a more lucrative new career, which was providing alcoholic beverages to those who desired them, notwithstanding their legal unavailability. Sometimes, he would even carry the hooch about in the big trunks that held the team's uniforms and equipment.

Back in Pittsburgh, where he hailed from — the Greenfield section, as you might imagine — Greenfield Jimmy Smith became a man of substance and power. He consorted with everybody, priests and pugs and politicians alike. He ran some speakeasies and, ultimately, the Bachelor's Club, which was the classiest joint in town — a "city club," so-called, as opposed to the numerous neighborhood clubs, which would let in anybody with a couple of bucks' annual dues and the particularly correct European heritage. But the Bachelor's Club was a plush place, and some of Pittsburgh's finest made a great deal of walking-around money by overlooking its existence. Even after repeal, the Bachelor's Club offered games of chance for those so inclined. It helped that, like so much of the Steel City constabulary, Greenfield Jimmy Smith was Irish.

The Bachelor's Club was located in the East Liberty section of Pittsburgh — or 'Sliberty, as it's pronounced in the slurred argot of the community. In a city of neighborhoods, before automobiles begat suburbs, 'Sliberty was known as a very busy place; people came to shop there. For action, though, it was probably not the match of Oakland, a couple of miles away. Most neighborhoods in Pittsburgh were parochial, with a single ethnic legacy, but Oakland had more of a mix and stronger outside influences as well, inasmuch as it embraced the University of Pittsburgh and Forbes Field (where the Pirates played), and the Duquesne Gardens, which must surely be the only boxing arena that was ever set right across the street from a cathedral, which, in this particular case, was St. Paul's.

The Gardens was an old converted carbarn — which, once upon a time, was a place where streetcars were kept when they were sleeping. Pittsburgh was strictly a streetcar town. That was how everybody got to the steel mills. Only in Pittsburgh, nobody ever said "carbarn." They said "coreborn." In Pittsburgh, even now, they don't know how to correctly pronounce any of the vowels and several of the consonants. Even more than the *a*'s, they mess up the *o*'s. A cawledge, for example, is what Pitt is; a dawler is legal tender; and, at that time, the most popular bawxer at the Duquesne Gardens was a skinny Irish contender from 'Sliberty named Billy Cawn, which, despite the way everybody said it, was, curiously, spelled Conn.

Greenfield Jimmy took a real liking to the kid. They had a lot in common. Somebody asked Conn once if he had learned to fight in the streets; no, he replied, it was a long time before he got to the streets from the alleys. Early in '39, after fifty fights around Pittsburgh and West Virginia and two in San Francisco, Conn finally got a shot in New York. "Uncle" Mike Jacobs, the promoter, brought him to Gotham in order to get beat up by a popular Italian fighter, a bellhop out of San Francisco named Freddie Apostoli. Only it was Conn who beat Apostoli in ten, and then, in a rematch a month later, with 19,000 fans packed to the rafters of the old Madison Square Garden on Eighth Avenue, he beat Apostoli in a fifteen-round bloodbath. As much as possible, then, the idea was to match the ethnic groups, so after Conn had beat the Italian twice, Uncle Mike sent him up against a Jew named Solly Krieger. And when the Irish boy beat Krieger in twelve, he was signed to fight Melio Bettina for the world light-heavyweight title the following July.

Suddenly, Conn was the hottest thing in the ring. "Matinee-idol looks," they all said, curly-haired, quick with a quip, full of fun, free, white, and (almost) 21. Money was burning a hole in his pocket, and the dames were chasing him. Right at the time, he took up with an older woman, a divorcée, and remember, this was back in the days when divorcée meant Look Out. He left her for a couple of days and came to Greenfield Jimmy's summer place down the shore in a Cadillac driven by a chauffeur.

Billy Conn was the cat's meow, and Smith was anxious for his wife and kids to meet him, too. Greenfield Jimmy wasn't just a provider, you understand, but also a great family man, and, they said, he never missed Mass. He thought it was really swell when Billy volunteered to take Mary Louise, his little daughter, out to dinner that evening. She was only 15, and for her to be able to go over to Somers Point and have a meal out with Sweet William, the Flower of the Monongahela, would sure be something she could tell the other girls back at Our Lady of Mercy Academy.

How would Greenfield Jimmy ever know that before the evening was over, Billy Conn would turn to the pretty little 15-year-old kid and say right out, "I'm going to marry you."

Mary Louise managed to stammer back, "You're crazy." She remembered what her father had advised her — that all prizefighters were punchy — only it surprised her that one so young and good-looking could be that way. Only, of course, he wasn't punchy. He had just fallen for the kid doll like a ton of bricks.

So now you see: It is Billy Conn who is the boxer in the club cellar and Mary Louise who is the blonde. By the time Greenfield Jimmy Smith (who prided himself on knowing everything) found out what was going on right under his nose, it was too late.

* * *

The Conn house is in the Squirrel Hill district. It has long been mostly a Jewish area, but the house was a good bargain at $17,500 when Billy bought it forty-four years ago because he wanted to stay in the city. Billy is a city guy, a Pittsburgh guy. Billy says, "Pittsburgh is the town you can't wait to leave, and the town you can't wait to get back to." They loved him in Gotham, and they brought him to Tinseltown to play the title role in *The Pittsburgh Kid,* and later he spent a couple of years in Vegas, working the Stardust's lounge as a greeter, like Joe Louis at the Dunes down the Strip. His son Timmy remembers the time a high roller gave the boxer $9,000, just for standing around and being Billy Conn. But soon the boxer grew tired of that act and came back to the house in Squirrel Hill, where, in the vernacular, he "loafs with" old pals like Joey Diven, who was recognized as the World's Greatest Street Fighter.

Pittsburgh may be a metropolitan area of better than two million souls, but it still has the sense of a small town. "Everybody's closely knitted," Diven explains. "A guy hits a guy in 'Sliberty, everybody knows about it right away, all over." Or it's like this: One time the boxer was trying to get a patronage job with the county for a guy he loafs with. But everybody was onto the guy's act. "Billy," the politician said, "I'd like to help you. I really would. But everybody knows, he just don't ever come to work."

Conn considered that fact. "Look at it this way," he said at last. "Do you *want* him around?" The guy got the job.

Pittsburgh, of course, like everyplace else, has changed . . . only more so. The mills are closed, the skies are clear, and Rand McNally has decreed that it is the very best place to live in the United States. Oakland is just another cawledge town; the warm saloons of Forbes Avenue have become fast-food "outlets." Where Forbes Field once stood is Pitt's Graduate School of Business, and in place of Duquesne Gardens is an apartment house.

It was so different when Conn was growing up. Then it was the best of capitalism, it was the worst of capitalism. The steel came in after the Civil War — Bessemer and his blasts — and then came the immigrants to do the hard, dirty work of making ore into endless rolls of metal. Then the skies were so black with smoke that the office workers had to change their white shirts by lunchtime, and the streetlights seldom went off during the day, emitting an eerie glow that turned downtown Pittsburgh into a stygian nightmare. At the time Conn was a kid, taking up space at Sacred Heart School,

H. L. Mencken wrote of Pittsburgh that it was "so dreadfully hid-
eous, so intolerably bleak and forlorn that it reduced the whole
aspiration of a man to a macabre and depressing joke."

The people coughed and wheezed, and those who eschewed the
respiratory nostrums advertised daily in the newspapers would,
instead, repair to the taprooms of Pittsburgh, there to try to cut the
grime and soot that had collected in their dusty throats. The Steel
City was also known as "the wettest spot in the United States," and
even at seven in the morning the bars would be packed three deep,
as the night-shift workers headed home in the gloom of another
graying dawn, pausing to toss down the favored local boiler-
maker — a shot of Imperial whiskey chased by an Iron City beer.
An Iron and an Imp.

And then another. Can't expect someone to fly on one wing.

Conn's father, Billy, Sr., was such a man. He toiled at Westinghouse for forty years. Eventually, Billy would come to call his old
man Westinghouse instead of Dad. But even in the worst of the
Depression, Billy, Sr., kept his job as a steam fitter, and he was proud
of it, and one day he took his oldest boy down to the plant, and he
pointed to it and said, "Here's where you're gonna work, son."

Billy, Jr., was aghast. "That scared the shit out of me," he says.
Shortly thereafter he began to apprentice as a prizefighter, and
when he got to New York and began to charm the press, he could
honestly boast that his greatest achievement in life was never having worked a day.

The mills meant work, but it was a cruel living, and even so recently as the time when Conn was growing up, two-thirds of the
work force in Pittsburgh was foreign-born. "People think you gotta
be nuts to be a fighter," he says now.

Well?

"Yeah, they're right. I *was* nuts. But it beats working in those
mills."

The immigrants who were shipped in from Europe to work in
the mills mostly stayed with their own — the Galway Irish on the
North Side, the Italians in the Bloomfield section, the Poles and
Balkans on the South Side, the Irish in 'Sliberty, the Germans on
Troy Hill. Harry Greb was German, but his mother was Irish, which
mattered at the gate. Promoters liked Irishers. A good little light-
weight named Harry Pitler, Jewish boy, brother of Jake Pitler, who
would play for the Pirates and later become a Brooklyn Dodger

coach, took the Irish handle of Johnny Ray to fight under. Jawnie Ray, one of Erin's own.

Everybody fought some in Pittsburgh. It was a regular activity, like dancing or drinking. It wasn't just that the men were tough and the skies were mean; it was also a way of representing your parish or your people. It wasn't just that Mr. Art Rooney, promoter, or Mr. Jake Mintz, matchmaker, would pit an Irishman against a Jew or a Pole versus an Italian, or bring in a colored boy the white crowds could root against at Duquesne Gardens. No, it was every mother's son scuffling, on the streets or at the bar rail. It was a way of life. It was also cheap entertainment.

Greenfield Jimmy Smith, as we know, enjoyed fighting all his life. So did Billy Conn, Sr., Westinghouse. Nearing 50, he was arrested and fined a five-spot for street-fighting only a few weeks before his son fought for the heavyweight title. Just for kicks, Westinghouse used to fight Billy all the time. When Westinghouse came to New York to watch his boy in the ring one time, Billy told the press, "My old man is a fighting mick. Give him a day or two here, and he'll find some guys to slug it out with."

Billy fought even more with his younger brother Jackie, who was an absolutely terrific street fighter. One time Jimmy Cannon wrote that "if the ring in Madison Square Garden were made of cobblestones," it would be Jackie Conn, not Billy, who would be the champion of the world. A night or so after Cannon's tribute appeared in the paper, Jackie came strolling into Toots Shor's. He was dressed to the nines, as usual. Jackie fancied himself a fashion plate, and he regularly rifled his brother's wardrobe. So Jackie took a prominent seat at the bar, and he was sitting there, accepting compliments and what-have-you from the other patrons, when a stranger came over to him and asked if he was Jackie Conn, the street-fighting champion of the world.

Jackie puffed up and replied that indeed he was, whereupon the stranger coldcocked him, sending Jackie clattering to the floor of Toots Shor's Saloon. "Now I'm the champion," the guy said.

Still, everybody says that Joey Diven was the best street fighter who ever lived. There are stories that he would, for amusement, take on and beat up the entire Pitt football team. Joey is a decade younger than Billy, in his fifties now, working as an assistant to the Allegheny County commissioner. He is a big, red-faced Irishman. That's unusual because most ace street fighters are little guys. Does

Billy Martin come to mind? Big guys grow up figuring nobody will challenge them, so they don't learn how to fight. Big guys break up fights. Little guys are the ones who learn to fight because they figure they had better. Billy always told his three sons, "Don't fight on the streets, because you'll only find out who's good when it's too late."

But Joey Diven was good and big. So first the other Irish pretenders in the neighborhood — the champion of this street or that bar — would come by to find him at the Oakland Cafe, where he loafed, and when he was done beating all those comers, the champs from the other neighborhoods would come over and insult him, so as to get into an inter-ethnic fight.

Insults were automatic. People routinely referred to one another, face to face, with the racial epithets we find so offensive today. For fighting, it was the dagos and the Polacks, the micks and the jigs, and so forth. Sticks and stones. Before a fight with Gus Dorazio, when Dorazio was carrying on at the weigh-in about what color trunks he would wear, Conn cut the argument short by snapping, "Listen, dago, all you're going to need is a catcher's mitt and a chest protector." It was late in Conn's career before he took to using a mouthpiece, because, like his hero Greb, he got a kick out of insulting the people he fought.

On the street, stereotypes prevailed all the more. Usually that meant that everybody (your own group included) was dim-witted, everybody else practiced poor hygiene, everybody else's women were sluts, and everybody but the Jews drank too much and had the most fun. Were the Irish the best fighters? Joey Diven says, "Ah, they just stayed drunk more and stayed louder about it."

One time Joey Diven was working as a doorman over at the AOH on Oakland Avenue. The AOH is the Ancient Order of Hibernians. You needed a card to get into the place, which was located on the third floor, or, as Joey explains it, "Up twenty-eight steps if you accidentally fell down them." This particular night, a guy showed up, but he didn't have a card, so Joey told him to take off. "Come on, let me in, I'm Irish," the guy said. Joey said no card, no admittance, and when the guy persisted, Joey threw him down the steps.

Pretty soon there was a knock on the door again. Joey opened it. Same guy. Same thing: no card. "Come on, let me in, I'm Irish." Joey threw him down the steps again.

A few more minutes and another knock. And get this: It was the same guy. What did Joey do? He ushered him in, and said, "You're right. You must be Irish."

What made Joey Diven such a good street fighter was that he held no illusions. Poor Jackie Conn (who is dead now) was different. He thought he could be as good as his brother in the prize ring. Jackie was on the undercard a night in '39 when Billy defended against Gus Lesnevich, but the kid brother lost a four-rounder. The failure ate him up so, he came apart afterward in the locker room. Just before Billy went off to fight Lesnevich, he had to soothe Jackie and make sure the brother would be taken to the hospital and sedated. Diven was different. "Ah, I didn't ever have the killer instinct like Billy in the ring," he says. "You see, even though Billy's such a God-fearing man, he could be ruthless in the ring. That's why Billy was so good."

Still, Joey will razz Billy good. For example, he says that Conn always was a rotten drinker — "Three drinks, and he's talking about the Blessed Mother or Thomas Aquinas." He also kids Conn that, when he travels, he still sleeps with all his valuables tucked into his pillowcase. Once when they were staying together in Vegas, Billy got up in the middle of the night to take a leak, and Joey was awakened by the sound of change rattling in the pillowcase. Billy was taking his nickels and dimes with him to the bathroom.

"Hey, Billy," Joey said. "You didn't have to take the pillow to the toilet. There's nobody here."

Conn stopped, "*You're* here," he said.

Joey had a lot of fun with Billy. They had a lot of fun street-fighting. It wasn't ever vicious. In those days, nobody ever drew guns or knives or even clubs. Nobody was loco with drugs. You could do all the same stuff Billy did in the ring — gouging and biting and that type of thing, plus the friendly name-calling — all the things that made up what used to be known as *a fair fight.* "No booting, though," says Joey.

"And it never took more than four or five minutes. Somebody would get in one good shot, and that would wear you out pretty quick, and after that there'd be a lot of mauling and rassling, and then it was history." It wasn't at all like in the movies, where the fights go on forever no matter how many times people get clobbered. "As soon as a guy said he'd had enough, that was it. No more," Joey says. That was the code. "Then you'd go back into the joint together and buy each other a drink, maybe even end up getting fractured together." An Iron and an Imp, twice. Do this again for both of us. One more time.

That was the sort of environment young Billy grew up in in 'Sliberty — scrapping with everyone in the neighborhood, running errands for the bootleggers over on Station Street, filching pastries from the bakery wagon to put a little something extra on the family table. There were four younger brothers and sisters. To help make ends meet, Billy's father didn't altogether shy away from working with the bootleggers; the authorities estimated there were 10,000 stills in the Pittsburgh area during Prohibition. Westinghouse sometimes brewed beer in the family bathtub. For Mrs. Conn, the former Marguerite McFarland, the most devout of Catholic women, this made it nearly impossible to ensure that cleanliness would take its assigned runner-up spot to godliness. "Be patient, woman, the beer'll be ready in a few days," Westinghouse would chide his wife as she fretted over her dirty-necked tykes.

Billy adored his mother. He was the one who named her Maggie, and it was that — not Mother or Mom — he called her as he grew older. He always gives nicknames to the people he loves the most. Maggie had come over in steerage from County Cork when she was a young girl, and she never did lose all of her brogue. She grew plump, but with her magnificent skin and blue eyes in a beautiful face framed by black hair, she was a colleen to the day she died. She lavished all that she could upon her oldest, and she was not frightened when he told her he wanted to be a boxer. She knew how hard it was in the mills, and when Westinghouse gave the boy gloves one Christmas, Maggie made him some fine, Celtic green trunks.

Billy Conn leans back in his chair in the club cellar and takes a deep drag on his cigarette, and this is what he says: "Your mother should be your best friend."

Maggie's boy did have one other talent besides boxing and loafing, and that was art. He could draw, and if he were growing up in Pittsburgh today, when Irish boys stay in school and don't lace on gloves, no doubt he would become an artist or a draftsman of some sort. But he never pursued drawing, never even played team sports. His children — Timmy, Billy, Susan, and Mike — all had to learn games from their granddad Greenfield Jimmy, and they still like to laugh at their old man, the former champion of the world, because he throws like a girl.

He stayed two years in the eighth grade at Sacred Heart before one of the sisters suggested that he give up his seat to someone who might use it to greater advantage. He departed school then, but it didn't matter because already, as he puts it, "I was going to cawledge at Jawnie Ray's." That was in 'Sliberty. Ray had retired from fighting, but he ran a gym so he could keep himself in bootleg whiskey. It came in milk bottles and cost 15 cents a pint.

The first time Billy ventured into the gym, Ray was amazed at how tiny and smooth the boy's face was. And Billy couldn't have weighed more than 80, maybe 85, pounds. But Jawnie let him audition in the ring, and he saw the instincts and the courage right off. So he let Billy work around the gym, tidying the place up, fetching him his booze, earning the occasional chance to spar.

One day a bunch of older neighborhood toughs confronted Billy as he came back to the gym toting a pint of moonshine. "What are you, a messenger boy for the rummy?" one of them said, and they jostled and taunted Billy.

He pulled himself up as tall as he could, and he hollered back, "You bums! Someday, I'm gonna be a champeen!"

They laughed, and he went on inside and gave Ray the moonshine. Billy came to call him Moonie for his addiction, and Moonie called him Junior. "All right now, Junior," Moonie would say, swilling the rotgut, "keep your hands up and punch straight." This was the shell defense Jawnie Ray taught. "Moonie was quiet, but he was a Michelangelo as a teacher. Hell, I didn't know he drank until one day I saw him sober. You know how it is — no Jews drink. I get the one who does. Only I tell you one thing, Jawnie Ray knew more about bawxing drunk than anybody else did sober."

Conn stayed with Ray in the gym three years but never was allowed to engage in an official fight. That was because Ray didn't believe in amateur fisticuffs. If you were going to chance being busted in the kisser, then you should make a dawler off it. Also, what could you learn from some amateur? During one period in the late thirties and early forties, the Pittsburgh area gave the world five champions, and Conn got to practice against a lot of talent in the gym. When Joe Louis came to town to fight Hans Birkie, Conn made a buck holding the spit box for the Brown Bomber. It was the first time he ever saw the man with whom he would be linked forever in boxing history.

Finally, when he was 17 years old, Ray drove him down to Fairmont, West Virginia, where he went four rounds against an experienced 24-year-old named Dick Woodwer. There were probably 300 fans at the armory, and Woodwer outpointed the novice. Conn's share was $2.50.

Ray gave him four bits. "Hey, Moon, what is this?" Billy said. "I get two and a half."

"We gotta eat," Ray said.

"Yeah, but how come we're both eating out of my share?"

"You were the one who lost," said Ray.

They never had a contract, but no other man ever managed Billy Conn. He even told the mob to back off when it tried to muscle in.

In the beginning, Ray had Billy fighting somebody somewhere every two weeks or so. Fairmont, Charleston, Wheeling, Johnstown. It was nickel hamburgers, 15-cent moonshine, and 16-cent-a-gallon gas that kept them going. "You tell kids that nowadays, they're sure you ran into too many of Joe Louis's blows," Billy says. And nowadays it's not just the prices that are different. A prospect is brought along against handpicked roundheels on Sunday afternoon TV. After ten bouts everybody gets to fight for the championship of something or other. Conn was barely out of West Virginia after ten fights, and even after fourteen he was hardly .500; then he had to win or draw thirteen in a row before he was allowed a ten-rounder. It was against Honeyboy Jones.

But he was learning. Always, he learned. Even when he fought for championships, he seldom won any of the early rounds. "They don't matter," he says. They counted, but they didn't matter, because that was the time you picked up the other guy's style. And Ray put him in against everybody, every style.

Near the end of 1936, when Conn was still only 18, Ray threw the boy in against the older Fritzie Zivic. "He put an awful face on me," Billy says, and he still honors Zivic, a Pittsburgh guy, by calling him the dirtiest fighter he ever met. But Billy outpointed Zivic and moved out of the welterweights.

A few months later, he won his twenty-third in a row over a red-haired black powerhouse named Oscar Rankins, who knocked Billy down in the eighth with such a stiff blow that, says Conn, "I didn't know I'd won till I read it the next day in the paper." Years later, when Joe Louis heard that Conn had fought Rankins, he said to Billy, "The people who managed you must not have liked you very much. Nobody would let *me* fight that sonuvabitch."

Conn's favorite photograph in the club cellar is a wirephoto of himself bandaged and stitched after he won the rematch with Freddie Apostoli. The headline reads: IF THIS IS THE WINNER, WHAT DOES THE LOSER LOOK LIKE? Conn howls at that, and to this day he speaks with greatest affection about the fighters who did him the most damage.

Damn, it was fun. After he beat Zivic and made big money, $2,180, Conn bought himself a brand new Chevy for $600. When he whipped Bettina for the title, he said, "Gee, I'm champion. Now I can eat regular." Then he went back home to Pittsburgh and out to 'Sliberty. "I hadn't been around the corner for a long time," he says. But now he made a point of going back, and he found the guys who had ridiculed him when he had just been starting out, running errands for Jawnie Ray. They were loafing in a bar. "Remember the messenger boy you laughed at?" he asked, and they nodded, cowering. Billy brought his hands up fast, and they ducked away, but all he did was lay a lot of big bills on the hardwood. "Well, all right," Billy said, "stay drunk a long time on the light-heavyweight champeen of the world."

He bought Maggie anything she wanted. He gave her champagne, the real stuff. She loved champagne. He bought presents for his younger brothers and sisters, and for the dames he found and who found him. He was even interviewed by a New York fashion editor on the subject of how a woman should be turned out.

"I guess these women's fashions are O.K.," Conn declared. "That is, except those dizzy hats and the shoes some of them wear. . . . I wouldn't wear a boxing glove for a hat, but some girls do. . . . Plaid dresses are pips. I think plaid looks swell on any woman, and I like any color as long as it's red. . . . Some evening dresses are pretty nice, if they're lacy and frilly and with swoopy skirts. But most girls look too much like China dolls when they're dressed in evening dresses. But what the hell! They're going to dress up the slightest chance you give 'em. And I'm for giving 'em every chance."

"We're just a bunch of plain, ordinary bums having a good time," Jawnie Ray explained. He and Billy would scream at each other and carry on constantly. "I'm glad we ain't got a contract, you dumb mick sonuvabitch," Jawnie would holler, "because maybe I'll get lucky and somebody even dumber than you will steal you from me." "Yeah, you rummy Jew bastard," Billy would coo back. It was like that, right to the end. The last time Billy saw him, Jawnie was at death's door in the hospital, and Joey Diven and Billy were visiting him.

"C'mon, you guys, sneak me outta here for some drinks," Jawnie Ray pleaded from the hospital bed.

"Moonie," Billy replied, "the only way you're gettin' outta this place is with a tag tied on your big toe."

Sometimes Westinghouse joined the traveling party, too, and on one occasion, coming back from Erie, he and Jawnie Ray got into a first-class fight. As Conn described it in a contemporary account, "My old man swung. Jawnie swung. When it was finished, Pop had a broken nose and Jawnie had lost a tooth. That made them pals."

Yes, sir, it was a barrelful of monkeys. They all loved to throw water on one another, too, and to play practical jokes with the telephone and whatnot. Eventually, when Jackie had grown up enough to come on board, it made it even more fun because then Billy had a partner to scuffle with. Billy would always go after Jackie when he caught him wearing his clothes. One time Billy was voted Best-Dressed Sportsman of the Year, so, Billy chuckled, that must have made Jackie the Second-Best-Dressed Sportsman of the Year.

The day before Conn defended his crown in Forbes Field against Bettina in September of '39, Billy found out that Jackie had been joyriding with his pals in Billy's new black Cadillac, so he put out a $300 bounty on his brother, and when he caught up with him he thrashed him bare-knuckled in the garage. "OK, get it over," Jackie said when he had positively had enough, and he laid out his chin for Billy to paste him square on it. Billy popped him a right, and Jackie was sliding down the wall clear across the garage when Jawnie Ray and Uncle Mike Jacobs and the cops burst in, all of them in disbelief that Billy would get into a fraternal dustup right before a championship fight. They were much relieved to discover that the blood all over Billy was only Jackie's.

Billy wiped himself clean and outpointed Bettina in fifteen. He was the toast of Pittsburgh and the world, as well. The *New York Daily News* rhapsodized: "The Irishman is indeed a beauteous boxer who could probably collect coinage by joining the ballet league if he chose to flee the egg-eared and flattened-nose fraternity." When Conn fought in New York, Owney McManus, who ran a saloon in Pittsburgh, would charter trains, and hundreds of the Irish faithful would follow Conn to Gotham — the Ham and Cabbage Special, they called it — and loaf on Broadway, even if it meant that maybe when they went back to the mills in Pittsburgh they'd be handed a DCM.

A DCM is a Don't Come Monday, the pink slip.

When Conn fought in Oakland, at the Gardens, the streetcars would disgorge fans from all over the Steel City. Pittsburgh's street-car lines were almost all laid out east-west, except for one, which ran north from the mills along the river. It was called the Flying Fraction because it was number 77/54 — a combination of two east-west lines, the 77 and the 54 — and it went right past both the Gardens and Forbes Field. Three rides to a quarter, and if you were getting off for the fights you got a transfer anyhow and sold it for a nickel to the people waiting, so they could save 3 cents on their ride home.

Photos of Conn went up in all the bars where those of Greb and Zivic were to be seen, and in a lot of other places where the Irish wanted strictly their own hero. And now that Billy had grown into a light heavyweight and had beaten all of them, it seemed like the only one left for him to fight was the heavyweight champion, the Brown Bomber himself. There wasn't anybody Irish in the country who wasn't looking forward to that. And by this point, there probably wasn't anybody Irish in Pittsburgh who hadn't seen Billy Conn fight, except for Mary Louise Smith.

"I've never seen a prizefight in my life," she said just the other day. Mary Louise just never cared very much for Billy's business, even when he was earning a living at it.

"You didn't miss anything," Billy replied.

But even if she hadn't seen him work, she was in love with him. She had fallen in love with the boxer. He gave her a nickname, too: Matt — for the way her hair became matted on her brow when she went swimming down the Jersey shore. She was still only a kid, still at Our Lady of Mercy, but she had become even more beautiful than she had been at that first dinner, and the sheltered life Green-field Jimmy had imposed upon her was backfiring some. Billy had the lure of forbidden fruit. "I was mature for my age," Mary Louise says, "something of a spitfire. And I guess you'd have to say that when my father didn't want me to see Billy, I turned out to be a good prevaricator, too." She sighs. "Billy just appealed to me so."

"Ah, I told her a lot of lies," he says.

They would sneak off, mostly for dinners, usually at out-of-town roadhouses, hideaways where they could be alone, intimate in their fashion, staring into each other's blue eyes. It was so very innocent. He was always in training, and she was too young to drink, and kisses are what they shared. That and their song, "A

Pretty Girl Is Like a Melody." Well, Billy made it their song, and he would request it from the big band on Saturdays when they would get all gussied up and go dancing downtown at the William Penn Hotel, which was the fanciest spot in Pittsburgh. And he was the champion of the world, and she was the prettiest girl, dressed all *lacy and frilly and with swoopy skirts.*

Even if Greenfield Jimmy didn't know the half of it, he could sense that it was getting out of hand. Mary Louise played Jo in *Little Women* at Our Lady of Mercy, and he liked that; he wanted her to be an actress, to be something, to move up. He liked Billy, he really did, and he thought he was as good a boxer as he had ever seen, but he didn't want his daughter, his firstborn, marrying a pug. So Greenfield Jimmy sent Mary Louise to Philadelphia, to a classy, cloistered college called Rosemont, and he told the mother superior never to let his daughter see the likes of Mr. Billy Conn.

So Billy had to be content sending letters and presents. When he came into Philly for a fight, he had twenty ringside tickets delivered to Rosemont so that Mary Louise could bring her friends. The mother superior wouldn't let any of the young ladies go, though, and when Billy climbed into the ring and looked down and saw the empty seats, he was crestfallen. His opponent that night was Gus Dorazio, and despite Billy's lipping off at the weigh-in, Billy was even slower than usual to warm up, and the fight went eight rounds before Billy won on a KO.

Greenfield Jimmy was pleased to learn about these events and that Mary Louise was going out with nice young men from the Main Line, who went to St. Joseph's and Villanova, who called for her properly and addressed her as Mary Louise, and not anything common like Matt. Greenfield Jimmy sent her off to Nassau for spring vacation with a bunch of her girlfriends, demure young ladies all.

As for Billy, he went into the heavies, going after Louis. "We're in this racket to make money," Jawnie Ray said. Billy had some now. He rented Maggie and the family a house on Fifth Avenue, an address that means as much in Pittsburgh as it does in New York. One of the Mellons had a mansion on Fifth with sixty-five rooms and eleven baths. "The days of no money are over, Maggie," Billy told his mother. She said fine, but she didn't know anybody on Fifth Avenue. Couldn't he find something in 'Sliberty? "Bring your friends over every day," Billy told her.

Maggie was 40 that summer, a young woman with a son who was a renowned champion of the world. But she began to feel a little poorly and went for some tests. The results were not good. Not at all. So now, even if Billy Conn was a champion, what did it mean? Of the two women he loved, one he almost never got to hold, and now the other was dying of cancer.

Conn's first fight against a heavyweight was with Bob Pastor in September of 1940. Pastor irritated him. "I hit him low one time," Billy recalls. "All right, all right. But he just kept on bitching. So now, I'm *really* gonna hit him low. You know, you were supposed to do everything to win." He knocked Pastor out in thirteen, then he outpointed Al McCoy in ten and Lee Savold in twelve, even after Savold busted his nose in the eighth.

All too often now, though, Conn wasn't himself. He couldn't get to see Mary Louise, and worse, Maggie was becoming sicker and weaker, and almost every cent he made in the ring went to pay for the treatment and the doctors and the round-the-clock nurses he ordered. "His mother's illness has Billy near crazy at times," Jawnie Ray explained after one especially lackluster bout. Between fights Billy would head back to Pittsburgh and slip up to see Maggie, and, against doctor's orders, he would bring her champagne, the finest, and the two of them would sit there on an afternoon, best friends, and get quietly smashed together. They were the happiest moments Maggie had left.

June 18, 1941, was the night set for the Louis fight at the Polo Grounds, and Uncle Mike Jacobs began to beat the biggest drums for Conn, even as Louis kept trooping the land, beating up on what became known as the Bums-of-the-Month. Incredibly, 27,000 people — most of them coming off the Flying Fraction — showed up at Forbes Field to watch Conn's final tune-up in May, against a nobody named Buddy Knox.

Everywhere, the world was swirling, and that seemed to make even everyday events larger and better and more full of ardor. Even if Americans didn't know what lay ahead, even if they told themselves it couldn't happen here, that foreign wars wouldn't engage us, there may have been deeper and truer instincts that inspired and drove them as the year of 1941 rushed on. It was the last summer that a boy hit .400. It was the only summer that anyone hit safely in fifty-six straight games. A great beast named Whirlaway, whipped by Eddie Arcaro, the little genius they called Banana

Nose, ran a Derby so fast that the record would stand for more than twenty years, and he finished up with the Triple Crown in June. That was when the Irishman and the Brown Bomber were poised to do battle in what might have been the most wonderful heavyweight fight there ever was. And all this as the Nazis began their move toward Russia and Yamamoto was okaying the attack on Pearl Harbor.

The pace was quickening. Mary Louise was as impetuous now as the boy she loved. It couldn't go on this way anymore. On May 28, a couple of days after he beat Knox, Billy drove her to Brookville, way north out of Pittsburgh, and took out a marriage license. DiMaggio got a triple in Washington that day, at Griffith Stadium, to raise his streak to thirteen. Mary Louise was 18 now, and Greenfield Jimmy couldn't change her plans any more than he could her heart, but she and Billy were good Catholic kids, and they wanted to be married in the Church, and that meant the banns had to be posted.

So Greenfield Jimmy heard, and he fulminated, "I'm just trying to raise a decent family, and I know where these boxers end up." He said he would punch Billy's lights out, and Westinghouse said he would rattle Greenfield Jimmy's cage first. Greenfield Jimmy went directly to the rectory where the bishop lived in Pittsburgh. He banged on the door and said there had better not be any priest anywhere in Pennsylvania who would marry his flesh and blood to the pug.

It worked, too. The next Saturday, Billy left his training camp and went to a nearby parish named St. Philomena's. He and Mary Louise had someone who had promised to marry them at the altar at 9:30 A.M., and an excited crowd had gathered. But the priests wouldn't buck Greenfield Jimmy, and, after a couple of hours of bickering, somebody came out and told the people there wouldn't be any June wedding this day.

Billy went back to prepare to fight the heavyweight champion. DiMaggio got three singles against the Brownies that afternoon.

The next time Billy left camp, a few days before the bout, he flew to Pittsburgh to see his mother. He probably didn't realize how close to the end she was, because she kept the news from him. "Listen, I've got to live a little longer," Maggie told everyone else in the family. "I can't worry Billy."

He couldn't bring her champagne this time. Instead, he brought her a beautiful diamond bracelet, and he gave it to her. "Maggie," he said, "this is for you." She was so sick, so weak, so in pain that she could barely work up a smile, but she thanked him the best she could. And then she pushed it back.

"Oh, it's so beautiful, Billy," she said. "But don't give it to me. Give it to Mary Louise." And Maggie told him then that he was to marry her, no matter what Greenfield Jimmy said, because he was her boy and a good boy and as good as any boy, and because he loved Mary Louise more than anyone else in the world.

Billy nodded. He kept his hand wrapped around the bracelet. He couldn't stay much longer. Just these few minutes had tired Maggie so. He kissed her and got ready to leave. "Maggie," Billy said, "I gotta go now, but the next time you see me, I'll be the heavyweight champion of the world."

Maggie smiled one more time. "No, son," she said, "the next time I see you will be in Paradise."

Tuesday, the seventeenth, the day before the fight, DiMaggio made it an even thirty in a row, going 1 for 4 against the Chisox across the river in the Bronx. That night, Billy slept hardly at all. And he always slept. Sometimes he would even lie down in the locker room while the undercard bouts were being fought and doze right off just minutes before he had to go into the ring. But this whole night he barely got forty winks. And he wasn't even worrying about getting in the ring with Joe Louis. He was worrying about Maggie and Matt.

At the weigh-in the next morning Louis, who had trained down because of Conn's speed, came in at 200. Conn tipped 169. That made Uncle Mike a bit nervous. It was already 17 to 5 for the champion in the betting, and this weight spread was making the bout look like homicide. Uncle Mike announced Conn's weight at a more cosmetic 174 and Louis at 199½.

Conn went back to his hotel to rest, but the Ham and Cabbage Special had just got in, and all the fans, wearing leprechaun hats and carrying paper shamrocks and clay pipes, came over to see him, and when a bunch of them barged right into his room, Billy went outside and loafed with them.

Finally, Jawnie got him back to his room, but who should come storming in, wearing a zoot suit and smoking a big cigar, but Jackie. Naturally, he and Billy started wrestling each other all over the suite, driving the trainer, Freddie Fierro, nuts. People can get hurt wrestling. At last Fierro was able to separate them, but Billy still couldn't sleep, so he looked in on Jackie and saw him snoring with his mouth open. He called down to room service, ordered a seltzer bottle, and squirted it right into Jackie's mouth. You can bet that woke Jackie up.

Jackie chased Billy into the hall. Billy was laughing, and he wasn't wearing anything but his shorts. That was how Billy spent the day getting ready for the Brown Bomber. Just a few miles away, at the Stadium, DiMaggio went 1 for 3 to stretch it to thirty-one.

Back in Pittsburgh the Pirates had scheduled one of their few night games for this evening, June 18. They knew everybody wanted to stay home to listen to the fight on the radio, so the Pirates announced that when the fight began, the game would be suspended and the radio broadcast would go out over the PA. Baseball came to a halt. Most of America did. Maybe the only person not listening was Maggie. She was so sick the doctors wouldn't let her.

Billy crossed himself when he climbed into the ring that night.

And then the Pirates stopped, and America stopped, and the fight began. Louis's eighteenth defense, his seventh in seven months.

Conn started slower than even he was accustomed to. Louis, the slugger, was the one who moved better. Conn ducked a long right so awkwardly that he slipped and fell to one knee. The second round was worse, Louis pummeling Conn's body, trying to wear the smaller man down. He had thirty pounds on him, after all. Unless you knew the first rounds didn't matter, it was a rout. This month's bum.

In his corner, Conn sat down, spit, and said, "All right, Moon, here we go." He came out faster, bicycled for a while, feinted with a left, and drove home a hard right. By the end of the round he was grinning at the champ, and he winked to Jawnie Ray when he returned to the corner. The spectators were up on their feet, especially the ones who had bet Conn.

The fourth was even more of a revelation, for now Conn chose to slug a little with the slugger, and he came away the better for the exchange. When the bell rang, he was flat out laughing as he came back to his corner. "This is a cinch," he told Jawnie.

But Louis got back on track in the fifth, and the fight went his way for the next two rounds as blood flowed from a nasty cut over the challenger's right eye. At Forbes Field in Pittsburgh the crowd grew still, and relatives and friends listening downstairs from where Maggie lay worried that Billy's downfall was near.

But Conn regained command in the eighth, moving back and

away from Louis's left, then ripping into the body or the head. The ninth was all the more Conn, and he grew cocky again. "Joe, I got you," he popped off as he flicked a good one square on the champ's mouth, and then, as Billy strode back to his corner at the bell, he said, "Joe, you're in a fight tonight."

"I knows it," Louis replied, confused and clearly troubled now.

The tenth was something of a lull for Conn, but it was a strategic respite. During the eleventh, Conn worked Louis high and low, hurt the champ, building to the crescendo of the twelfth, when the *New York Herald Tribune* reported in the casual racial vernacular of the time that Conn "rained left hooks on Joe's dusky face." He was a clear winner in this round, which put him up 7–5 on one card and 7–4–1 on another; the third was 6–6. To cap off his best round, Conn scored with a crushing left that would have done in any man who didn't outweigh him by thirty pounds. And it certainly rattled the crown of the world's heavyweight champion. The crowd was going berserk. Even Maggie was given the report that her Billy was on the verge of taking the title.

Only later would Conn realize the irony of striking that last great blow. "I miss that, I beat him," he says. It was that simple. He was nine minutes from victory, and now he couldn't wait. "He wanted to finish the thing as Irishmen love to," the *Herald Tribune* wrote.

Louis was slumped in his corner. Jack Blackburn, his trainer, shook his head and rubbed him hard. "Chappie," he said, using his nickname for the champ, "you're *losing*. You gotta knock him out." Louis didn't have to be told. Everyone understood. Everyone in the Polo Grounds. Everyone listening through the magic of radio. Everyone. There was bedlam. It was wonderful. Men had been slugging it out for eons, and there had been 220 years of prizefighting, and there would yet be Marciano and the two Sugar Rays and Ali, but this was it. This was the best it had ever been and ever would be, the twelfth and thirteenth rounds of Louis and Conn on a warm night in New York just before the world went to hell. The people were standing and cheering for Conn, but it was really for the sport and for the moment and for themselves that they cheered. They could be a part of it, and every now and then, for an instant, *that* is it, and it can't ever get any better. This was such a time in the history of games.

Only Billy Conn could see clearly — the trouble was, what he saw was different from what everybody else saw. What he saw was himself walking with Mary Louise on the boardwalk at Atlantic City, down the shore, and they were the handsomest couple who ever lived, and people were staring, and he could hear what they were saying. What they were saying was: "There goes Billy Conn with his bride. He just beat Joe Louis." And he didn't want to hear just that. What he wanted to hear was: "There goes Billy Conn with his bride. He's the guy who just *knocked out* Joe Louis." Not for himself: That was what Mary Louise deserved.

Billy had a big smile on his face. "This is easy, Moonie," he said. "I can take this sonuvabitch out this round."

Jawnie blanched. "No, no, Billy," he said. "Stick and run. You got the fight won. Stay away, kiddo. Just stick and run, stick and run. . . ." There was the bell for the thirteenth.

And then it happened. Billy tried to bust the champ, but it was Louis who got through the defenses, and then he pasted a monster right on the challenger's jaw. "Fall! Fall!" Billy said to himself. He knew if he could just go down, clear his head, he would lose the round, but he could still save the day. "But for some reason, I couldn't fall. I kept saying, 'Fall, fall,' but there I was, still standing up. So Joe hit me again and again, and when I finally did fall, it was a slow, funny fall. I remember that." Billy lay flush out on the canvas. There were two seconds left in the round, 2:58 of the thirteenth, when he was counted out. *The winnah and still champeen.* . . .

"It was nationality that cost Conn the title," the *Herald Tribune* wrote. "He wound up on his wounded left side, trying to make Irish legs answer an Irish brain."

On the radio, Billy said, "I just want to tell my mother I'm all right."

Back in the locker room, Jawnie Ray said not to cry because bawxers don't cry. And Billy delivered the classic: "What's the sense of being Irish if you can't be dumb?"

Maggie lasted a few more days. "She held on to see me leading Joe Louis in the stretch," Billy says.

He and Mary Louise got married the day after the funeral. The last time they had met with Greenfield Jimmy, he said that Billy had to "prove he could be a gentleman," but what did a father-in-law's blessing matter anymore after the twelfth and thirteenth rounds and after Maggie's going?

They found a priest in Philly, a Father Schwindlein, and he didn't care from Greenfield Jimmy or the bishop or whoever. As Mary

Louise says, "He just saw two young people very much in love."
They had a friend with them who was the best man, and the cleaning lady at the church stood in as the maid of honor. DiMaggio got
up to forty-five that day in Fenway, going 2 for 4 and then 1 for 3
in a twin bill. Greenfield Jimmy alerted the state police and all the
newspapers when he heard what was going on, but Billy and Mary
Louise were on their honeymoon in Jersey, man and wife, by the
time anybody caught up with them.

"They're more in love than ever today, forty-four years later," Michael Conn says. He is their youngest child. The Conns raised three
boys and a girl at the house they bought that summer in Squirrel
Hill.

That was it, really. DiMaggio's streak ended the night of July 17
in Cleveland. Churchill and Roosevelt signed the Atlantic Charter
four weeks later, and on November 26 the first subs pulled away
from Japan on the long haul to Pearl Harbor. By then Billy was
shooting a movie. It was called *The Pittsburgh Kid*, and in it he
played (in an inspired bit of casting) an Irish fighter from the Steel
City. Mary Louise was so pretty the producers wanted at least to
give her a bit part as a cigarette girl, but she was too bashful, and
Billy wasn't crazy about the idea himself. Billy did so well that the
moguls asked him to stay around and star in the life story of Gentleman Jim Corbett, but the house in Squirrel Hill was calling. And
Mary Louise was pregnant. "We were just a couple of naive young
kids from Pittsburgh, and we didn't like Hawllywood," she says.

Joey Diven says that if Billy doesn't care for somebody a whole
lot, he'll have them over to the house, take them down to the club
cellar, and make them watch *The Pittsburgh Kid*.

After Pearl Harbor, Conn fought three more times. Nobody knew
it then, but he was done. Everything ended when he hit Louis that
last big left. The best he beat after that was Tony Zale, but even the
fans in the Garden booed his effort, and he only outpointed the
middleweight. It didn't matter, though, because all anybody cared
about was a rematch with Louis — even if both fighters were going
into the service.

The return was in the works for the summer, a year after the first
meeting. It was looked upon as a great morale builder and diversion for a rattled America. The victories at Midway and Guadal-
canal were yet to come.

Then, in the middle of May, Private First Class Conn got a three-day pass to come home to the christening of his firstborn, Timmy. Art Rooney was the godfather, and he thought it would be the right time to patch things up between Greenfield Jimmy and his son-in-law, and so he and Milton Jaffe, Conn's business adviser, arranged a christening party at Smith's house and they told Billy that his father-in-law was ready to smoke the peace pipe.

On Sunday, at the party, Greenfield Jimmy and Conn were in the kitchen with some of the other guests. That is where people often congregated in those days, the kitchen. Billy was sitting up on the stove, his legs dangling, when it started. "My father liked to argue," Mary Louise says, "but you can't drag Billy into an argument." Greenfield Jimmy gave it his best, though. Art Rooney says, "He was always the boss, telling people what to do, giving orders." On this occasion he chose to start telling Conn that if he was going to be married to his daughter and be the father of his grandson, he damn sight better attend church more regularly. Then, for good measure, he also told Billy he could beat him up. Finally, Greenfield Jimmy said too much.

"I can still see Billy come off that stove," Rooney says.

Just because it was family, Billy didn't hold back. He went after his father-in-law with his best, a left hook, but he was mad, he had his Irish up, and the little guy ducked like he was getting away from a brushback pitch, and Conn caught him square on the top of his skull. As soon as he did it, Billy knew he had broken his hand. He had hurt himself worse against his own father-in-law than he ever had against any bona fide professional in the prize ring.

Not only that, but when the big guys and everybody rushed in to break it up, Milton Jaffe fractured an ankle and Mary Louise got herself all cut and bruised. Greenfield Jimmy took advantage of the diversion to inflict on Conn additional scratches and welts — around the neck, wrists, and eyes. Billy was so furious about blowing the rematch with Louis that he busted a window with his good hand on the way out and cut himself more. The *New York Times,* ever understated, described Conn's appearance the next day "as if he had tangled with a half-dozen alley cats."

Greenfield Jimmy didn't have a single mark on him.

Years later, whenever Louis saw Conn, he would usually begin, "Is your old father-in-law still beating the shit out of you?"

In June, Secretary of War Henry Stimson announced there would be no more public commercial appearances for Louis, and the champ began a series of morale-boosting tours. The fight at the christening had cost Louis and Conn hundreds of thousands of dollars and, it turned out, any real chance Conn had for victory. Every day the war dragged on diminished his skills.

The legs go first.

Conn was overseas in Europe for much of the war, pulling punches in exhibition matches against regimental champs. One time, the plane he was on developed engine trouble over France, and Billy told God he would do two things if the plane landed safely.

It did, and he did. Number one, he gave $5,000 to Dan Rooney, Art's brother, who was a missionary in the Far East. And number two, he gave $5,000 to Sacred Heart, his old parish in 'Sliberty, to build a statue of the Blessed Virgin. It is still there, standing prominently by the entrance.

Conn was with Bob Hope at Nuremberg when V-E day came. There is a picture of that in the club cellar.

Then he came home and patched up with Greenfield Jimmy and prepared for the long-awaited rematch with Louis. It was on June 19, 1946, and such was the excitement that, for the first time, ringside seats went for $100, and a $2 million gate was realized. This was the fight — not the first one — when Louis observed, "He can run, but he can't hide." And Joe was absolutely right. Mercifully, the champion ended the slaughter in the eighth. In the locker room Conn himself called it a "stinkeroo," and it was Jawnie Ray who cried, because, he said, "Billy's finished."

As Conn would tell his kids, boxing is bad unless you happen to be very, very good at it. It's not like other sports, where you can get by. If you're not very, very good, you can get killed or made over into a vegetable or what-have-you. Now Billy Conn, he had been very, very good. Almost one-third of his seventy-five fights had been against champions of the world, and he had beaten all those guys except Louis, and that was as good a fight as there ever was. Some people still say there never has been a better fighter, a stylist, than Sweet William, the Flower of the Monongahela. But, of course, all anybody remembers is the fight that warm June night in the year of '41 and especially that one round, the thirteenth.

One time, a few years ago, Art Rooney brought the boxer into the Steelers' locker room and introduced him around to a bunch

of white players standing there. They obviously didn't have the foggiest idea who Billy Conn was. Conn saw some black players across
the way. "Hey, blackies, you know who Joe Louis was?" They all
looked up at the stranger and nodded. Conn turned back to the
whites and shook his head. "And you sonsuvbitches don't know
me," he said.

But really he didn't care. "Everything works out for the best," he
says in the club cellar. "I believe that." He's very content. They can't
ever get him to go to sports dinners so they can give him awards
and stuff. "Ah, I just like being another bum here," he says. "I just
loaf around, on the corner, different places." Then Mary Louise
comes around, and he falls into line. He never moved around much,
Billy Conn. Same town, same house, same wife, same manager,
same fun. "All the guys who know me are dead now, but, let me tell
you, if I drop dead tomorrow, I didn't miss anything."

He's standing over by the photograph of Louis and him, right
after their first fight. He still adores Louis, they became fast friends,
and he loves to tell stories about Louis and money. Some guys have
problems with money. Some guys have, say, problems with fathers-
in-law. Nobody gets off scot-free. Anyway, in the picture Louis has
a towel wrapped around a puzzled, mournful countenance. Conn,
next to him, is smiling to beat the band. He was the loser?

Billy says, "I told Joe later, 'Hey, Joe, why didn't you just let me
have the title for six months?' All I ever wanted was to be able to
go around the corner where the guys are loafing and say, 'Hey, I'm
the heavyweight champeen of the world.'

"And you know what Joe said back to me? He said, 'I let you have
it for twelve rounds, and you couldn't keep it. How could I let you
have it for six months?'"

A few years ago Louis came to Pittsburgh, and he and Conn made
an appearance together at a union hall. Roy McHugh, the columnist
for the *Pittsburgh Press,* was there. Billy brought the film of the '41
fight over from Squirrel Hill in a shopping bag. As soon as the fight
started, Louis left the room and went into the bar to drink brandy.
Every now and then Louis would come to the door and holler out,
"Hey, Billy, have we got to the thirteenth yet?" Conn just laughed
and watched himself punch the bigger man around, until finally,
when they did come to the thirteenth, Joe called out, "Good-bye,
Billy."

Louis knocked out Conn at 2:58, just like always, but when the lights went on, Billy wasn't there. He had left when the thirteenth round started. He had gone into another room, to where the buffet was, after he had watched the twelve rounds when he was the heavyweight champeen of the world, back in that last indelible summer when America dared yet dream that it could run and hide from the world, when the handsomest boy loved the prettiest girl, when streetcars still clanged and fistfights were fun, and the smoke hung low when Maggie went off to Paradise.

*   *   *

One of my earliest recollections is, at the age of seven, being allowed to stay up to some ungodly hour to listen to the second Louis-Conn fight on the radio. Since I knew that neither of my parents cared about boxing, this always provided me with a personal insight into how much the nation must have been involved in those two boxing matches. When a friend of mine, a Hollywood publicity agent named Milt Kahn, suggested to me that Billy would make a good story, that childhood memory was called back. Actually, what Milt thought was that eventually Billy's story would make a good movie, and, in fact, after the piece about Billy appeared in Sports Illustrated, *my agent sold the rights to a movie producer. Nothing's ever come of it, though.*

I told Billy in advance that probably nothing would ever come of it. I explained to him how they just buy things in Hollywood; they seldom make things except stuff for teenagers with monsters in them. So, we got a couple thousand dollars apiece, and Billy called me up when his check arrived. "Hey, Frank," he said, "it's better than a kick in the ass, right?" I felt like I was Moonie, and Billy and I had just shared a good gate in Wheeling or Johnstown or somewhere.

This next story was suggested to me by the first editor I worked with regularly at Sports Illustrated, *Jerry Tax. Something more than half the pieces I do are my own ideas; the balance come from editors. I had never met Tony DeSpirito, but jockeys fascinate me as much as any athlete. Perhaps it is because I am very tall that jockeys, so small, especially impress me as they do. As a group, baseball pitchers are also particularly intriguing to me, but jockeys are the ones I like the best.*

The Kid Who Ran Into Doors

1975

T HE phenoms we know about. But forget them. They were overrated, that's all, and we cannot cry about water finding its own level, at their having to go on to pumping gas or selling mutual funds. After all, they had their day in the sun, even if it was only a hazy day of spring; that is a freebie, one more day in the limelight than the rest of us will get. No, the ones to weep for are those who honestly had it but were denied a lifetime of fame by some sad, unlikely fate. Tony Lema died one way, Harry Agganis and Ernie Davis another. Who knows how good Connie Hawkins might have been? Herb Score could have rewritten all the record books, page after page. But for injuries Pete Reiser and Lew Hoad might have made us forget Cobb and Tilden.

And Tony DeSpirito, the late Tony DeSpirito. Most people don't even know the name anymore. Others had forgotten it until it flashed fuzzily before them, an old tune we danced to at the beach one summer, when the word came the other day that he had died, age 39. His mother found him on a Monday morning on the couch in the little apartment he rented in Riverside, Rhode Island. For reasons nobody understands, he choked to death. That's what the autopsy determined. Probably there were too many parts inside him that were just too busted up or worn down. But only 39, that just doesn't seem fair. Especially after all the spills that nearly killed him with his boots on, all the horses' hooves running over him. He had the last rites twice. And he would come back; but each time he rode again there was something else diminished, if never the courage.

What a waste. The late Tony DeSpirito could have been the best there ever was on a horse, the very best. He knew that himself. When he visited his children, who had been too young to see him when he was great, sometimes he would laugh and say, "I'm the king. I am. Nobody could ever do on a horse what your father did." And there was no braggadocio to it. It was almost teasing. He just wanted his children to know, for the record. He would laugh. "The king, Donna. Your father was the king."

Even from an outside hole he could drive a horse out of the gate and put it on the engine, or from off the pace he could finish as well as Garrison or Arcaro or Cordero or any man who ever lived, and in between he rode so straight and beautifully, absolutely classically. The old-timers say you could have put a glassful of water on the late Tony DeSpirito's back, and he would win by a nose in the last jump and never spill a drop. That is what the old-timers say.

In 1952, when he was 16 years old, he won 390 races, more than anybody ever had before him. Everybody thought he was 17, but he had lied about his age when he quit school and went to the track. He wasn't 17 till Christmas Eve that year. He would have ridden more than 390 winners, but before he got close to the record he would just take off his mounts a day here and there and get in his latest Cadillac, of which (by the best family estimates) he owned seventeen in one year's time, and go pick up some tall, big-breasted, grown woman and spend the afternoon with her.

And when people talk about the late Tony DeSpirito that wondrous year, what above all is the first thing they say, the very first thing? It is that he was brought up special from Miami to be on *Ed Sullivan* after he broke the record. That certifies it, his greatness. From age 17 it was never so good again, and all bad luck. He was just on *Ed Sullivan* the one time.

Willie Shoemaker is 43 years old. He broke DeSpirito's record the next year, 1953. This year, 1975, Shoemaker is still in perfect shape, body and mind. He has no weight problem and expects to ride another decade or more. Why not? He hits a golf ball straight for better than 200 yards and plays tennis with people like Burt Bacharach. He has had the same agent all his life. His money is in a safe place. He is not just liked and respected but damn near sainted. Not long after Mrs. DeSpirito found her oldest son dead in Riverside, Willie Shoemaker won the Belmont on Avatar; and he is having one of the better seasons of his twenty-six-year career. Willie

Shoemaker, like anyone else, does not know why it is that these things happened to him and those things happened to the late Tony DeSpirito. He just says, "Some people go through doors, Tony ran into them."

Tony's mother has read about him in the paper so many times that she plays it back. She says, "Tony was just a hard-luck kid." Have you ever before heard a mother say that her son was a hard-luck kid? Probably not. But there is nothing much else to say unless you want to talk about the doors.

In the early 1950s DeSpirito in the East was considered the equal of Shoemaker in the West. And DeSpirito was said to have more potential because he was stronger. DeSpirito was the one they compared to Arcaro more often; Arcaro himself thought the kid from New England would be his heir. Many people still refer to DeSpirito as "the kid." It is not that it was a nickname; they just say it unconsciously. He is 39 years old, dead in the ground, and he is still *the kid.* "Oh, you want to talk about the kid." "Lemme tell you about the kid." "I knew the kid some twenty-odd years." And so forth.

This is what happens when you scale the top at age 16, and then can't ever outdo it. Athletes get frozen in time. They get attached to a certain year. People say, "Oh, yeah, that was his year." "That was Walt Dropo's year." "That was Dick Kazmaier's year." "Wasn't that Tom Gola's year?" Nobody ever says this about other people. Nobody once ever said that 1776 was Thomas Jefferson's year. Maybe just athletes have years — and very few of them; usually just the kids. Willie Shoemaker never had a year. But 1952 was the late Tony DeSpirito's year, and when we are all dead, the lot of us, when things are even, he will be able to say that he had the one thing very few others had. Maybe that is why nobody ever heard him rail at the misfortunes dealt him. At least he had a year in his hip pocket.

He came from Lawrence, Massachusetts, a mill town on the Merrimack River, a place out of the textbook chapter on the industrial revolution. For him it was six miles from Rock, which is across in New Hampshire and formally named Rockingham Park. His father is a little man, too. He wanted to be a rider, but never could work it out; he was out of a job at the mills when his boy started riding a great many winners around New England that spring. Mr. De-Spirito spent the balance of 1952 signing papers for the various

Cadillacs; all the business with the excise taxes was a real mess, he says.

It is fascinating that everybody but one who knew the kid back then says how mature and precocious he was. For example, Pee Wee Gervais, his valet for most of 1952, says, "Tony really grew up quick. He learned the fast life pretty quick." Bob Aiello, his best friend, says, "Tony was a sixteen-year-old boy who was a fifty-five-year-old man." Everybody — his parents, his friends, other riders — echoes this feeling. The one person who disagrees completely is his first wife, Doris. She shakes her head and laughs that anyone could ever have thought he was grown up. "Listen, Tony was small," she says, "but he was the biggest, bravest man I ever knew. But what did he know? What did *we* know? We were just a couple of kids. That's all he was, a kid." We think kids are men for doing the things well that would make grown men kids again if they could do them. The late Tony DeSpirito could pick up a tab, take home a broad, trade in a Caddy, and switch sticks in the stretch; so much for growing up.

The amazing thing, really, is that it didn't mess him up. It didn't. It cost him plenty of easy money, but it never did go to his handsome head. Aiello, who is now the clerk of scales at Lincoln Downs, says, "Sixteen years old, he could write his own ticket. I'll tell you, it was more than I could have handled. He's making three, four thousand a week. The toast of the town. Women chasing him. He's taking bows wherever he goes. He's on *Ed Sullivan*. And always the entourage, the fair-weather friends. Sixteen, he knew all the wheeling and dealing."

That is the occupational hazard (such as it is) of being a great athlete. The ones like Shoemaker, the ones who avoid getting caught up in it, they are the exceptions. The late Tony DeSpirito wasn't anything out of the ordinary, and maybe he was a classic case; it all happened so quickly and ended so fast. And also, he was carved larger than life, a regular folk hero in his part of the world.

New England is a singular place. Everybody thinks of the South as the most distinctive American region, but since air conditioning, the people in Atlanta and Richmond are from Cleveland, and the other way around. There was never any cult about New England. In the South the thinkers wrote about the South, and glamorized it; in New England the thinkers started schools. At the time DeSpirito came to prominence, New England was a place unto itself, and it still is. The people prize their own.

The North End of Boston is Italian. There are still dyed-in-the-wool Yankee fans in the North End, this affiliation going back to Joe DiMaggio and Frankie Crosetti, when the Red Sox didn't have any good *paisanos.* When DeSpirito got hot, the whole North End came in on him, and then the whole city and then New England. It wasn't just the broads, understand. The kid had the whole place at his feet.

You still will have a hard time in Beantown betting with a bookie if you want to bet more on place or show than win. This goes back to 1952 and the late Tony DeSpirito. He was on so many good horses and riding them so well that he was almost a lock to finish in the money on certain mounts. He had a one-armed agent named Wingie, so called because of his unfortunate dismemberment, who could pick and choose the best stock, and about the only time the kid didn't get the horse that figured was when another trainer could make it exceptionally appealing, laying a bill across Wingie's existing palm. So wagerers were putting fifty, say, on DeSpirito to win, and then backing that up two, three hundred place or show. People were betting the late Tony DeSpirito who had never bet so much as a bingo card at the parish hall before. The books were getting handled. They couldn't even win when he lost because everybody was saving. That's when they said you could only wager fifty to show if you wagered fifty to win.

The entire New England racing economy went on a DeSpirito standard. The books had to play "the comeback window." This is a term for a corrective device to deal with perverse betting. Say a horse named Irish Mother is entered on St. Paddy's Day at Suffolk. Obviously every Irishman in town is going to get five down with his bookie. Suppose Irish Mother is 20 to 1 at the track, where there isn't so much hunch money coming in. But away from the oval, maybe a quarter, a third of the books' take is on Irish Mother. At 20 to 1 they'll be wiped out if the hunch filly scores. So they have to take a lot of Irish Mother money and run it out to the mutuels, to the comeback window, and bet it on Irish Mother in order to get the odds down. Well, the kid was an Irish Mother all year. Every day the bookies had to go out to the track and feed the comeback window just to stay square.

Playing to his audience, an old racetrack announcer named Babe Rubenstein stopped calling the horse and would call the boy, instead — and where did you ever hear of that before? De-sper-EE-to, he pronounced it, and it stuck, even though the family says

De-SPEER-it-to. People can still remember Babe Rubenstein suddenly shouting, ". . . and here comes Tony DeSpirito, flying on the outside like the wind!"

Oh, what a time it must have been for a 16-year-old boy.

Having done it all, at 17 he got married. Nelson Eddy sang at the wedding. The bride was the former Doris DeCristoforo, the daughter of the chef at the Latin Quarter, the big Boston nightclub. Doris was 18, pretty, stacked, brunette, and a virgin. The last was especially important to the kid. "I was a nice girl," Doris says. "That's why he married me." They went to Niagara Falls on their honeymoon because that was the thing to do. It snowed, and Doris got pregnant with Donna right off the bat. And they bought a trailer to go to the tracks in. Then one day Tony took Doris into a bar and ordered two J&B Scotches, hers tall with soda to cut the taste. "If you're going to be married to me, you've got to learn to drink what I do," he said.

When Doris was home with the babies he would occasionally tie one on, bust up a Caddy, maybe even get arrested for drunken driving, but it wasn't booze that did in the late Tony DeSpirito. Fast living was just his style. "As sharp as he was, he was always the type of boy who only lived for today," Bob Aiello says. "Tony was just a leave-it-or-like-it guy." He drove the big cars like his horses. Once he went out to get some Chinese food. This story sounds too good to be true, but it is. He smashed up his Caddy on the General Edwards Bridge coming back, climbed out of the wreck, hailed a cab, and brought Doris the Chinese food while it was still steaming. He came through the front door smiling, actually smiling, holding aloft the food containers he had salvaged from the crash.

He made something like $150,000 the first year — 1952 dollars — and a bunch thereafter before he got hurt. For as long as they were married, good times and bad, Doris says there was never a day he didn't carry $3,000 to $4,000 in his pocket. And he could be touched. A racetrack scuffler came up to Aiello a few days after DeSpirito died and said the kid had lent him a ten, who did he pay it back to? This fellow wasn't going to short a regular guy like DeSpirito, even dead. The kid never really lost his money. He just dribbled it away, here and there, on this and that. His only real investment venture was a restaurant named Carl's Duck Farm near Boston, which he ran with his father-in-law, the chef. That cost him a bundle. The late Tony DeSpirito would come in some nights and get rid of all the paying customers so he could sit around and drink with his buddies. Most of the money just faded away, and he never regretted a penny of it.

Some of it, of course, went on the ladies. The kid was a doll. His ex-wife says he was 5'3". "Come on, Mom," says Mark, his son, who is 16 now, small and handsome like his father with exactly his mannerisms. "You know he was only five-two." She smiles sheepishly. DeSpirito was not hung up on his height. Like Shoemaker, who is even smaller, he was perfectly proportioned, so he looked taller than he was. With his dark good looks he was even called Brando, and he had the beautifully muscled body of a boxer. So, while there were always women, they didn't hurt his career any more than the drinking. Popular opinion aside, seldom do the ladies do an athlete in. It is not being with a lady that harms athletes. In fact, look at it this way: When an athlete is with a lady he is not out drinking with the boys. It is *the chasing* of women that is wearing, but the late Tony DeSpirito, like other sports stars, didn't have to do any chasing.

Doris realized early on that he was cheating on her. Hurt and embarrassed, she didn't press it at first. Later, whenever she would question him, he would put on a little-boy look and play innocent. "He'd always tell me he was 'a victim of circumstance,'" Doris says. "It was all the guy's fault he was with, that sort of thing." She pauses and smiles at the memory. "He would actually say, 'victim of circumstance.' He'd say, 'But, Doris, I'm a victim of circumstance.'"

The ladies ruined only his marriage. It was the horrible accidents that destroyed his greatness on the track. He had too much courage — and not enough luck. He took a spill at Lincoln in 1953, and they thought he had injured a disk. He rode 311 winners that year. In 1956 they finally discovered he actually had broken his back in three places. He was almost killed when he was trampled on in the Beldame Stakes at the old Aqueduct in 1955. He came back and was almost killed when his mount broke a leg at Laurel in 1956. He came back again and was almost killed at Rock in 1958. All told, there were nine spills. He came back again and would have been dragged to death at Suffolk in 1960, but another jock, Henry Wajda, who was later killed himself at Rockingham Park, grabbed DeSpirito and held him up, just off the hooves on the first turn.

Over the years the kid lost a kidney and his spleen. He broke ribs and his back and jaw and lacerated his brain. There was so much surgery, so much pain, and a lot of painkillers that sometimes got confused with the J&B. At 22 he called himself "washed up"; at 25 he said, "The pain, I got to call it quits." Another day he rode once more, vowing to be a jockey for "as long as I can climb on a horse." The new injuries aside, the back always troubled him and, as he got older, the weight as well. He was so muscular that he had no fat to lose. All that went was the greatness. "I can't get out of a horse what I used to," he admitted. He even quit for a year and a half and sold real estate in Florida, but he came back to what the jocks call "the whites," for the color of their work pants.

When Doris left him he went right out and married again, and after he and Ginny had a little boy, that marriage broke up, too. It truly hurt him that the second divorce kept him away from his 2-year-old, little Tony. DeSpirito hadn't had any childhood himself, and he realized for the first time that he hadn't experienced his first family's growing up, either, because he was always riding or a victim of circumstance. It hit him all the harder when his younger sister, Barbara, died suddenly last year of a rare blood disease. She was 35.

In hardly more than a year Mr. and Mrs. DeSpirito lost their only daughter and their oldest son, both in their thirties. Mr. DeSpirito, with a bad heart and a bad leg (a horse kicked him in 1959, when he was trying to be a trainer), forces a smile and says, "I always thought I'd be the first one up there, but it turns out they'll be waiting for me."

There is the one boy left, young Barry. His parents are very proud of him. He lives nearby, visits often and, as Mrs. DeSpirito points out, "He's salaried." He wanted to be a jockey himself once, and during one of his retirements Tony acted as his brother's agent. But Barry wasn't that good, and, besides, Tony tried another comeback himself. Barry found his way back to the real world. Tony finally quit again for what was supposed to be the absolute last time two years ago and became a $45-a-day placing judge and general factotum around the racing secretary's office at the Rhode Island tracks. "Oh, Mother of God, I kissed the ground when he went on that judging," Mrs. DeSpirito says.

Maybe the late Tony DeSpirito was never scared out there himself, but he terrified the women in his family. They knew he was just a hard-luck kid. Even when he and Doris had bad arguments, when they had fights about his women, she would cry, "Tony, Tony, don't ever leave to ride before you kiss me good-bye."

His mother was even more scared. It was good that she didn't know he was planning another comeback. Mrs. DeSpirito went down as low as 72 pounds after Barbara died, and she says that after Tony died, "I'd have gone to the booby hatch" if she hadn't had Barbara's three boys to take care of, to occupy her.

They are tiny people, the DeSpiritos. In the mornings, when the grandchildren are at school, they sit around the living room and smoke cigarettes and watch the game shows. In the afternoon, when the boys come home, it is livelier around the house, jumping and noisy again, almost exactly as it must have been with their own three kids twenty-five years ago before Tony quit school and went to Rock.

He was getting ready to start all over again this summer. He had been itchy when he was sitting in high school, and now he was itchy sitting in a puff job where they give you a pair of binoculars, call you an official, and then you play second fiddle to a television camera. Of course he wanted to come back. You cannot expect an athlete to swear off performing. Reporters clustered around Shoemaker after his Belmont, but they didn't have all day because he was up in the ninth race, too, some inconsequential allowance route. They asked him why he kept on riding. "I enjoy what I'm doing," he replied, easy enough. "I love it."

A couple of days later, at Lincoln Downs, a jock named Norman Mercier, who has been riding about as long as Shoemaker, although you never once heard of him, came back after winning the first race, $1,500 claiming maidens. Why did DeSpirito keep on trying to ride? "How many people have a job which they really love what they're doing?" Norman Mercier said. "That's why I'm still here. That was what Tony lived for." It's the same with Shoemaker.

All the time, as he worked as an official at the tracks, DeSpirito would get away now and then and go down to the jocks' room to have coffee with the other boys. He was a quiet man, sometimes moody. The other jocks, even the kids who knew little but the legend, always deferred to him and liked him because he never put on airs even though "he had been to the races and back."

In a TV world of superlatives, of greats and alls, dynasties and supers, athletes themselves tend to go the other way, to employ the most prosaic language to indicate the extreme. Thus, in team sports, the greatest compliment an athlete can pay another is to say that he is "a player." At the tracks, making the big time is merely "going to the races." And this in the jocks' room at Lincoln:

"Oh, Tony was a rider," says one.

"Tony was a *race* rider," says another.

And that is precisely what the late Tony DeSpirito was. Other people, though, always expect athletes to move on to other things. Why? Because we are envious that they get to keep on playing games? If Willie Shoemaker wants to ride until he's 60, what's it to us? Why shouldn't the kid try to come back? "In Tony's mind there was never any doubt that he was the greatest rider who ever lived," says Bob Aiello. "Never a doubt." So what is making weight and a bad back when you feel that way about the one thing you can do in life? DeSpirito began to jog and bicycle to get fit. He figured to break in at Calder in Miami this summer. He prepared to move out of his apartment, the one he died in. "Well, I guess I'll go back to the whites," he told a couple of friends, and proudly.

DeSpirito had been feeling poorly off and on. He spent a couple of weeks in the hospital last winter. He would run a temperature, and they couldn't figure out why. Also, strong as he always was, there was an irony. "The one thing he couldn't ever do was ride steady, steady, steady, seven, eight, nine races a day like a lot of guys can," says Pee Wee Gervais. But there was no inkling, no premonition of death. If anything, DeSpirito was actually looking ahead for once in his life. He was going back to the whites and he was going to try to get Doris to come back with him, too.

He would always barge into her house as if they were still married, come in, make himself a J&B, use the phone, take over. One of the last times he came by, Doris was up in the bathroom, coloring her hair. That didn't stop him. He got all three kids together, and they went up and talked to her. She knew exactly what he was doing; he was trying to make it all a real family again — the five of them, Doris and Tony, Donna, Rosemarie, and Mark. The kids had told her that their father was trying to enlist their support to help get her interested in remarrying him. Doris says he even bought her a big two-pound box of chocolates once, "like a kid on a first date." In the bathroom, as she went on coloring her hair, he suddenly blurted out, "You know, Doris, you did a wonderful job of bringing these kids up." He had never said that before.

But he was going back to the whites, and if he could get his nice girl back, too, why everything would be just like before, when he was so very young, standing on the threshold of being the greatest rider of all time. But of course he was 39 now, fighting weight and all the injuries, the bad back. The kid couldn't come back, not really. But maybe just a winner every now and then to tease him: *And here comes Tony DeSpirito on the outside, flying like the wind!*

He had no chance of getting Doris back. But it's kind that he never learned that. He wouldn't have understood, anyway. Doris was never an athlete. She never had a year. She had a family instead and is salaried, and she has grown up since it snowed in Niagara Falls.

The Best
Against the Best
at Their Best

1986

As they approached the tee at the seventy-second hole, Alfie Fyles, Tom Watson's caddie, spoke up. "Go for the jugular," he said, and Watson broke a small grin and nodded his head and asked for his one-iron. This was it, at last; this would be the final hole in what, even then, people were calling the greatest golf match ever. Watson had gone head to head with Jack Nicklaus — the young lion, the challenger of this decade, versus the golfer of the ages — in the first British Open ever played on the Ailsa course at Turnberry, on the Ayrshire coast of Scotland, by the Firth of Clyde, off the North Channel of the Irish Sea. It was July of 1977; Nicklaus was 37, still in his prime, and Watson was 27, the new Masters champion, just coming into his.

On this last hole, Watson's tee shot drifted a bit left, but still clear of the bunker that sat 260 yards out. It was "awfully perfect," said Watson, so Nicklaus didn't hesitate.

For the first time on this hole he yanked out his driver and called up his power. It was incredible what he and Watson had done: identical 68–70s the first two days, matching 65s the third day, playing almost stroke for stroke together the final two rounds, pushing each other higher and higher, driving the gallery into a happy frenzy. They were a shot apart coming to the last hole, but still, either one of them could *ten*-putt the eighteenth green and finish runner-up. The winner's 268 would be the best score in British Open history by eight strokes. Two men had never played golf like this before, side by side.

The instant Nicklaus finished his swing he knew he had tried too hard and had hit the ball too full. The eighteenth fairway bent left just past the bunker Watson had missed, and Nicklaus wanted his drive to drift that way. Unfortunately his drives had been sailing to the right all day, and once again his tee shot flew that way, through the crook in the fairway, into rough as deep as there was anywhere on the course. Nicklaus turned the driver in his hand like a baton, took the offending club end, and banged the handle down angrily to the turf as he stomped off the tee. To think it would end like this. It had to finish in glory. Nobody should *lose* this match. He or Watson, either one, OK, but this was a match one of them had to *win.*

Watson walked over to check on Nicklaus's lie. At first he wasn't sure that the ball was even playable; it was buried deep in tall grass, only inches from a prickly strand of gorse. Would Jack be able to bring a club back, much less muscle the ball out? Watson decided Nicklaus would just be able to negotiate a swing, and he returned to his own ball, which lay perhaps 180 yards from the pin.

"What do you think?" he asked Alfie. The caddie fingered the seven-iron. Watson stared at him quizzically.

"What? You know I can only carry one-sixty, one-sixty-five with a *six.*"

"The way your adrenaline's pumpin', Tom. . . ." was all Alfie said, and his man took the seven. Watson hit it full-blooded to the pin, thirty inches from the cup.

It surely must be over now.

Nicklaus grasped his eight-iron. He took it back right through a branch of the gorse bush, macheted it down with a superhuman swat, and sent the ball and a massive divot flying out. Somehow the ball found the right side of the green, thirty-two feet from the flag. It was impossible. Right away Watson knew — *knew* — that Nicklaus was going to make that putt for a birdie.

Nicklaus strode off. Barely had he turned heel than the Scots rushed over and reverently began dropping coins in the gash in the ground where Nicklaus's ball had lain, bribing the god of chance for a good putt. Pennies went onto the spot, twopenny coins, tenpenny pieces, even some old shillings. The pile began to resemble those cartoons of the pot of gold at the end of the rainbow.

Watson tried to fight his way through the rabble that swarmed onto the fairway. People were scrambling, bumping, tussling. Alfie got knocked down, pitched full forward. At the last moment he reached out and broke his fall, but he strained his left wrist, and as Watson broke through the mob, he looked back and was shocked to see his caddie's wrist already swelling. Until then, Alfie had been a pretty fair player himself, "a bit of a hustler." But even after the knot went down, the wrist stayed stiff, and he never again played a hole of golf. Alfie has carried, all told, for six victorious British Opens, and no other caddie has won more than half as many. After being so close to the perfection of those two men those days at Turnberry, maybe it was meant that no mortal should himself ever play again.

Nicklaus studied his putt, right to left, down into a dip and up. It was thirty-two feet on the seventy-second hole of the British Open, with his rival lying less than a yard from the hole. Watson turned to Alfie and whispered, "You know, I believe Jack'll make this." Alfie looked at Watson as if he were mad. "I *expect* him to make this," Watson declared.

"Fine, and so you can make yours."

"Mmmm," was all Watson said back. If Nicklaus birdies, thirty inches looks like thirty miles.

Nicklaus struck the ball and started it on its path. Even before it was halfway, Alfie could see that Watson was right. Impossibly, incredibly, it was a birdie. "Good god," Alfie thought. "Tom's dead right. The bloody ball is going into the hole."

Although the British Open was first played in 1860, only fifteen courses have been used in the rotation — what the British call the "rota." Turnberry has long been generally recognized as the best links on Scotland's west coast, but not until 1977 had it ever been tapped for the Open. Part of this was circumstance, for Turnberry — *Tonbrrry,* the Scots say — though only fifty miles from Glasgow, is isolated down the coast, with the only close lodging at the Turnberry Hotel itself. The hotel is a magnificent old building, built on a hill, looking out onto the golf course below and the firth beyond, its long, burnt-red roof visible from almost everywhere on the links except, perhaps, from the depths of the sixty-six well-like bunkers that are scattered around the course.

Inconvenience aside, Turnberry would surely have entered the rota earlier, except that twice it had to go to battle. In the Great War it served as a flight training station for the Royal Flying Corps and Commonwealth Flying Units, and then in World War II it was all but ripped apart and reassembled as an air base, with eighteen-inch-deep runways laid down where the Scots had hit second shots out of the fescue and buttercups. After World War II, when the whole useless place — hotel and acreage, the lot of it — could have been had for £10,000, the course was knitted back together. Now only here and there do bits and pieces of tarmac remain alongside the gorse. Otherwise, all that is left of Turnberry's noble other life is the monument on the knoll overlooking the twelfth green, on which the names of the brave lads who flew off from the old links, never to return, are listed. Besides the English and the Scots, there were Aussies, South Africans, Americans, and Canadians.

The Turnberry lighthouse stands just a fairway beyond the monument. By all that is holy in British golf, the courses ordained for the Open must lie by the sea, on sandy soil the land has reclaimed from the god Neptune. These are the undulating links courses, literally linking those two realms of nature that make up God's blue-green earth. Curiously, though, while St. Andrews and Muirfield, Carnoustie and Royal Troon — all the fabled Scottish links — reside by the sea, they are folded into the land in such a way that the sense of water can be lost. Turnberry alone is one with the deep. From the fourth hole to the eleventh, the course clings to the firth coastline like a wet suit, and from almost everywhere on the course wee boats are visible below the dunes, with whitecaps breaking and winds blowing trenchant and briny.

On the best of days it's possible to see beyond the Mull of Kintyre, all the way to Ulster in Northern Ireland. The greater, looming presence, however, always belongs to Ailsa Craig, ten miles out at sea and 1,113 feet high. It is a massive rock that stands at the mouth of the firth as if it were the helmet top of a monster Norse warrior god who will, if piqued, finally bestir himself from the sea floor, then stomp across the links and the heather.

The Scots say, "If ye can see Ailsa Craig, it's gaun to rain. If ye canna see it, it's already raining." The Scots also say, "If it's nae rain and it's nae wind, it's nae golf," and while that obtains on any links, Turnberry is the model. On the odd day when there is no wind, without what is known as the Tonbrrry Giant, the course, sans trees and tricks, is defanged. Like some large, toothless animal, it could still box your ears and gum you something fierce, but it could never take a bite as big as an 85 out of Gary Player's hide, as it did at a tournament in 1972 when the Giant blew in. In that tournament, as the wind picked up round by round, Peter Townsend posted a progressively revealing 65–70–75–80. The next year, during the same tournament, a huge hospitality tent was lifted clean off its moorings and blown away. There have been days at Turnberry when rain, hail, sleet, and snow have arrived sequentially, each at gale force, and at times the Giant howls so ferociously that fairways cannot be reached with a driver. On most parts of Turnberry the gorse has been tilted over by the prevailing winds, left as if it were cowering in fear.

But the wind lay still in the summer of '77 when Nicklaus and Watson arrived. Everything was askew. The previous two summers had been absurdly hot and dry, and then that winter there had been too little moisture, which further inhibited growth. At that time, too, a bizarre Scottish heat wave swept in, discombobulating man and sheep. In the gallery, many of the Scotsmen went without shirts, their unaccustomed bare skin glowing a bright pink. This being the land of wool and cashmere, there literally wasn't a T-shirt to be found, and some of the fans actually stripped to their underwear. Ailsa Craig shimmered like some misplaced Club Med isle.

Into this alien Scotland came Nicklaus, who was posted as the 6-to-1 favorite even if he was suffering what, for him, had been a regular depression. Although he had been the PGA Player of the Year the past two years, he had actually gone six majors in a row without a victory. To help put an end to this nonsense, Nicklaus eschewed the use of a British caddie and brought with him his American aide, Angelo Argea, an imposing man with silver steel-wool hair and a menacing, mustachioed countenance.

The affable Alfie Fyles came up from near Liverpool to — as his fading ilk still puts it — caddie *to* Watson. Alfie had caddied to Gary Player for more than a decade before shifting his allegiance to the young Watson two years before. It was a fortuitous pairing. Watson had been tagged a choker by captious critics, but though he arrived at Carnoustie in '75 too late for a practice round, he won his first major title there — in a playoff, to boot. Given that Watson was in a strange land, unprepared, accomplishing something he had never managed under the best of circumstances back home, Alfie assumed that he must have played a role of some consequence indeed in the young Yank's triumph.

British caddies have always presumed a more significant, distinguished role than their American counterparts, who, often as not, have been viewed as little more than necessities, on the same order, say, as pinsetters in a bowling alley. British caddies have always had their opinions solicited, and usually valued, even by the grandest and most savvy of golfers. For one thing, the elements are forever shifting in Britain. But much of the status of caddies has to do with the differences between the two societies. In America it's considered beneath oneself to labor as an athletic domestic, yet the British, comfortable with the gentleman-servant relationship, saw that men could make an honorable career out of toting other men's bags. Except for time out as a seaman in the Royal Navy, Alfie has caddied for about half a century.

Alas, there are fewer such stalwarts all the time. Long John, the Wasp, the Lawyer, the one-armed Wingy Eugene, the similarly handicapped Halifax Wingy (who lost his hook in some heavy rough once), Johnny One-Blank (who did have all his limbs but lacked an eye), Mad Mac, Laughing Boy, Yorky Billy have all gone. And disappearing just as rapidly is the caddie's Cockney argot, which featured a rhyming code. A Vera Lynn, for example, meant a gin, a Gregory Peck a check. A beehive was a five (usually used in association with cherry picker, which meant a knicker, which was itself a slang word for pound; thus a caddie with a beehive cherry picker had a £5 note). And St. Louis Blues was shoes, Holy Ghost was toast, and sizzle and strife meant the missus.

But the career boys are a dying breed. "All you've got is your bag-carriers now," Alfie sneers. "All they can do is give the golfer a weather report — not the right club." Nothing sets Alfie's blood to boiling more than the familiar sight of a man who calls himself a caddie throwing grass up in the air to detect the wind direction. In Alfie's view, you might as well have a homing pigeon asking a bobby to show him the way back to the house. "Once it was all eyeball," he explains. Caddying is telling your man to use a seven-iron to carry 180 yards when the most he can hit a six is 165. That is caddying, eyeball.

And in a world today where Americans expect to have a little piece of home wherever they go — the English language and the baseball scores, McDonald's and MasterCard — most American pros bring their caddies over to Scotland for greater security. Watson and Alfie are the exception. And even they had one great falling out, right at the beginning, after Alfie eyeballed Watson to his first major, at Carnoustie in '75. When he went up to the Watsons' room to get his pay, Alfie was so furious at the figure Watson gave him that he threw the Gregory Peck down on the floor. "You must need this more than me," he snapped. Linda Watson was livid, and Alfie told Watson to have her leave, that he worked for Tom, not for his wife. But Watson wouldn't budge, so Alfie picked the check off the floor — "before Tom could take me literally" — and left in disgust.

The next summer Watson brought his American caddie over to help him defend his title at Royal Birkdale, and he missed the 54-hole cut. Both the Watsons began to seek rapprochement after that, and Alfie was waiting for Watson when the Yank arrived at Turnberry. They've been together every July since then, and Watson has the finest British Open record — five championships — of any American.

In 1977 it wasn't until Friday, the third round — when Nicklaus and Watson were first paired together — that they began to outdistance the field. Indeed, when they started off that midday, both having shot par 70s the morning before, they were a stroke behind Roger Maltbie, and there were sixteen contenders within four shots of the lead.

But on that third day Nicklaus and Watson would both shoot 65s — six birdies and a bogey apiece — and on Saturday they would move off into a realm by themselves. The pattern was set at the first hole, too, when Nicklaus struck a wedge to within three feet and made a birdie. Always, over the last two days, Nicklaus would draw ahead and Watson would fight back. On Friday, Nicklaus was two strokes ahead, playing the eighth hole, called Goat Fell, when the overcast skies turned electric. Both men were on the green, but Watson wanted to take cover immediately.

Nicklaus, the senior, prevailed, though, and Watson reluctantly went along, but as soon as they both putted out, parring, the golfers and their caddies scurried down to find shelter among the rocks on the beach. Only when they were protected by an overhang did it occur to Alfie that water made the best conductor, so back up the cliff they hustled to take refuge in a BBC trailer. Watson and Nicklaus didn't say much to each other, but rarely does either talk on the course. When the storm passed they put on sweaters and proceeded to the forbidding ninth tee, the one stuck out on an overlook, the one that Herbert Warren Wind has described as "out of a Gothic novel."

They both parred there and sank long birdie putts on ten. Nicklaus took his only bogey of the round with a bad putt on fourteen, and when Watson sank a twenty-footer on fifteen, they were level once again. Nicklaus should have gained a stroke on seventeen, but he missed an eagle putt and, like Watson, had to endure a mere bird. Both parred eighteen. Nicklaus 31–34, Watson 33–32. Both: 203 for fifty-four holes, seven under par.

Curiously, it still wasn't viewed strictly as a duel. There was Ben Crenshaw, of whom great things were expected, only three shots back, at 206. Nicklaus was near the height of his powers, but even if Watson had won at Carnoustie in '75 and had edged Nicklaus at the Masters three months earlier, there remained something unsubstantial about him. In time Watson would tote up eight majors, but the "quitter" charge still lingered then with Watson, as even now he is being written off early, after only two years of struggling. "It has the same flavor," he says, biting off the words. Pause. "The same smell." Then, too, even at his best, Watson was neither awesome nor mysterious, and while he was invariably described as having "a Huck Finn look," Huck's playful, mischievous aspect was missing. Besides, the British had never held it against Nicklaus, the way the Americans did, that he eclipsed Palmer, so there were more cheers for Jack.

Nobody knew then how great a force Watson would become in the British Isles. "Tom's a good thinker," Nicklaus says, "and you have to think well over there to win. You're playing in adverse conditions, and there are just a lot of our guys who can't do that for seventy-two holes."

Watson would also develop a peculiar facility for playing his best down the stretch against Nicklaus — better even than emotional characters like Trevino and Palmer, who could sway a crowd. In his entire career, Nicklaus says, "my hardest loss" remains the '82 U.S. Open, when Watson beat him straight up by chipping in from off the seventeenth at Pebble Beach. Watson never let Nicklaus's majesty intimidate him. Three months before Turnberry, at the Masters, playing in adjacent twosomes, Watson was on the thirteenth fairway when he saw Nicklaus raise his putter toward him after he sank a birdie on the green ahead, as if to say, *Take this.* In fact, Nicklaus was only exulting, but Watson upbraided him for his seeming hot-dog action as soon as they encountered each other off the last green. Nicklaus, stunned, didn't have the foggiest idea what he was being accused of, and Watson finally backed off, embarrassed but undaunted.

Watson is not an easy man to characterize. Principled and sensitive, he also bears the rap of being a know-it-all. He is one of the few athletes left who still smoke. While most other golfers play out of planned Sunbelt subdivisions, Watson went off to Stanford to school and has returned to his native Kansas City to celebrate his family, the Royals, and the seasons. Some days in January or February, he's the only person playing at the Kansas City Country Club. "It's cleansing," he says. After that, Turnberry and the other links may not seem quite so beastly.

The fans at Turnberry were jostling for places when the two men teed off in the final pairing late Saturday morning. It was a bright, sunny day, but for the first time all week a brisk wind was coming steadily, broadside off the firth. Nicklaus wore a pale yellow sweater with dark blue slacks, while Watson chose a sea-green sport shirt, which he wore with checked light-green-and-orange trousers and a wide, white belt that was the fashion at that time.

It's funny, looking back. Today, at 36, Watson is nearly the age that Nicklaus was then. Watson now appears, naturally, older than he did in 1977. The Huck Finn business is behind him. Plus, looking back, that wide, white belt locates him firmly in time. On the other hand, Nicklaus, a renowned 46 now, looks almost the same as he did in '77. Examining the old pictures, and then studying the men today, one gets the impression that Nicklaus has stood still for a decade while Watson has been catching up.

On this occasion Nicklaus and Watson were playing a final round *together* for the first time, and it almost appeared decided on the second hole, named Mak Siccar, when Nicklaus sank a ten-footer for a birdie and Watson, playing indifferently from off the green, bogeyed. A two-stroke swing. Nicklaus went up three just two holes later, when he rolled in a twenty-footer at Woe-be-Tide. But Watson remained foolish enough to think he could still win. "In 'eighty-two, the time I beat Jack at Pebble Beach, I was lucky," he says. "I was driving the ball all over, but the gallery packed down the rough, and I knew the course. Turnberry was different. It had an element of a Texas summer to it and I was the same way — very calm inside the boiler, so to speak. I could feel the heat, but only as if it were around me."

As for Nicklaus, even if he was three strokes ahead, he wasn't taking anything for granted. "If I'm playing Tom Watson, I know I have to win," he says. "With somebody else against you, maybe you feel they'll lose instead."

And sure enough, Watson steadied and started to fight back. On the fifth, Fin' me Oot, he hit a five-iron to sixteen feet and popped it in. Never again would there be a three-stroke margin, although there could have been on the very next hole, Tappie Toorie, a long par-3, for Watson put his three-wood in a bunker. He splashed out to six feet and eyed the putt nervously. Nicklaus had his par assured. Then Watson asked Alfie for his opinion. In all their British Opens together — before and since — this was the only occasion when Watson, one of the finest putters of his era, ever asked Alfie for help on the green.

Shaking, Alfie stood behind his man and allowed that it seemed to him that it would break left at the last. It did just that. "Good line," was all Watson said as they walked off to seven, the 528-yard Roon the Ben. The tee there is elevated, the beach almost straight down, sixty feet below. Both drove to the left, but Nicklaus drove well beyond Watson, leaving himself only a three-iron. Watson pondered his plight. "What do you think, Alfie?" he asked.

"Everything you got, Tom."

"A driver?"

"If you can lift it."

"Yeah, OK," Watson said, and he took out the driver, used it on the fairway, and put the ball on the green — "my best shot of the day." And it was he, not Nicklaus, who made birdie. He had two of the three strokes back.

On the eighth he got the tie. It was a twenty-foot putt, dead center. "It was lucky," Watson says. "It had the line but not the touch. If I had missed at all, it would have gone six, seven feet by."

Except for the wives and girlfriends and accountants of the other golfers, there wasn't a fan on the course who wasn't in the last gallery. They kicked up such a dust cloud chasing down the ninth fairway that Nicklaus fought his way over to Watson and said, "Tom, this is getting out of hand." The junior man agreed, so Nicklaus went to the gallery marshals, and the two players sat down on their bags for several minutes until the crowd was brought to heel. The damn thing was getting like a football match at Wembley.

Maybe the disruption upset the golfers. The picturesque ninth was, in sum, their worst of the thirty-six holes they played with one another, Watson taking a bogey, Nicklaus only saving par with a twelve-foot putt. And then, just like that, when Nicklaus sank a twenty-foot birdie putt on twelve, under the monument, the great champion was two ahead again, and there were only six holes left.

So, OK, Watson broke serve right back. On the difficult two-tiered elevated green at the thirteenth, Tickly Tap, Watson ran in a twelve-footer, and now he was only a stroke back and the crowd was beside itself again, reinvigorated, scurrying this way and that down the sides of the fourteenth fairway, so that Watson, with the honor, had to pause before he hit his drive.

Watson did get a squeak at the hole on fourteen, but he missed his seven-footer, and they went to fifteen with Nicklaus still one stroke ahead. It's the last par-3, 209 yards, Ca Canny, which means Go Very Carefully, bunkered on the left, with a great drop off the right of the green. Predictably, the flag for the final day had been put far right, too, and so Watson played prudently to the left, but his ball drifted too far that way, off the green, between two traps. "Damn," said Watson after the shot. Nicklaus instantly realized he could absolutely, finally, put Watson away, and he went for the stick. He hit right on line, too, with an uphill putt for a reasonable birdie try and a two- or maybe three-stroke lead.

Though he was well off the green, Watson took his putter. He practiced this sort of shot regularly — the old "Texas wedge" — and, in fact, he had also already played a similar easier version off the twelfth green. Here, he was a full sixty feet away, but he hit much too hard, about seventy feet's worth. Only the cup got in the way. Slam dunk. Watson jumped high in the air. Somehow, Alfie had the presence of mind to glance over at Nicklaus. He was just reaching down to put his ball back on his mark when Watson's ball swooped in, and Nicklaus literally rocked back, as if he had been coldcocked. More even than any of the great shots he himself hit at Turnberry, this is the one Nicklaus best remembers to this day. And when he missed his own putt they were tied again.

The Scottish sky would hold the light for hours yet, till 11:00 or so, and just now, late in the afternoon, for the first time was it starting to slant low. Standing on the sixteenth tee, Watson felt the rays on his freckled face, and he sensed the moment, what he and Nicklaus were doing, and he couldn't help himself. He couldn't help but smile, and when he did, he turned to Nicklaus and he said, "This is what it's all about, isn't it?"

Nicklaus smiled back beatifically, and then they both struck magnificent drives and strode off down the fairway. They both liked it that they were head to head, *mano a mano,* in the manner of most other sports, where your opponent is more flesh and blood and not the turf and the trees. Nicklaus dolefully recalled his second British Open, at Royal Lytham in 1963, when, standing on the eighteenth tee, he could see Phil Rodgers and Bob Charles come off sixteen; he didn't hear any cheers so he assumed they had both parred, and he played it safe on the last hole — only to lose by a stroke to Charles because, in fact, both Charles and Rodgers had birdied sixteen, but the wind was blowing the other way and had carried the cheers off with it.

Nicklaus and Watson were still tied after sixteen, Wee Burn. Seventeen, Lang Whang, the short par-5, was an obvious birdie hole, the one where Nicklaus should have had an eagle the day before. As was the pattern, Watson drove straight down the middle while Nicklaus went a bit right. Watson then unloaded a three-iron, which rolled around in a ringlet, ending up only twelve feet away for a chance at an eagle.

And that was when Nicklaus gave way. He was the one who made the kind of shot everybody else in the field had been making all four days. He botched a four-iron. It stayed right and, while it did stop a few yards short of a bunker, it left him in the scarred rough, fifty feet or so to a green that sloped away, five or six feet below. For the first time, Watson arrived at a green as if he were stalking it, and realizing how difficult his rival's plight was, he turned to his caddie and uncharacteristically cracked, "I've put a nail in his coffin now, haven't I, Alfie?"

So Nicklaus promptly played a perfect chip, running the ball out of the rough, down to within four feet of the pin, and then Watson, shaken, missed his eagle try. They were both putting for routine birdies in order to go to the seventy-second even.

It was Jack Nicklaus who missed his.

He played it to break, but it went right through the break, a hair to the left.

And that was when Alfie said, "Go for the jugular," and Watson took out his one-iron. At last, after seventy-one holes, at last he had the lead, and Jack Nicklaus was in his lee.

Minutes later, though, Watson's premonition that Nicklaus would sink his birdie putt at eighteen proved to be correct, and the roars of amazement reached a crescendo even before Nicklaus's ball tumbled in for his birdie: 68–70–65–66, eleven under. The nearest competitor besides Watson was Hubert Green at one under; and no one else had ever shot better than four under in 105 other British Opens. Only, of course, if Watson sank his two-and-a-half-footer, if he made his birdie, he would finish 68–70–65–65, twelve under.

Watson did not hesitate. He could not let the crowd rule. "All right, I'm ready to win this thing now," he said to himself, and he sized up the putt as Nicklaus raised his arms to quiet the mob. Still there were, in fact, the odd lingering whistles and sighs when Watson brought his putter forward and tapped the ball firmly. Alfie watched. It was not short. Tom Watson was never short then. It was not straight either.

But it was straight enough.

The ball plunked into the right side of the cup, and the greatest golf battle ever was over. Watson raised his hands to the crowds, putter high, and he was almost dazed when Alfie reached his man and embraced him. Then, there was Nicklaus before him, looking Watson square in the eye and telling him, "I'm tired of giving it my best and not having it be good enough."

Watson was almost too stunned to reply. "Thanks," was all he could manage. Remembering that, still a bit ashamed at how tongue-tied he had been, Watson drew on a Winston and shook his head. "I'm not very good at words in situations like that." But Nicklaus had understood. He put his arm around Watson's shoulders, squeezed him affectionately about his neck, and escorted him off the green that way, as if he were the winner and Watson the vanquished.

Then at the ceremony, Nicklaus said in public, so graciously, what he had first said to Watson alone. "I gave you my best shot," the greatest player said, "and it just wasn't good enough. You were better." And then, too, a final, very British understatement: "It was well played." The Mona Lisa was well painted. Hamlet was well written.

A day's work done, Nicklaus went to dinner. His memories of Turnberry are not nearly so vivid as Watson's. "I couldn't take you around that course if I had to," he says. But then, he figures he has played 500 courses. "I just don't remember a whole lot when I lose. But you've got to understand: I don't remember a whole lot about the ones I win, either; only, when I win people keep bringing them up, so I'm not allowed to forget. But what's to say here? I shot a sixty-five–sixty-six and another man shot a sixty-five–sixty-five. Well done." It's not Nicklaus but his wife, Barbara, who remembers how touched they were when they came into the dining room a bit later and the whole place, people at every table, rose and applauded him, the runner-up. Well done.

Watson, with Linda and a couple of friends, arrived a few minutes later, and once more the entire dining room rose and applauded. Watson went over to Nicklaus and spoke briefly to him. He came back to his own table and said he had told Nicklaus "what a wonderful speech Jack gave." Linda hurried to assure her husband that he had given a fine speech, too. "No, my speech was awful," Watson said, and he shrugged. He had forgotten, perhaps, how eloquent he had been on the sixteenth tee. That *was* what it was all about, wasn't it?

Then, when dinner was finished, Watson went into a small ballroom where a dance band was playing, and he walked over to the leader and requested a song. "It'll be 'Blue Skies,'" Linda said. And it was "Blue Skies." That was his father's favorite song. His father taught Tom to play golf. Tom took Linda in his arms and they danced to his father's song.

It was late, but the light lingered. The manager of the hotel had sent a bottle of champagne to the Watsons' room. They sipped it and talked of the wonders of this day. No matter what else Tom Watson would ever do in golf — and he would do much more — history had embraced him now, for he had beaten the best at his best, best to best.

The Watsons' room was on the top floor, and from there, under the red roof, with the last of the sun's rays falling behind the Mull of Kintyre, they could see down and across Turnberry. It was still below, except that here and there a Scotsman or two strolled the links, taking the unusual tropic air. It was as if the universe had been turned upside down, and dark was light and up was down and the people below were like stars sprinkled above in the heavens.

And then downstairs, outside on the promenade, a lone piper began to walk, playing his pipes, the Scottish melodies drifting up to where Tom and Linda sat drinking champagne. And they looked at each other and began to cry.

"I think it was at that time that I really fell in love with the game," Watson said, reminiscing. And now, just like that, just simply remembering, he began to mist up again. For a long time, then, he simply sat there, the tears welling up from the glorious days past into his eyes. He knew he was crying, he was told he was crying, and still he made no effort to brush away the tears.

"I'd always loved golf, but now it was a new type of love I could have," he said, and without disturbing them he let the tears keep rolling down his cheeks so that they could reflect the memories of Turnberry past, tinting them with his pride and joy.

*   *   *

I wrote the story of the Nicklaus-Watson duel almost a decade after it happened, and I chose to write it without revealing the winner till the end of the piece, because even though it was about a British Open, I was fairly confident that, except for dyed-in-the-wool golf fans, the vast majority of people who read the story wouldn't remember who won. I came to that decision when they asked me to do the story and I couldn't remember who won.

This next piece, about Jimmy Connors's growing up, infuriated Jimmy when he read it. The story came out just before the 1978 U.S. Open, and Connors punished me by refusing to talk to the other members of the press who were covering the Open. About two years later, I was sitting in the Palm Court of the Plaza Hotel, when an old friend and associate of Gloria Connors's approached me. He just wanted to tell me, he said, that while Mrs. Connors also hated the story when she read it the first time, she eventually came to appreciate it and to see herself better for it. I consider that especially high praise.

Raised by Women to Conquer Men

1978

A man who has been the indisputable favorite of his mother keeps for life the feeling of conqueror, the confidence of success which often induces real success.
— *Sigmund Freud*

JIMMY CONNORS was the indisputable favorite of his grandmother as well, and so, he is most abundantly infused with this magic milk. It surges through his veins, suppressing every doubt and every defeat. And why not? The two women had promised him the world, and, just so, he grasped it in 1974: only 21, but already champion of all he surveyed, Alexander astride Bucephalus astride the globe. He won the Wimbledon final with the loss of but six games, Forest Hills with the loss of but two. Wise men in tennis sat about and seriously contemplated whether he would win every major title for, say, the next decade.

Conqueror was what he was, too, because Connors did not merely win. He assaulted the opposition, laid waste to it, often mocked it, as well, simply by the force of his presence. The other players feared to go against him, because the most awesome legend that can surround any athlete sprang up about Connors: The better any mortal played against him, the better Connors became. So, he became invincible upon the court, because no man could beat him, and he was inviolate off the court, because his mother had told him so.

Two months ago, on July 8, Connors lost the 1978 Wimbledon final, winning only seven games against an ascendant Bjorn Borg. Since 1974 Connors has played in seven major finals and lost six.

What has happened is disillusioning for Connors and his mother. They speak of the latest rack and ruin by Borg in hallucinatory terms, and Jimmy fitfully retreats to the glorious conquests of yore: "They'll be talking about 'seventy-four when I'm dead. . . . Don't forget what I did in 'seventy-four. . . . Nobody can ever take 'seventy-four from me." On and on like that. And the greatest irony is that '74 will be devalued if he does not triumph over Borg in '78, because this year Borg can win the Grand Slam and the Davis Cup — and as extraordinary as '74 was, Connors did not achieve that. For history, then, what would '74 become but a real good year a kid had just before Borg became great?

And that was so long ago — 1974. Since then Connors's father has died, and his surrogate father — his manager, Bill Riordan — has become estranged from him. His only male instructor, Pancho Segura, has been discharged. His engagement to Chris Evert, the one sweet love of his life, was called off, nearly at the altar. Looking back, it all began to unravel then, the loss of dear ones and tournaments alike. A kind of incompleteness has come to plague Connors. In the big tournaments, the ones he shoots for, he virtually never loses until the finals. What is it there? What seizes him at the last step? There is a flaw somewhere, something that denies him consummation in his life.

"It happened so fast," Chris Evert says. Oddly, she and Jimmy have matured more in the difficult ways of their love than they have as players in a simple game. "There was no emotional foundation, nothing to fall back on," Evert says. "You must never forget that he made Number One when he was twenty-one, and now he's not Number One. That makes him so defensive. You see, he's still a champion. He isn't Number One, but he hasn't lost the qualities of a champion."

In retrospect, Arthur Ashe may have dismantled the invincible Jimbo by upsetting him in the 1975 Wimbledon final. Although he won Forest Hills in 1976, Connors has never really been the same since. In the months before the Ashe match, in the period after Jimmy and Chrissie broke up, Connors had already begun to self-destruct — ballooning in weight, running imperiously over good people and firm obligations. But by Wimbledon time he was

primed, and all the more forbidding for the callousness he had displayed.

Now rampant upon the court, he did not lose a set in the early
matches at Wimbledon. In the semifinals he came up against Ros-
coe Tanner, who has the best service in the game. That day Tanner
was serving at his very best — yet Connors obliterated him 6–4,
6–1, 6–4. *New York Times* correspondent Fred Tupper, an able —
and restrained — tennis authority for several decades, wrote in
awe, "Did anybody ever see a ball hit so hard? . . . Connors'
performance today staggers the imagination and confuses the
memory."

Incredibly, Connors rose to this majesty despite a secret leg injury — something called an interior compartment syndrome —
which he had suffered in his opening match. After beating Tanner,
Connors went to Chelsea Hospital, and as he lay on the examination table, the doctors called Riordan aside and told him that the
damage to the leg was growing dangerous, and the final could only
be played at the risk of crippling Connors, perhaps of ending his
career. Riordan broke the news to Connors, who replied that it was
the final of Wimbledon and he had to play. Riordan then turned to
leave, and Connors called plaintively to him.

"Bill," he said, "don't tell Mom."

Connors and his mother shared a hotel room (they are as frugal
as they are close). She knew he was going for treatments, but not
that he was putting his playing life — the one she had created for
him — on the line.

Ashe beat him badly. There was no evidence that Connors was
at a physical disadvantage, but he played as if in a daze. Ashe
changed his style for the match, as Borg would come up with new
tricks for him years later — but Connors could not, or would not,
adjust. There were no alibis afterward. There never are. Although
often crude and ill-mannered upon the court, Connors is almost
always a gracious sportsman once the game is done. But Ashe had
belled the cat. The conqueror that the mother and the grandmother had carefully fashioned was exposed. Riordan, who did not
tell Mom, was banished by the end of the summer; Chrissie and
Segura were already gone. And also departing soon enough was
that unshakable confidence, the mystical armor his mother had
spent a childhood dressing him in.

Two months after the Ashe defeat, Connors lost another final, to

Manolo Orantes at Forest Hills. By now he was indulging himself with groupies and food, taking both to excess. Under tension, Connors gorges himself. At tournaments, *in training*, he will devour four or five large meals a day. At that time, in '75, lost and depressed, he gained thirty pounds. One day in Acapulco he saw himself in the mirror — "a spare tire, fat face; I only had slits for eyes." He reached for the phone. "After I called my mom, I lost eighteen pounds in the next two weeks," he says.

And so he started back; but something was never recovered from that night at Chelsea Hospital and the next afternoon on Centre Court. By this summer of 1978, even before he fell to Borg, other players had begun to see in Connors a pathetic parody of his old self. "Jimmy's always exuded such confidence," Ashe says, "and real or not, it seemed all the more intimidating because it was cocooned in that aura of bravado and brashness. But now even that seems specious. He's scared about something. I don't know what's happened, but he's not the same."

"The kid is psyched," says Riordan. At Wimbledon this year, Riordan took Borg at 7 to 1 to win in straight sets and cashed in big against his Jimbo.

Gloria Thompson Connors proudly points out that she and her mother are the only women ever to have developed a men's champion. Whatever more Jimmy achieves, theirs was an amazing accomplishment, and no one should be surprised at the obvious — at how much the mother lives for the son and how much he depends on her. Naturally, if this were not so, it never could have worked.

Of the other major influences upon Jimbo, Segura was merely brought in as a retainer, a male totem, to help Connors "think like a man" on the court, while Riordan was tapped as something of a necessary evil in the shattered times after the grandmother, Bertha Thompson, died in 1972. Bertha was known as Two Mom, a name bestowed on her by Johnny, the older of the two Connors children. Johnny had originally been cast as the future champion, but, as Gloria has noted many times, he lacked the requisite "guts." The second boy, the left-hander, did not. Eerily, it was Jimmy whom Gloria was carrying when she personally cut and cleared the land behind their house to build the tennis court that would give meaning to her life.

This sporting monument at 632 North Sixty-eighth Street, East St. Louis, Illinois, is now grown over, in disrepair. But then, so is the whole town run down, forgotten by the whites who abandoned it. But while East St. Louis was never fashionable, while it was always the other side, when Gloria Thompson was growing up there it was a well-kept blue-collar borough, the municipal manor of Mayor John T. Connors.

That was Jimmy's grandfather. Mayor Connors had one son, Big Jim, a good-looking, well-liked fellow of no particular abilities. He was sent off to Notre Dame and, back home, was provided with the sinecure of running the toll bridge that spanned the Mississippi into St. Louis at the other end of Sixty-eighth Street.

Gloria's father, Al Thompson, was chief of the city parks police. Hers was a disciplined, rock-ribbed upbringing. As the Connorses were open and genial, so were the Thompsons tight and skeptical, even suspicious. Jimmy Connors got his athletic genes from the maternal side. Al Thompson had been a middleweight boxer and a lifeguard, and when he and Two Mom were courting, they shared their love this way: He taught her to swim, she taught him to play tennis. They had one child, and the happiest times of Gloria's life were spent at Jones Park, which she recalls as a nearly idyllic place where she would swim in a sand-bottomed pool and then skip past a beautiful lagoon to the tennis courts. "Believe me," she declares earnestly, "I never went to a country club as nice as Jones Park." The remark is not offhand. Tennis was a country-club activity, and the Thompsons, the cop's family, insular by nature, grew even more defensive as tennis brought them into contact with the swells across the river.

Says a St. Louisan who has known the family for many years, "Gloria was taught, 'They're all out to get us,' and that's what she taught Jimmy. His mother is the only person he trusts. They're really not comfortable with anybody else. They have such over-powering loyalty to each other that they're incapable of any lasting outside relationships. Their own relationship is spooky. I swear, it's always been like there was a tube going from her veins into his." One of the first things mother and son bring up (independently) is that she can correct his game over the telephone merely by sensing what has gone awry.

Gloria was a fine athlete in her youth, but there was no evidence then of the drive and single-mindedness that would consume her on behalf of her son. Pauline Betz Addie, a world tennis champion in the mid-1940s, says, "It's impossible for me to believe these accounts of Gloria today — hard and mean. Never. She was the sweetest, most ingenuous, lovely person." She was pretty, too, a good catch. Surely no one in the world photographs worse than Gloria Connors. In fact, she is a lovely woman, gossamer feminine, all grace and poise. The good-timing mayor's boy, who had had his eye on Gloria since childhood, wooed her, married her, and they settled in the trim little red brick house on Sixty-eighth Street.

This marriage of opposites never worked. Big Jim died of cancer last year, and both Gloria and Jimmy stoutly uphold his memory, but from all objective accounts, theirs was a house divided by tennis. Big Jim learned of his son's engagement to Chrissie over the radio. When Jimmy won Wimbledon in '74, he couldn't be bothered to take his father's congratulatory phone call. Gloria explains it this way: "My husband enjoyed being around people in the evenings, and, of course, he had to take care of Johnny. We all had to sacrifice. You see, we more or less had to part ways if Jimmy was to play the tournaments he had to. Two Mom and I had a job to do."

Unlike that of Johnny, now a teaching pro in Atlanta, Jimmy's interest in competitive tennis never flagged. "I've been known as a pushy stage-door [sic] mother, but my biggest problem was to stop him from playing tennis," Gloria says. "He's always been the same. Why, he couldn't wait to kick the slats out of his playpen and get started in life. *But always a homebody.* Johnny would like to spend the night at other boys' houses. Not Jimmy. He was so happy just being in his own home. You know, he was so much like his grandmother especially. Why, we were a team. We were three peas in a pod."

Soon everything was devoted to Jimmy's tennis potential. It was Gloria's pleasure to become, as she describes it, "a human backboard." No detail was overlooked. On the boys' circuit, free tournament housing would be declined, and the team would spend money it really couldn't afford to spend to stay in a motel, so that Jimbo would not get chummy with the children he had to beat. In St. Louis, Gloria would transport him about to clubs, soliciting good adult players to hit with the child. Those who lacked the zeal for this pastime were dismissed as snobs. At the same time, those pros who took an interest in the boy and sought to help his game were suspected of trying to "steal" him from his mother.

Two Mom told Gloria, "Don't bring anybody else into the picture. You made him, Glo. Don't ever hand him over to anybody." If there is one thread that weaves most prominently through the whole fabric of the relationship, it is this one. And yet, contrary to what is generally assumed, Mrs. Connors does not appear to be motivated by selfishness. No, she is simply and utterly devoted to this son, and she is convinced that no one else can serve him so well as she.

"Yes sir, we fought it," Gloria says. "But if no one would play with Jimmy, *he had me.* I played him every day — every good day — of the year, every year. And we played hard. We taught him to be a tiger. 'Get those tiger juices flowing!' I would call out, and I told him to try and knock the ball down my throat, and he learned to do this because he found out that if I had the chance I would knock it down his. Yes sir. And then I would say, 'You see, Jimbo, you see what even your own mother will do to you on a tennis court?'"

Ah, but off the court he was pampered: bikes and go-carts, a pony. More important, he was spoiled emotionally, always shielded from life's little adversities. This arrangement remains in force to this day. Connors is about as difficult to reach as any public figure in the country; he has been protected for so long that he will go to almost any lengths to avoid personal confrontation off the court; by his own admission he finds it constitutionally impossible to say no. He avoids contention in real life as he seems to seek it on the court.

It is all bizarre and contradictory. Once Connors has been treed, he is not only wonderfully genial, but he also seems to enjoy himself. In paid personal appearances, he is charming, considerate of strangers and supplicants to a fault. He will never refuse an autograph. Children adore him, and he seems happiest of all in the haven of their innocent affection.

But now it seems the price of a lifetime of the Connors insularity must be paid upon the court. Connors seems incapable of making hard decisions — even to honestly assess, much less change, his game or strategy. Out there, on the concrete garden, only the tiger was formed — and his only response is to salivate more tiger juices. That very quality of his mother's that protected him, that let him gain the world championship, now appears to be vitiating him. "Wouldn't you be different with your mother around all the time?" Ilie Nastase says. "I don't mean better or worse, I just mean very different."

Nastase was once very close with Connors. Then, at their TV

challenge match in 1976, Nastase was wounded by some tiger-juice insults that Connors hurled at him, and last year, in a match at Caesars Palace — where Connors had never been beaten in a dozen outings — Nastase was prepared. When Connors began abusing him, Nastase stopped him dead by saying, "You don't want to fight. Go get your mother." Connors, shaking, was beaten for the first time on that court.

Acknowledging the incident, Nastase adds beseechingly, "Hey, don't get Gloria mad at me." For, notwithstanding Pauline Addie's tender memories, Mrs. Connors is feared. She is feared as a zealot, for being an implacable advocate for her son. When, after months of negotiations, Riordan obtained the unheard-of guarantee of $500,000 for a single match — a figure so large even CBS considered it obscene and refused to divulge it — Gloria's first response was that it should be a million. Last year a three-man round-robin among Borg, Vilas, and Connors was set up for television. Michelob was bankrolling it for $1 million: $500,000 for the winner, $300,000 for the runner-up, $200,000 for show. At worst, two hundred grand for losing two exhibitions over a weekend. "Isn't there something else?" Mrs. Connors said to the promoter, Gene Scott. "There has to be an extra two hundred fifty thousand for Jimbo." Michelob, aghast at this hubris, walked.

Such examples are legion. The possibility that somebody somewhere might "use" Jimbo haunts the Connors entourage. What makes this all the more fascinating is that neither Gloria nor Jimmy gives a tinker's damn about money. In all their lives, they have been extravagant only with their love and loyalty for one another.

In her devotion to him, Gloria makes sure that everyone pays in some way to use Jimbo — the press in the currency of delay and exasperation, which it can least afford. She is herself, frankly, "scared" of the press, and she has a right to be, for she is never treated sympathetically, and often savagely. Jimmy's image may be as negative, but the press is hardly to blame; his cockiness and vulgarity, the strut and bluster, are visible enough that they do not need to be filtered through newspaper columns in order to produce a bad public taste.

But poor Gloria: The existing impression of her derives more from deep-seated biases. People who don't know Mrs. Connors from Mrs. Calabash just plain don't like the idea of her. She is, first of all, dead correct in what she has perceived: that she is viewed as a stage mother, and that Americans do not approve of that species. It is dandy for Mickey Mantle's father to instruct his son to switch-hit, but only a pushy dame like Judy Garland's mother would shove that poor kid onto the stage. Moreover, in our affluent society, parents who lavish stereos and Toyotas upon their children are approved of, while those who only devote their time and talent are eyed suspiciously; they make other parents feel guilty. This is all the more so with Gloria, because as a coach she comes in the wrong sex. She and Jimmy are also victims of sexism.

To be sure, it is an unusual relationship. To be sure, Gloria is on guard in private, and Jimmy is obnoxious in public. Guaranteed, they will find a way to louse up public relations. And yet, for all the negative consequences that this unusual relationship might encompass, nobody ever pauses to acknowledge the greater truths: that this relationship contains an extraordinary amount of love, and that this relationship made Jimmy Connors champion of the world.

By now they expect no quarter. Having been cross-examined on their relationship for so long, they are both defensive — as Nastase proved consummately — and they both have pat answers. They maintain that all final decisions are Jimbo's, and both will intimate archly that people who are offended by their relationship probably have very unhappy family histories themselves. Says Jimmy, "The people who talk meanly about my mom and me are just a lot of people who are jealous. Wouldn't most people like to love their mom or dad the way I do?" He always adds the "or dad" when making this point.

As important as Gloria has been to her son, she has never really been isolated with him until now. Two Mom was a constant presence for the first two decades. "Our right arm," as Gloria always refers to her, Stonewall Jackson to her Lee. Jimmy is just as emphatic. "Both my mom and my grandma gave me my blood." So much was Two Mom on the road with Gloria and Jimmy that the family took to calling Al "Lonesome Pop," and, after Two Mom died (while in Los Angeles, with Gloria), Lonesome Pop suggested it might be more appropriate for Gloria to take his cemetery plot next to Two Mom's.

One of the reasons why Riordan, the outsider, could come to exert such authority for a time was that he was, in effect, Two Mom's legacy. She had admired him, and suggested to Gloria that if they ever did need a male specialist off the court, he might fill the bill. Riordan, who is in bitter litigation against the family now, is a non-person in their eyes who tried to take over tennis by "using" Jimmy as the wedge, but the fact cannot be avoided that he was a major male influence in Jimmy's life at precisely that time when he was leaving adolescence and becoming a public figure. With legal suits that became a crusade approaching paranoia, Riordan probably brought a surfeit of contentiousness into the life of a boy already brimming with antagonisms.

But Riordan did provide Connors with a close, influential adult male figure for the only time in his life — and it showed. Away from the tennis establishment, Connors exhibited an ease and good humor that he has never again shown. Granted, some of his comic material came with lines written, inflection indicated, by Riordan, but the public image was of a dead-end kid who could stop and laugh at the world and himself. Since Riordan's leavening influence has disappeared, this breezy Cagney figure has hardened into a surly and sour wise guy — the bluster and forced antics culminating in the mortifying episode at Forest Hills last year when Connors ran around the net onto the other side of the court and erased a ball mark that his opponent, Corrado Barazzutti, was citing as evidence of a bad call.

Jimmy was so at home with Riordan because he obviously could see much of his father in him. Like Big Jim, hanging around the Stop Light Restaurant back home, telling stories, having some Scotches, laughing with the gang — *My husband enjoyed being around people in the evenings* — Riordan is a social animal, in search of any crowd to which he can distribute his blarney and sly jests out of the corner of his mouth. He really fit in: a conservative Catholic, devoted to tennis, with a strong wife and tight family ties. "Bill was a father image for Jimmy," Chris Evert says. "He put a lot on the line for this guy. I don't mean just his reputation. Jimmy put his emotions up for Riordan."

Playing, competing, with a racket in his left hand, Jimbo is more a Thompson than a Connors — in a sense, he is Jimmy Thompson. Has any player ever been more natural? But then, in an instant, he wiggles his tail, waves a finger, tries to joke or be smart, tries too hard — for he is not facile in this way and his routines are forced and embarrassing, and that is why the crowds dislike him. He is Jimmy Thompson no more. He is trying so hard to be Jimmy Connors, raised by women to conquer men, but unable to be a man, to be Big Jim or Bill Riordan. He is unable to be one of the boys.

Connors says he "holds no grudges" against Riordan, but there is no question but that the older man took something valuable of Jimmy's when he was sent packing. "So much of it goes back to Jimmy's growing up, to the way people back home treated him," Evert says. "This was all inside him, and then he confided in Riordan, put his emotions on the line for him, and now he feels betrayed. So now his attitude is: You see, it is true. It is. I can't trust anybody."

Then, Riordan gone, body and soul, Connors's real father died of cancer a year and a half ago, on January 30, 1977. Jimmy was holding Big Jim's hand at the end. At the time, Connors's traveling companion was Marjie Wallace, a former Miss World, but she did not enjoy Gloria's favor and faded from Jimmy's life shortly after his father died, and there has been no serious new romantic interest since then.

Last year Connors was sometimes convoyed about by a hard-nosed phalanx of Gilbert and Sullivan bodyguards, but they have been superseded, mercifully, by Lornie Kuhle, an affable 34-year-old Las Vegas teaching pro. Kuhle is a favorite practice partner and a devoted friend ("You know what Jimmy is? He's just a good American kid"), but obviously he cannot harvest the emotional ground that lovers and fathers have turned and planted.

So Gloria's universe expands. Now she is everything to Jimmy: mother (he calls her "Mom" in that capacity), coach ("Coach"), best friend and business manager ("Glo"). So totally involved are Gloria and Jimmy with one another that, since it was knocked down to a two-person operation, the mother and son have engaged in some dreadful arguments; shouting matches in hotel rooms, Jimmy using some four-letter names that tennis people have been embarrassed to overhear. Both mother and son dismiss these episodes as healthy outbursts. "Look, I can cut it for you," Connors says. "First, she's my mom — you know, the one who creates you. She's my mom first and always will be. But she's my coach and my friend too, and if we scream at each other sometimes, that just clears the air. That's good among friends."

Only Evert appears to be in a position to exert a major influence on Connors. She fills all the necessary criteria. She is female, which he prefers — "I'd rather be friends with a woman than a man any day" — and she is enduring. All of the Connors family intimates must stand the test of time. Besides, it is obvious by now that Chrissie and Jimmy can't get each other out of their systems. That doesn't necessarily mean that they will marry someday. It just means they can't get each other out of their systems.

In fact, what has emerged from a teenage infatuation is a tender, understanding adult affection. "We fell in love when we were so young," says Chris, "before we were friends. Jimmy has always worked harder on the court than anyone, but he's always been completely pampered off. His mom thinks he deserved it that way. So you must be very attentive to Jimmy. And I don't want to sound harsh, please, because much of this also applies to me, to athletes in general. So when we were together, each of us was thinking about ourselves. It's very tough for Jimmy to give on those occasions, because he gives so much on the court, and you come to expect it off. And then, of course, most of the time you *do* get it off the court. Imagine us, two kids, so young, in love for the first time, each expecting the other to give." She shakes her head.

With Chris, with any woman, Connors feels more relaxed "because I'm never in competition with them." Besides, as he was schooled to be a tiger on the court, so was he taught to be a gentleman off, and nowhere is this more evident than in his relationships with women. He believes in ladies, old-fashioned manners, and modesty. The well-publicized itinerant liaison with Marjie Wallace might be viewed as something of a baffling interlude, because the family background, as Mrs. Connors volunteers, was very puritanical. She herself had a "girls' academy" upbringing. Jimmy spent several years in parochial schools, and, indeed, the ostensible reason for Two Mom being drafted as an extra escort was that the family considered it scandalous that a married woman would journey about alone, with only a child. In private conversation, Jimmy can go literally for hours without so much as a "damn" escaping his lips, and in the men's locker room he is known for his obsessive modesty, never appearing without a towel held primly about his waist.

So here, perhaps, is the greatest contradiction of all between the public figure and the private man: a genuine personal prudery contrasted with the grotesque machismo and vulgarity he flaunts upon his stage. Connors's court pantomimes are invariably sexual, his imprecations obscene, his attempts at comedy and his belligerent statements sexual or scatological. For a time he and Nastase used to drift into a mincing "queer" act. Jimbo was going to show the world that he is not some sissy or mama's boy, but that he can be as coarse and crude as any father's son.

Not even Riordan could fathom these upside-down transformations. "Jimbo was so thoughtful," he says. "He always called his mom. Whenever he saw me, he'd ask about Terry, my wife. When I first sent him to Europe, he clung to me at the airport. 'Bill, please don't leave me,' he said. He was such a child. And we had such fun. I could make Jimmy laugh.

"But then all of a sudden, out of the blue, he'd be obscene, and I'd just get lost then, because it was so distasteful to me. And I never understood any of that in him, because it doesn't fit. Which is strange, because that's how he is on the court, that's what people see the most. But it's not his dominant side — not at all. And I could forget it and go on being fond of him because we had so many good things, so many good times, and there should have been so much more of that ahead."

One day, when Jimbo was 11 or 12, Gloria and Two Mom took him out to the backyard court and told him it was time to abandon his childish two-handed backhand and start learning to hit backhands with one hand. This had always been their intention. The two women watched the child hit one-handed for a couple of days, and then Two Mom said, "Let's put it back, Glo. By the time he's nineteen or twenty he should be able to tear tennis apart with the two-handed backhand." Two Mom, as usual, was right as rain.

Still, as great as Connors's backhand is — one of the three or four best shots in tennis history — what always set the kid apart was his ability to be offensively unorthodox; he scores best from defensive situations, especially with the return of serve. No one ever used an opponent better against himself. No wonder players hated to face him.

For power, Connors learned to literally throw himself at the ball. His main source of strength comes from his thighs; it is his secret, a perfect, fluid weight transfer. And then, finally, he grew adept at what is known in tennis as hitting the ball on the rise — meeting the ball as it comes off the court, before it bounces to its apex. That is the ultimate attack, taking it on the rise, a man spitting back bullets. It speeds up the game infinitesimally in time, exponentially in fact, by putting constant pressure upon the other man. To hit on the rise requires three essentials: excellent vision (Connors's is 20–15), superb coordination (he even slugs with a trampoline-like steel racket), and utter confidence.

And so the Connors all-court game grew as a whole, each part advancing with all the others, and one day, when he was 16, only five years before he was to win Wimbledon, he beat his mother. He came to the net apologetic, and said, "Gee, Mom, that hurt. I didn't mean to do that."

Gloria almost cried. "No, no, Jimmy," she said. "Don't you know? This is one of the happiest days of my life."

But now it seems that everything thereafter has been anticlimactic. Even 1974 just came naturally, in the wake. Nothing ever changes. To even acknowledge that changes might be considered would, it seems, repudiate all that Gloria and Two Mom did with a child many years ago. For example, Connors's serve has always been relatively weak, and Borg exposed it at Wimbledon as an outright liability. But when Jimmy and his mother worked out for a week after that defeat, no special attention was paid to his serve, to his forehand approach, or to any other of the weaker elements of his game. "His serve is good enough for me," Gloria says emphatically, peeved. "We just worked on the overall game. Borg just had one of those days, like Jimmy did in 'seventy-four against Rosewall."

Unfortunately, Borg and Connors only meet in the finals, on Saturdays and Sundays, and those appear to be the two particular days Borg has. Besides, even if Borg did just happen to get hot at Wimbledon, the real crux of the matter is that even just a year ago, under no circumstances could Borg have ever routed Connors in straight sets. But Borg has worked on his game, and it has matured. Borg, the machine, the robot — "The Clone," his colleagues call him — he, not the exciting, bombastic Connors, has put variety and spice into his game.

Connors is so locked into the past he cannot bear to change even his practice routines. Practices are rugged and spirited physically, but they only amount to "hits" against lesser players. In Los Angeles, Connors's regular sparring partner is Stan Cantor, a middle-aged movie producer; on the road, he hits against Kuhle. Dick Stockton, who has known Jimmy since childhood, says, "To improve, you must practice against players of your own ability and you must work on the individual parts of your game. If Jimmy really wanted Kuhle to help him, he'd have him hit three hundred balls in a row to his forehand approach. But Jimmy can't change. He only knows one way."

And that is precisely what Connors himself says, again and again, as a point of pride. "It isn't me if I don't play the way my mom taught me. . . . My mom gave me my game, and she taught me one way, that lines were made to be hit. . . . My mom and my grandma were the *only* ones who ever touched my game, and they taught me to play one way. There's no other way."

And as with style, so with intensity. Connors boasts, accurately, admirably, "I peak every time I play." He loved to hear Riordan, an old racetrack buff, tell stirring tales of Bill Hartack, the cantankerous jockey who was famous for two things: fighting the establishment and riding every race as though it were the Kentucky Derby. "My mom taught me she'd rather have me play correctly for thirty minutes, her way, than play messing around for two hours," Jimmy says. "Play thirty minutes right, then I could go ride my pony or minibike." Thus, even practice games against Cantor or Kuhle are conducted as vendettas, with growling and curses. Every shot is for real. As ever, there is Gloria across the net. *You see, Jimmy, you see what even your own mother will do to you on the court?*

Just as Connors must give his all in every match, so does he exhibit uncommon physical courage. In 1977 he played all of Wimbledon with a broken left thumb. When an X-ray technician brought the news, he said, "Well, Mr. Connors, I guess you won't be playing tennis for a few weeks." Connors sneered, "You want to bet, sucker?" They put on a splint that dug in so hard the blood was gushing down his arm. The Connorses came back for another splint; they never told a soul, there would be no excuses, and he went to 6—4 in the fifth set of the finals, to that very last step, when, as ever, it was not his thumb that kept him from winning.

And yet, in contrast, since 1974 Connors has defaulted from almost twenty tournaments, often with the most transparent excuses of ill health at the eleventh hour. "Why should I let someone make a name off of me, beating me when I'm not right?" Connors snaps. Nobody uses Jimbo. What he does not say is what is apparent, that whereas he needs a physical excuse to get him off the hook, he is "not right" for psychological reasons. If there is not enough animosity on tap, not enough tiger juices flowing, then Connors does not dare to even venture into competition.

We should remember that 1974, his year, was swollen with

vitriol and tension — and he was near unbeatable. And what of this year, of 1978? At the time Borg laid waste to him, it was hard to find a player who did not mention how Connors had mellowed, become friendlier. Bill Norris, a tennis trainer and an old friend, says, "Jimmy's found an inner peace. He's much more aware of other people's feelings."

"Jimmy was brought up to win on hate," says a top player, a contemporary. "How long could anyone keep winning on hate?" If Connors's game is locked into the past, if it remains exactly the same, it may, nonetheless, have diminished in one almost imperceptible way: hitting the ball on the rise. To the keenest eyes, Jimbo does not appear to be taking the ball quite so soon. He has either lost the confidence to perform this feat, or somewhere deep inside a little bit of the killer instinct has paled, and he is giving the poor guy on the other side a chance, an instant more of breathing room. And the balls are coming back.

Borg, though, so bland, so unflappable, is a special problem. Connors tries to dislike him. He tries to hate him. Give Jimbo that. For years he would snarl that Borg had "no guts," and he always goes chasing after him. After Wimbledon, Jimbo vowed, "I'll chase the son of a bitch to the ends of the earth." And in the weeks that have followed, that charge has been embellished: "I'll be waiting for him. . . . I'll dog him everywhere. . . . Every time Borg looks around he'll see my shadow."

But the problem is that it is not Bjorn Borg who is the target. It is his own man that the boy is chasing. Jimbo will be 26 next week, and the boy and his mother can only go so far. There must be the man to accept the harsh truths, so that once again he can win finals, win other people. If ever Jimmy Connors would stop trying to be something else, if only Jimmy Connors would again take the ball on the rise, the way he once did, crushing it, crashing forward, taking no prisoners, what a dreadnought he would be. Why, that would make 'em forget '74 — and serve 'em right!

But no one knows if he is capable of the necessary changes. What we do know is that only one mother has made a men's champion, but that no mother has ever kept a man champion.

"As well as I know Jimmy," Chris Evert says, "a lot of times I don't know what goes on in his head. But if he still has me baffled, I know that he's still got himself baffled, too. Jimmy might know himself better if he would ever spend some time soul-searching. But he won't.

"He's always had to hate the men players to be at his best. But they don't hate him anymore. A lot of them have even come to like him. So he's got to find a new motivation, and that's going to be very hard for Jimmy."

It is strange that as powerful as the love is that consumes the Connorses, Jimbo has always depended on hate in order to win. And all along that must have been the hard way. There is no telling how far a man could go who could learn to take love on the rise.

I'm one of the few in my profession who can't tolerate boxing. It's a great sport to write about, and many of the people in it are terrific — witness Billy Conn — but boxing's really quite evil of itself, indefensible, and in contradiction to all that our Judeo-Christian ethic holds. I can never understand some of my colleagues, who count themselves among the most liberal of men, who always fret about baseball or football players losing a few thousand dollars on their pension plans, but who never seem to be troubled that boxers maim and kill one another for the amusement of others and the profit of creeps like Don King.

When I write something like "The Anglo Meets the Indian," I'm vain enough to think that, immediately, the scales will fall from people's eyes and they will see the light. But, of course, it never works that way. My feeling is now that boxing will just fade away, unmourned. Not enough people are hurt by it to stir up the politicians, but fewer and fewer poor people are foolish enough to box, so there are fewer and fewer fights of any consequence, and fewer and fewer fans. Thank God, the spiral for boxing is all down, but, alas, a lot more kids, like one of the good boys in this fight, will have to die before boxing is gone for good.

A hundred years from now, I'm sure, boxing will seem to be as barbaric and immoral as slavery appears to us now.

The Anglo
Meets the Indian

1982

DUK KOO KIM died in Las Vegas on November 17 of brain injuries he suffered in a fight with Boom Boom Mancini four days before. Kim's death attracted a lot of attention because he was fighting on network television for some alphabet world championship. To this day, though, the most celebrated boxing death remains Benny Paret's, and it happened way back in 1962. Paret, the welterweight champion, was battered by Emile Griffith as the world's most famous referee watched, apparently mesmerized by the brutality. Plus, it was all on a Gillette fight night. Look sharp. Feel sharp. Be sharp.

Normally boxers don't get much ink for dying, unless they do it while fighting for a title and on a network. For example, if you walk into the Civic Auditorium in Albuquerque, New Mexico, you'll see only one photograph in the lobby. It's over by copies of such patriotic memorabilia as the Declaration of Independence, the Japanese surrender document, and Jackson's letter after he won the Battle of New Orleans. That lone photograph hangs high. It's of Victor (Vito) Romero, and under the picture it says "1960–1980." This is because Romero, age 20, died on August 21, 1980, from injuries he'd suffered in the Civic Auditorium ring three days before. But while Romero is dead, he isn't counted as a genuine boxing death, because he was fatally injured while sparring. So he's not listed among the 353 boxers who have been killed in fights since 1945. Even local boxing historians say that the last boxing death in New Mexico before 1982 occurred in 1956, when John Anthony Lopez was killed in the Golden Gloves in Roswell.

If only boxers would wear headgear, safe, protective headgear,
the argument goes. But Charles Love succumbed in Louisville, Kentucky, this past October 16, after a fight with Darryl Stitch, a sophomore at the University of Louisville. Love, an Army private from
Milwaukee, was, like Stitch, wearing headgear when he was killed.
He didn't even get knocked off his feet. It was quite enough that
his brain got pummeled while he stood up. He was 19 years old,
wearing protective headgear. Love was one of six fighters who died
after official bouts in '82. Maxwell Myaica was a South African black
killed by another South African black at Bhekuzulu Hall, Umlazi,
Natal Province, on November 11, a couple of days before Kim
went down. Naoki Kobayashi had died a few weeks before, after
Yoshsimu Oyama knocked him out in Tokyo. Andy Balaba of the
Philippines was the WBA's second-ranked flyweight when he died
in Seoul on May 11, four days after fighting Shin Hee Sup. Balaba
was 28 years old and gunning for a title shot. Doctors removed 100
cubic centimeters of blood from around his brain, but it was too
late, and so his body was taken from South Korea back to the island
of Mindanao, where his three small children watched his remains
go into the ground. Six months thereafter, Duk Koo Kim's body was
returned to South Korea. Days later, he was married posthumously
to his girlfriend, and two months after that, his mother, still de-
spondent over his death, drank a bottle of pesticide so that she
might kill herself, which she did.

All of these fighters came from poor families. One of the most
emotional arguments made on behalf of boxing — usually by
people who don't box — is that if the sport didn't exist, poor boys
couldn't grow up to be Sugar Ray Leonard or Larry Holmes, with
big houses and investment portfolios. It's their choice. Nobody
makes these boys bash their brains in for our amusement. If we
buy tickets and cheer them on, they might well become million-
aires.

The problem is, very few poor young fighters ever do grow up
to be Leonard or Holmes. Instead, every year, a number of them
grow up to be corpses, to be Andy Balaba or Maxwell Myaica or
Charles Love or Duk Koo Kim or Naoki Kobayashi. Or perhaps as
bad — who knows? — they grow up to be Shin Hee Sup or Chris
Naidoo or Darryl Stitch or Boom Boom Mancini or Yoshsimu
Oyama. They grow old with blood on their hands.

On Lincoln's Birthday 1982, under the photograph of Vito Romero, Benjamin Davis and Louis Wade walked into the Civic Audi-

torium in Albuquerque to fight each other in the semifinals of the New Mexico Golden Gloves, 132-pound novice class. You could not hope to meet two nicer boys. One would help kill the other in the ring that night.

Benjie and Louis had never met one another, but Louis had seen Benjie fight the night before, in the first round of the tournament. That had been the first fight that Benjie had ever fought. Louis, who had been granted a bye in the first round of the competition, had participated in only two previous bouts.

On the tournament's opening night, a Thursday, the crowd had been sparse, so Louis had been able to move down to ringside to watch the bout that would determine his opponent for the following evening. Louis had a special interest in the boy fighting Benjie, Anthony Tapia, who came from Los Lunas, which is just a few miles up Interstate 25 from where Louis lived, in Belen. Louis had heard that Tapia was looking forward to mixing it up with him. But if Louis was primarily interested in Anthony Tapia, he was impressed by the way Benjie fought. Although the two were almost identical in size, in the same weight class, Louis thought that Benjie seemed taller than himself, and heavier. Indeed, Benjie did cut an imposing figure: His shoulders were wide, his waist a mere ribbon, his limbs all sinewy muscles, lithe and long. What Louis didn't know, though, was that Benjie was six years older than he was. Louis was only 16, but Benjie was a man of 22. That was two years over the age limit for the novice class, but the Golden Gloves wasn't too picky about little details like that. Other things the tournament couldn't be bothered with were the pre- and post-fight physicals it was required to provide.

But then, neither Benjie nor Louis had ever spent so much as a night in a hospital. And both were good-looking, even handsome. Louis's brown hair was somewhat long, but always neatly combed, drawn down over his forehead toward his clear green eyes. He had a glimmering kind of smile. "Just plain well liked by everyone," says Casey Cordova, who was his boxing coach. "No one could help but like Louis." It was the same with Benjie. Phil Belone, his brother-in-law, who works for the Department of Indian Affairs, says: "Benjie? Warm and mischievous. A little Dennis the Menace in him, you know. But always happy. An admirable guy with just so many friends."

Benjie's hair was a bit curly, a silky black, and his dark eyes shone, even when viewed through his big oval eyeglasses. His smile was accented by his copper Navajo skin. He talked a lot, and his family kidded him about that, because as Navajos are the first to acknowledge themselves, they're supposed to be reticent.

Benjie and Louis never said a word to one another. They saw each other in the locker room shortly before they fought, but Benjie had never laid eyes on Louis and had no idea who he was, and even though Louis had watched Benjie fight the night before against Tapia, he didn't recognize Benjie with his glasses on. So they never exchanged a word. Just blows. Even when the referee, Roger Rodriguez, had them touch gloves at the start, they didn't say anything. And in the fight itself, they never uttered a word for the two minutes of the first round and the fifty-seven seconds of the second. The bout was scheduled to go three, but it didn't last that long, because this turned out to be a fight to the death, and that came at 0:57 of the second.

It's too bad that Benjie and Louis never got to meet in the proper way, for they would have liked one another. There was the age difference, and one was Indian and the other, as they say in New Mexico, Anglo, but they had plenty in common. Despite being as small as they were, they'd both tried football and basketball. Benjie was a rodeo champion, while Louis had just joined a rodeo club. They were attractive and popular, with boys and girls alike. Both were poor, too, with parents who had divorced. They were average students, but they worked hard and were proud of their accomplishments in the classroom. They were conscientious, dependable at what jobs they could find. They were all-American boys. A lot of people cared about them. But here they were, alone, prepared only to hit each other, to entertain a few thousand people who had come to pass the time on a Friday evening, on Lincoln's Birthday, watching brave boys rattle each other's young brains.

Both fighters had received their first boxing gloves as presents. Benjie's brother Raymond gave him a pair when he was 10, while Louis got a pair from his father, Sonny, the Christmas he was 13. They were red and white, without laces, and Louis took a real shine to them and used them to slug it out with his pal, Melvin Maldonado. But it was several years before Louis decided to pursue boxing more seriously. One day he just went over to Becker Street in Belen, to a place where Casey Cordova taught boxing. Louis told Cordova that he'd like to learn to be a fighter.

"Ever box before?" Cordova asked.

"No, not really. But my daddy used to box in the Army."

"Well, OK, glad to have you try," Cordova said. There wasn't much to the building. It had been a bar when Cordova's father owned it, and half of it was still devoted to bingo on Friday nights. There wasn't even a ring in the room, just the essentials — a big bag and a speed bag and kids who liked to mix it up. Cordova has trained eighteen state champions, including two of his own sons, although he'd never boxed himself. But he was a good athlete, and when he went to barber school in L.A., he started hanging out at the Olympic Gym, which was across the street from the school, giving free haircuts to the trainers and managers and whatnot. Casey runs the Sportsman's Barber Shop, three chairs, in Albuquerque, when he's not teaching kids boxing in Belen.

You wouldn't call Belen a suburb of Albuquerque, although it's only half an hour from downtown and a number of Belen's residents work there. Louis's stepmother, Evelyn, for example, has a job at Motorola in Albuquerque. But Belen has always had an identity of its own, right back to when it was first settled, in 1741, and it even calls itself the Hub City, which seems like conceit for a place so small. But Belen is the center of what's around, agriculture, and it has always been a railroad town, too. Belen means Bethlehem in Spanish, and it's about fifty-fifty Anglo and Hispanic. There are hardly any Indians in that valley, where the Rio Grande cuts through.

In February, the time of year when Louis drove up to the Golden Gloves, the land is bare and brown, scrubby. The telephone poles stand out more than anything God provided. The valley needs the spring.

Pinehaven, Benjie's town, is the other way, northwest from Albuquerque, close on the Arizona line, a few miles from the Navajo reservation that spreads across the top of each state. Benjie was born on the reservation and had lived in the vicinity, either just on or just off the reservation, all his life. Gallup is the main town in the area, right on fabled old Route 40, offering, surely, more Indian souvenirs per capita than anyplace else. "Indian Jewelry!" the neon signs blink, and lots of establishments also hire bona fide Indians to come in and weave blankets right on the site, for the edification of tourists.

The Indian area is high, a mile or more in altitude, and, at least in the winter, the diverse terrain is pleasing to the eye. There are trees on many of the mesas, full-boughed evergreens, and best of all, when there's some snow, it clings to the needles in the high dry air and makes it look as if powdered sugar had been sprinkled all around. It was so nice out that last day, before Benjie went to Albuquerque to box, that he talked his girlfriend, Debbie, into taking the day off from work, and they drove deep into the reservation, past Sheep Springs, up to Washington Pass, where they could hold hands and look down on the only world they'd ever really known. There, one more time, Debbie tried to talk Benjie out of going off to fight. Maybe if the romance had been going on longer, Debbie could have won out, but Benjie had never been tied down long by any girl; he'd been going with Debbie only a couple of months, and he couldn't be swayed.

That day Louis was in school, at Belen High, where he was a junior. He would have to wear headgear when he fought in the Golden Gloves, because in New Mexico boxers under the age of 18 must wear headgear. Louis had split his two fights. His first time out, in the PAL tournament in Albuquerque, both Cordova and Louis thought he'd been jobbed, a hometown decision. That had been some months before, when Louis weighed only 103. Later, when he was up to 117, Cordova took him to Grants, which is where the Perpetual Ice Caves are, on the high road to Gallup, and this time Louis easily beat a kid from Milan. Had him bent over at the end. Wade, TKO, 3.

Cordova had no illusions about Louis, though. "He was a mediocre fighter," he says. "He could never go anywhere with it. All Louis could do was jab. But he couldn't hurt anybody with those jabs. Trouble was, he always stood flat-footed, and he backed up all the time. A lot of times, I told him, 'Now look, Louis, I'll try and get you a fight, but I'll stop it if I have to.' And he understood. The last time, I said, OK, I'm going to let you go to the Golden Gloves, but I'm going to watch you close, and I'll stop it real fast if you start to get into any trouble."

The only thing was, the bingo on Becker Street was always held Friday nights, and Cordova was going to have to stay in Belen Friday and call the bingo while Louis was fighting either Anthony Tapia or Benjamin Davis in the Golden Gloves.

Of the nine children in Benjie's family — now ranging in age from 14 to 31 — he was born smack in the middle, number five. His mother, Katherine, 48, like many of her contemporaries, can speak only Navajo. There were so many mouths to feed that even when Benjie was in elementary school he had to be shipped away from home to attend a free government boarding school on the reservation. Even now telephones are a luxury up that way; paved roads are the exception. Four-wheel-drive pickup trucks — so many of them, it seems they must be the New Mexico state animal — the mud caked to their underpinnings, are requisite around Gallup. In winter, snow can make conditions even worse. In the cities — suburbs, too — old snow piles up on the sidewalks, growing dirtier there. But in the countryside, around the reservation, the snow doesn't get dirty. It just melts and makes the dirt dirtier.

Still, no question: Of the two boys, the Anglo, Louis, had had the harder life. His parents separated when he was very young, his mother all but fading from his existence, his father going off to Vietnam and then to Belen, where he remarried. Louis stayed with his paternal grandmother in Florida. He was going to rejoin his father in New Mexico sooner than he did, but the grandmother grew sick and she loved the little boy, so everybody decided it would be unwise to take Louis away from her. So he stayed in Florida until she died. He was eight when he came out to Belen, to his father's new family, with a stepsister three years younger and a half brother on the way.

One of the reasons Louis couldn't concentrate on boxing as much as he wanted to was that he had to devote a lot of his time to working. About the time of the Golden Gloves, one of the jobs he had was doing yard work for an elderly lady in town. He felt close to her. The closest adult in his whole life had probably been his grandmother, and the old woman he worked for must have reminded him of her. He told friends he would go visit the old woman when things weren't good at home, "when things close in on me."

What Louis liked best about boxing was the solitude, the road work, running alone. It wasn't the hitting. He wasn't street-tough. His aunt, Sylvia Burns, says, "If there was ever any confrontation, Louis would walk away from it." He was never in any trouble.

Not long before the fight, Louis also joined the rodeo club at Belen High. Rodeo is an individual sport, too. Louis hadn't chosen a rodeo event to specialize in by the time he had to go up to Albuquerque, though.

Benjie, however, was already very accomplished in rodeo. As a bull rider, he had finished second in the New Mexico high school

finals in 1978, which earned him a trip to the nationals, in South
Dakota. He lasted seven seconds on the bull he drew. Eight is the
limit you have to reach. The only reason Benjie got involved with
boxing was that the Indian rodeo circuit wasn't starting up again
for a few weeks. He had some time on his hands, that's all. Surely,
he wasn't any kind of troublemaker, no macho brawler. "Spit in Benjie's eye," Phil Belone, his brother-in-law, says, "and first he'd ask
you why you did that." *If there was ever any confrontation, Louis
would walk away.*

Benjie was always a hard worker, too. After he graduated from
high school at Wingate in '78, he took special vocational training
and became a heavy-equipment operator. But work for Indians was
scarce in the winter of '82, and Benjie met a guy named Dave Peterson on the reservation, in the Navajo hamlet where Debbie was
living. Peterson was coach of the Navajo Boxing Club. Benjie
started working out.

All he talked about, though, was how itchy he was for the Indian
rodeos to start again. He even got some lumber, and with two of
his brothers he planned to build his own rodeo arena, chute and
all, down in Pinehaven, where he'd lived with his father, Charlie,
since his parents' divorce.

The breakup had wounded Benjie. Unlike Louis, who never
really had a family, Benjie was used to a whole household. His folks
didn't split apart until he was a tenth-grader, and he brooded a lot,
longing for the time when he would have his own family. Louis
would go talk to the old woman when he needed someone. Benjie
got the same sort of solace from being around children. He loved
to play with his nieces and nephews. One day, not long before he
went to Albuquerque to fight, he took Ernessa, his sister Lena's
little girl, and held her on his lap, hugging her, for the longest time.

"Hey, what are you doing with my baby?" Lena said at last, laughing.

"Just practicing," Benjie said, flashing that gigantic smile of his.
"Just practicing for when I have my own."

He knew most of the family members wouldn't like it one bit if
they learned he was boxing. Benjie wrestled, played football at 130
pounds, learned the martial arts, broke a pony when he was only
six years old, rode some mean horses, and would jump on a 2,000-
pound bull's neck in a rodeo. But in those activities the potential
for danger is random. In boxing, the hurt is intentional.

Benjie did tell his younger brothers, Raymond and Augustine, what he was up to, but he also cautioned them, "Don't tell Mom." His sisters didn't know, either, and his girl didn't like it. But he told Debbie he couldn't let Coach Peterson down, couldn't let the team down. And so Benjie came down from Washington Pass, left Debbie behind, left the reservation behind, and went to fight in Albuquerque, on another one of those days when all the pickups were dirty and splattered.

At the motel where the Navajo team put up, Benjie took a room with Johnny King, his best friend in the club. Then they all went over to the Civic Auditorium. It had been built in 1957 but had become something of a white elephant, because all the top events in town play the Pit, the beautiful, 18,000-seat arena a couple of miles away on the University of New Mexico campus. The Civic seats only around 4,000, maybe 5,000 with the extra folding seats that can be put on the floor for boxing. The Civic is conveniently located, though. It's right off the Interstate, in the middle of town, and easy to spot because it shares its parking lot with St. Joseph's Hospital, distinguished by its deep blue cross, set high up in its white facing.

On that first night Louis wasn't much impressed by the Anthony Tapia–Benjamin Davis fight. Tapia was so worn out from his exertions in the first round that he couldn't even come out for the second. Casey Cordova was watching, too, and he didn't see anything for Louis to worry about; he was sure it wasn't going to make much difference that he had to be at the bingo in Belen Friday and wouldn't be looking out for Louis from his corner.

Still, come Friday morning, Louis was becoming nervous. He had permission not to go to school that day, but he couldn't sleep, and his friends were surprised to see him come to class. He stayed half the day.

By contrast, after winning his fight against Tapia, Benjie seemed at ease. Certainly he showed no concern that anything consequential was going to happen that evening — "and Indians usually have strong premonitions," Phil Belone says. As a matter of fact, although Benjie was usually an early riser at home, in the motel he slept late. It was past ten that morning before Benjie stirred, rubbed the sleep from his eyes, and said good morning to Johnny King.

*   *   *

There was a respectable crowd that night at the Civic Auditorium. The Navajo Boxing Club had come over from the motel as a group, Benjie included. Steve Pena, Cordova's assistant, had driven Louis up from Belen around six o'clock. There was no sense getting there too early. Davis versus Wade wouldn't be till the twelfth fight on the card.

So it was going on a quarter to nine when the two boys got the call, walked out into the smoky arena, climbed through the ropes, and looked at one another. They both wore gold tops, but Benjie, the Navajo, was in maroon trunks, Louis, the Anglo, in blue. And, of course, they both had on protective headgear.

The two boys moved to the center of the ring and listened to Referee Rodriguez's instructions. Lots of fighters will use this moment to try to intimidate the other fellow, but neither Louis nor Benjie was that kind of person. The whole thing was so incongruous — just their being in this position, having to hit each other. Louis did peer thoughtfully into the older boy's face, but even that little gesture seemed too much of a confrontation for Benjie, and he ducked his dark eyes.

The bell rang. This would be the third fight for Louis, the second for Benjie, and the last for them both. They came to blows.

Louis, though younger, clearly had more ring experience, and he gained the early advantage. He shot his long left out, again and again, bothering Benjie, scoring points, compensating for his flat-footedness, so that Benjie could not close on Louis. Jab, jab. Down in Belen, Cordova was calling off the night's bingo numbers: N-43, I-24, G-68, and so forth. Up near the reservation, the Navajos were pouring into Gallup from all around, pickups parading, the way they always do on Friday, payday. The town was lit up bright. Tacos! Mucho Munchies! Rooms $13.95! $12.95!! Indian Jewelry!!!

And now it was the middle of the first round, and Louis was scoring so well with the jab that he got a little confident. This time when he jabbed, clipping Benjie, he tried to follow with a right uppercut. It missed, though. Benjie slipped that punch, and he remembered the sequence. Moments later, when Louis tried the same thing again, Benjie was ready.

He couldn't duck the jab, but he was waiting, and when Louis tried the right, Benjie dodged it easily, cocking his own right fist as he did, and there was Louis standing flat-footed, his weight back. He was caught open, and the blow crashed hard into his face. Louis shuddered, pain rushing to his nose. In his three fights, in all his time in the ring, Louis had never felt a punch like that.

Perhaps if Benjie had been more experienced he could have finished off Louis before the bell. Of course, it's also a possibility that Benjie did know what to do, but he just couldn't manage to do it because his reaction time was dulled from blows he had taken from Tapia in the first-round match only twenty-four hours before. Whatever, Louis was able to get his jab going again.

Back in his corner after the first round, Louis mentioned how much his nose hurt, and he said he thought he would take it easy this round, conserve himself. Steve Pena nodded. He assured Louis that despite Benjie's one good punch, Louis had scored almost all the points in the first round with his jab. He was ahead, he could afford to take it easy for a round. Maybe then, the pain would be gone.

But almost as soon as the bell rang, Louis had to change his plan. He couldn't coast. Benjie didn't seem to put up any resistance at all. Jab, jab, jab. And this round, when Louis followed the jabs with crosses, they crashed home, Benjie's head snapping back. After the second of these combinations rang true, Benjie let his hands drop, and he just stood there. But the referee did nothing, and nobody threw a towel up through the smoke. The crowd yelled in appreciation. Louis waited for a signal to stop, but there wasn't any, so he poked Benjie with a left. Then a right. Another left. More raucous cheers. And now the Navajo staggered and fell across the ropes, his stomach against one of the strands. Again the Anglo held back. There was no sign from the referee, even though when Benjie struggled back and righted himself, Louis could see that his eyes were glassy. But Benjie was back on his two feet now, and the crowd was cheering, and Louis fired out one more time, another left. This time Benjie crumpled and fell in a heap to the canvas, his brain now swimming in blood, bruised and purple and of no more use to him.

Suddenly, Louis was scared about what had happened to Benjie. "I had seen the way his eyes rolled back in his head," he said. So, in a neutral corner now, Louis fell to a knee and prayed.

The referee took off Benjie's gloves and his shoes. The one doctor there climbed into the ring. Benjie needed oxygen. There was no oxygen in the building. He needed to get to a hospital. And there was St. Joe's right out the door, just across the parking lot, its blue cross shining down like a star, but there was no ambulance, not even a stretcher. They had to tend to Benjie where he had fallen.

After a few minutes, the referee went through the ritual of raising Louis's hand in victory. And then Louis left the ring. He remembers hearing someone say "Good fight" as he passed through the haze and the crowd. Pena drove Louis back home to Belen, but he couldn't sleep. He kept seeing Benjie on the canvas, "lying there with his eyes all white." Good fight. Wade, KO, 2.

It wasn't until past four in the morning that the cops could reach the Davis family. Even then, the only news at first was that Benjie had suffered an "accident," so the family members assumed it involved an automobile. Except for the two younger brothers, sleeping, none of the Davises knew about Benjie's boxing. His mother and his three sisters, Elsie, Lena, and Loretta, drove to Albuquerque, but they didn't learn about the boxing until they finally got to St. Joe's, around eight in the morning. It was already too late. Benjie had gone without a heartbeat for ten minutes or more. By the time they finally got him across the parking lot to St. Joe's, in an ambulance that had to be called, he was no more than a bunch of organs. The first night that Benjie ever stayed in a hospital, he slept there dead.

"What made it even harder," Phil Belone says, "is that there were no bruises on him. It just looked like he was lying there, sleeping." When the family finally decided to have the life-support machines turned off on February 17, after Valentine's Day had come and gone, they all went in to say their last good-byes. "We're Christians," Belone says. "We just believed that Benjie went to sleep in the ring and woke up in heaven."

On the seventeenth, Louis was drifting off in his own bed when his father and stepmother came into the room. Up to then Louis hadn't come to grips with the obvious truth. "I just thought it was a boxing injury," he says. Now his parents had learned the news, and they wanted Louis to hear it from them first. He took it hard. His stepmother gave him a sleeping pill, but it was hours before he slept. The next morning he didn't go to school, but instead rode aimlessly around on his bicycle. After a while it started to drizzle, and he went over to the house where his friend the old woman lived. She had heard the news, and asked him if he wanted to talk it out. No, Louis said, not even with her. Instead, he asked her if she minded if he raked some leaves. She said that would be fine, and so Louis spent the next few hours raking leaves in the rain.

By the time Benjie was buried five days later, on Monday, the twenty-second, George Washington's Birthday, the skies had cleared. It was uncommonly warm for February in Gallup. A lot of the people who overflowed the Christian Reformed Church hadn't even worn overcoats.

The service was conducted in English and Navajo. The eulogy was delivered by Raymond Pinto, a distant relative who had been Benjie's science teacher at Wingate High. "In Hebrew, Benjamin means son of my right hand," Pinto said. "It was always a fitting name, for Benjamin was always willing to help. He was a particularly loving son."

Then two of Benjie's cousins, Sharon and Cecil Benally, came up to sing "Amazing Grace." The church was hushed.

"Amazing grace! How sweet the sound . . .'" the cousins began, but after only a few more words Sharon began to cry, and soon she couldn't go on. Cecil moved closer to her, and without missing a note, he put his arm around her and held her as he kept on singing by himself:

> *"Through many dangers, toils, and snares;*
> *I have already come;*
> *'Tis grace hath brought me safe thus far,*
> *And grace will lead me home."*

Sharon had come up to sing with her brother, and now he was singing alone, while everyone out in the pews was, with her, crying.

> *"He will my shield and portion be*
> *As long as life endures. . . ."*

Cecil held steady to the end.

Three more cousins were among the pallbearers, along with Benjie's high school basketball and wrestling coaches and Andrew Chicharello's older brother. Andrew was Benjie's best friend, but, at the last, he couldn't bear to come, and so his brother took his place. The casket they carried was black with silver trim. Benjie lay inside on a Navajo blanket. He was wearing a Western-cut suit, and his black Stetson rested beside him.

He was put to rest under the warm sun in Sunset Memorial Park, just off Business Route 40, the main drag, at the western edge of

Gallup. Another time of year, Benjie might have been buried in a family place on the reservation, but in February the roads are usually so bad that it would be hard to get there, even for pickups with four-wheel drive.

"His was an honorable death," Phil Belone says. "Benjie died as an athlete."

While Benjie had still lain at St. Joe's, technically alive, Evelyn Wade, Louis's stepmother, had gone up there. The members of the Davis family whom she met told her to take the word back to Louis that no one blamed him. To this day the Navajos have only compassion for the Anglo, and everybody keeps assuring Louis that it was not his fault. Sometimes he believes that.

Louis's school was especially supportive. The teachers knew he hadn't ever had much of a male influence at home, and so, led by Ron Hodges, the principal, the men teachers rallied to him. There was also a middle-aged man in town whom Louis knew, and one day he asked Louis to come see him. He told Louis something that even the man's own children didn't know, that once, when he was young and working in an oil field, there was an accident that he was involved in and another boy was killed, and he had had to live with that knowledge all these years. And Louis and the man both began to cry, out of the pain that they shared.

There were no cruel taunts from the other students. Still, there are times when Louis walks by some kids and he hears the word *kill* mumbled, and he knows what they're talking about. "You almost forget it sometimes, until you see something, like when the Korean was killed," he says. "Then it comes back." And he tries to stifle his tears.

In the fall, for a few weeks, he tried boxing again. "But I guess I still haven't gotten far enough away from it," he says. "I started working out, but I just couldn't get into it." Just about everybody understands that, except for his father, who tells Louis that if he doesn't box again, he'll be a coward. So, not long ago, Louis moved in with other relatives.

It might help Louis to know that many people think the greater damage was probably done to Benjie in his first fight, on the Thursday. The fact that Benjie slept so uncommonly late Friday is a telltale sign of coma. Later in the day he complained to Johnny King of a headache. Even the most cursory examination would have resulted in Benjie's being prohibited from fighting Friday. But Louis is hard to convince. He saw the Thursday bout, and he's positive Benjie "just didn't get hit that hard."

Louis prays for Benjie. He goes to church more regularly now. He's a Pentecostal. Recently he enlisted in the Army for four years and will report for basic training shortly after he graduates from high school in June. It's best that he get away. "Maybe I'll try boxing again when I get in the Army," he says. "You know, after I let everything settle."

Cordova is against that. "You've got to be really mean in the ring to box well," he says. "Louis just isn't mean; he's too nice. He never wanted to hurt anybody."

And that makes two of them. When Katherine Davis talks about her son, the first word she chooses for Benjie is *baatei-abin,* Navajo for "gentle." She starts to cry. It has been a year now, and she has eight surviving children near her, but that doesn't help. "I was never sick before," she says. "Now I'm sick all the time." She wears an aqua-colored bandanna about her head, Indian jewelry upon her wrists and clothing. "*Baatei-abin,*" she says again. "Gentle. And always with a smile. That's how I think Benjie would want to be remembered."

But no one — none of the men, anyway — on either side wants to blame boxing for the tragedy. "I like boxing. It's my favorite sport," Louis says. Indeed everybody goes out of their way to absolve boxing. The Davis family is suing every principal, individual and corporate, involved with the fight, except Louis, but everyone denies any responsibility whatsoever for the events that took a healthy 22-year-old's life. Still, nobody is mad at boxing. It's only, they say so conveniently, as ever, the corruption within boxing that's accused of poisoning the sweet science. Corruption is the best thing boxing has going for it, because as long as it is there to divert attention, who will ever say no, it's not the corruption that corrupts but the science itself. Good fight. KO, 2.

Ernie Arviso, who is married to Benjie's older sister, Lena, brushes back the snow and scrapes away at the ice on the headstone that lies flush with the ground. Without headstones sticking up, it's easier to mow the grass. Lena picks up the flowers they left here last time, now withered, colorless in the cold. Ernie has cleared the ice away from the headstone enough now to read:

1959–1982. And above that: "Benjamin Davis." And above that: "In Memory of Brother and Son." That was what Benjie was; he never had the chance but to practice at holding his own child.

What could he have been — what else, anyway, besides a husband and father? "I think if he was still around, Benjie would be in the rodeo," Herman Arviso says. He is another brother-in-law, and he was a rodeo champion himself.

"The last time I spoke to Benjie, just before the fight, he was really excited about getting ready for the rodeo," Lena says.

"Oh yeah," says Herman. "He could've been a champ bull rider. He was that good."

Someone translates that for Benjie's mother, and Mrs. Davis nods and smiles and fingers the blanket she has just finished. Over in Pinehaven, though, no one ever bothered to try and complete the rodeo arena Benjie had started just before he went down to Albuquerque to fight another boy.

Now that Louis has given up boxing, he's concentrating more on rodeo. It's been months since Cordova last saw Louis, and he hasn't been by the room on Becker Street at all. In what spare time he has, Louis goes out to a rodeo arena known as the Sheriff's Posse. He looks the part, too. This day Louis is dressed in boots, Western shirt, jeans, a cowboy belt, bandanna, and rodeo club jacket. It's black with silver trim. He says he has a rodeo specialty now, too. It's bull riding. Just like what Benjie did.

What a shame it was that the two boys, the Anglo and the Indian, never knew each other except for two minutes and fifty-seven seconds one night in a boxing ring, pummeling each other's faces in the haze, for the roar of the crowd and something dark in all our souls.

TEACHING
THE GAME

The Depression Baby

1976

IN Al McGuire's office at Marquette, images of sad clowns abound. Pictures, all over the place, of sad clowns. Everybody must ask him about them. McGuire is touted to be a con, so the sad clowns have got to be a setup. Right away, commit yourself to those sad clowns, you're coming down his street. *Hey, buddy, why do you have a banana in your ear? Because I couldn't find a carrot.* Zap, like that. And yet, how strange an affectation: sad clowns. Obviously, they must mean something. It cannot be the sadness, though. Of all the things this fascinating man is — and clown is one — he is not sad.

Another thing he is, is street smart. McGuire has grown up and left the pavement for the boardrooms, so now when he spots this quality in others, he calls it "credit-card-wise." One time in a night-club, when the band played "Unchained Melody," all the 40-year-olds in the place suddenly got up and packed the floor, cheek to cheek. Nostalgia ran rampant. Right away, Al said, "Summer song. This was a summer song when it came out. Always more memories with summer songs."

Perfect. He got it. Right on the button. Of course, this is a small thing. A completely insignificant thing. But the point is, he got it just right. And this is a gift. It is McGuire's seminal gift, for all his success flows from it. The best ballplayers see things on the court. McGuire lacked this ability as an athlete, but he owns it in life. Most people play defense in life, others "token it" (as Al says), but there are few scorers, and even fewer playmakers, guys who see things about to open up and can take advantage. McGuire is one of life's playmakers. He perceives. He should be locked in a bicentennial time capsule so that generations yet unborn will understand what this time was really like. There will be all the computers and radar ovens and Instamatics, and McGuire will pop out from among them in 2176 and say, "If the waitress has dirty ankles, the chili will be good." And, "Every obnoxious fan has a wife home who dominates him." And, "If a guy takes off his wristwatch before he fights, he means business." And, "Blacks will have arrived only when we start seeing black receptionists who aren't good-looking."

Words tumble from his mouth. He's a lyrical Marshall McLuhan. Often as not, thoughts are bracketed by the name of the person he is addressing, giving a sense of urgency to even mundane observations: "Tommy, you're going to make the turn here, Tommy." "Howie, how many of these go out, Howie?" And likewise, suddenly, late at night, apropos of nothing, unprompted, spoken in some awe and much gratitude: "Frank, what a great life I've had, Frank."

This starts to get us back to the sad clowns. The key to understanding McGuire is to appreciate his unqualified love of life, of what's going on around him. e.e. cummings: "I was marvelously lucky to touch and seize a rising and striving world; a reckless world, filled with the curiosity of life herself; a vivid and violent world welcoming every challenge; a world hating and adoring and fighting and forgiving; in brief, a world which was a world." Al McGuire: "Welcome to my world." With him everything is naturally vivid and nearly everything is naturally contradictory, the way it must be in crowded, excited worlds.

So with the clowns. It is not the sadness that matters, or even the clownishness. It is the *sad clown,* a contradiction. By definition, can there be such a thing as a sad clown? Or a wise coach? "Sports is a coffee break," McGuire says. And Eugene McCarthy once observed, "Coaching is like politics. You have to be smart enough to know how to do it, but dumb enough to think it is important."

Now, if all of the foregoing has tumbled and twisted and gone in fits and spurts, that's what it is like being around Al McGuire. His business, making money (it includes coaching as a necessary evil), comes ordered and neat, hermetic — to use his word, *calculated* — but everything else veers off in different directions, at changing speeds, ricocheting. Actually, all of that is calculated, too, only we cannot always fathom to what purpose. For example, later on here McGuire is going to expound at length on how he is not only sick of coaching but how he no longer applies himself to the task, and how Marquette could be virtually unbeatable if he just worked harder. Now, these remarks were made thoughtfully and have been repeated and embellished on other occasions. Obviously, they are going to come back to haunt him. Other recruiters are going to repeat them to prospects. If Marquette loses a couple of games back-to-back, the press and the alumni and the students and even those warm and wonderful fans who don't have shrews for wives are going to throw this admission back in his face. And he knows this, knew it when he spoke. So maybe you can figure out why he said what he did. Probably it has something to do with tar babies. Somehow he figures that other people who slug it out with him in his world are going to get stuck.

People are dazzled by McGuire, by his colorful language and by the colorful things he does — riding motorcycles at his age, which is 48, or going off on solitary trips to the four corners of the globe. That stuff is all out front, hanging out there with the clown pictures, so people seize upon it and dwell on this "character." They miss the man. First off, he is a clever entrepreneur, a promoter, a shrewd businessman, an active executive of a large sports equipment company (vice-president of Medalist Industries). This interests him much more than the baskets. "And I have an advantage," he says, "because people have a false impression from reading about me. They expect one thing and suddenly find themselves dealing with a very calculating person. I scare them. I want to skip the French pastry and get right down to the numbers."

The fans and the press think of McGuire as the berserk hothead who drew two technicals in an NCAA championship game, or the uncommonly handsome, dapper sharpie, pacing, spitting, playing to the crowd, cursing his players, themselves attired in madcap uniforms resembling the chorus line in *The Wiz*. The fans and the press overlook the fact that McGuire's Marquette teams have made the NCAA or the NIT ten years in a row, averaging twenty-five wins a season the last nine, and they got there by concentrating on defense, ice-picking out victories by a few points a game. As a coach, you can't much control an offense: *They just weren't going in for us tonight.* A defense is a constant, seldom fluctuating, always commanding. Just because people see Al McGuire's body on the bench, they assume that is he, carrying on. You want to see Al McGuire, look out on the court, look at the way his team plays, calculating. McGuire will play gin rummy against anybody; he won't play the horses or a wheel in Vegas; he won't play the house. You play him, his game, his world. "People say it's all an act, and maybe it is," he says. "Not all of it — but I don't know myself anymore whether I'm acting. Not anymore. I don't know. I just know it pleases me."

The motorcycle, for example, gets involved here. McGuire adores motorcycling. Most mornings at home in Milwaukee, he rises at seven and tools around for a couple of hours on his Kawasaki. Before the regionals in Louisiana last year, he rented a bike and went to a leper hospital. So the motorcycle business is for real. Also, it is French pastry. Let us look at McGuire vis-à-vis more important things; for example, cars and women.

Now, most coaches adore automobiles and have no rapport with women. That is not to say that they don't like sex; it is to say that they tolerate women because women provide sex. But they don't enjoy the company of women. They don't like them *around.* This is what upsets them about women's athletics, not the money it's going to take from men's sports. Just that they're going to be around. On the other hand, American coaches are nuts about cars. Cars count. The most important thing to coaches is to get a courtesy car to drive around town in. This is the sign of being a successful coach. Almost any American coach will sign for $10,000 less if you give him the use of a $6,500 car.

Naturally, being one of the most famous and successful basketball coaches in the land, Al McGuire has a courtesy car. It is a Thunderbird. He gets a fresh one every two years. But, unlike other coaches, he has no relationship with his car. It doesn't mean anything to him. Last February, after a whole winter of driving the thing, 3,200 miles' worth, he still didn't have any idea how to turn on the heat. He had to be shown. And while he can whip around on his motorcycle, he is nearly incompetent as an automobile driver. While driving, he can become oblivious to the fact that he is driving. Sometimes he hunches over the wheel, sort of embracing it, and lets the car carry him and his country music along. Other times he takes both hands off the wheel to properly gesticulate. As a rule, he stops at all stop signs, including those that face down the other road of an intersection. This leads to some confusion in the cars behind the courtesy Thunderbird. Or sometimes, when a topic especially involves him, the car will sort of drift to a halt as he is talking. Just kind of peter out by the side of the road.

But as he does not fraternize with cars, so is he the rare coach who enjoys and appreciates women. This is not telling tales out of school. This has nothing to do with his marriage, which is going on twenty-seven years. This has to do with women generically. "I get along with women better than I do with men," Al says, simply enough. Whenever he talks to a woman he knows, he takes her hands gently in his and confides in her. But understand, the consummate calculator doesn't flash those green eyes just to be friendly. There are many ways to be credit-card-wise. "I've always believed that if you get women involved in anything, it will be a success," McGuire says. "Frank, most men in America are dominated by women, Frank."

He is not. He and Pat McGuire share a marriage that is not unlike the way he coaches. They do not crowd one another. In the twenty-six years he has been married, he has never used a house key. When he comes home, Pat must let him in. When it is late, which it often is, she is inclined to say, "Where have you been?" He replies, "Pat, were there any calls for me, Pat?" When Marquette is on the road, McGuire never sits in the game bus waiting for it to leave. He waits in a bar for the manager to come in and tell him everyone is aboard. Then, if someone was late, he doesn't know. "A lot of coaching is what you choose *not* to do, *not* to see," McGuire says. "That is hypocritical, of course, but it is also true."

This, however, is not to suggest that Pat McGuire puts up with him completely. Like her husband, she is not crazy about all kinds of surprises. This leads to the Al McGuire First Rule of Marriage: when you have something unsettling to tell your wife, advise her thereof just before you go into the bathroom. Thus, when Al decides to take off for Greece or the Yukon or any place where "I can get away from credit cards and free tickets," he announces the trip to Pat as he walks down the hall. "Yes?" she answers. "I'm going to Greece tomorrow for two weeks," he calls out. "What?" she says, afraid she has heard him correctly again. She has. Then he repeats the message and closes the bathroom door. This has worked, more or less, for twenty-six years. Is it at all surprising that his unorthodoxy has succeeded so well at Marquette for a mere twelve?

Now that you are more than somewhat confused, let us go back to his beginning. Al McGuire is influenced by his family and his heritage. He was born on September 7, 1928, in the Bronx but grew up in the Rockaway Beach section of Queens, where his family ran a workingman's bar. It was a club, a phone, a bank; they cashed paychecks. There were fifty-six saloons in seven blocks, meaning a) the McGuires had a lot of competition, but b) they were in the right business for that particular constituency. Al was named for Al Smith, then running as the first major Catholic presidential candidate. Al Smith was the quintessential New Yorker. He was fervently opposed to Prohibition, he wore a derby hat and said such strange words as "raddio" for what brought us *Amos 'n' Andy.* The namesake McGuire, removed from New York for two decades now, first in North Carolina, then in Milwaukee, still honors the other Al by talking Noo Yawkese. The *r*'s in the middle of many words evaporate. Thus, the fowuds play in the conner, whence they participate in pattuns. And there is the occasional awreddy and youse and den (for then), and the missing prepositions so reminiscent of that disappearing subway culture: down Miami; graduated high school.

McGuire also claims to have enriched the language. It was his interest in the stock market, he says, that brought the term blue chip into sports ("But I wasn't famous enough at the time to get credit for it"). Likewise, "uptick," for when a stock/team advances. Gambling, a familiar pursuit of his father's, an illness for his legendary older brother John, provided "the minus pool" (for losers), "a push" (a standoff), and "numbers," the word McGuire invariably uses for dollars. "What are the numbers?" is a common McGuire expression. Then, from the old sod, there are the adages: "Never undress until you die" (always save something, or, "Squirrel some nuts away"). "Congratulate the temporary" (live for the moment, or, "Go barefoot in the wet grass"). He has recently developed an interest in antiques, which he hunts down on his motorcycle forays, and promises us new terms from antiquing soon.

But it is his imagery, original and borrowed, that is the most vivid McGuire. Seashells and balloons: happiness, victory. Yellow ribbons and medals: success in recruiting. Memos and pipes: academia. Hot bread and gay waiters: guaranteed, a top restaurant. A straw hat in a blizzard: what some people, like the NCAA, will provide you with. Even a whale comes up for a blow sometimes: advice to players who can't get their minds off women. Hot lunch for orphans: a

giveaway, some sort of PR venture. French pastry: anything showy
or extraneous, such as small talk or white players. Keepers: good-
looking broads (you don't throw them back). Closers: people who
get by the French pastry and complete a deal, e.g., yours truly, Al
McGuire. Guys who charge up the hill into a machine gun: most X-
and-O coaches; see also "Brooks Brothers types" and "First Communion guys." Welcome to my world: come uptown with me.

Moreover, McGuire has begun more and more to turn nouns into
verbs. Thus, to "rumor it out" is what a smart executive does when
he keeps his ear to the ground. And: "Guys like Chones and Mem-
inger magnet kids for us." Or: "You've got to break up cliques or
you'll find players husband-and-wifing it out on the court." Or: "If
you haven't broken your nose in basketball, you haven't really
played. You've just tokened it."

It is the custom at Marquette to let teammates fight, to encourage fights, for that matter, until the day the season opens. McGuire
lets them go a minute. One day he stood there, biting his lip for
the required time while an older player beat his son Allie, a pretty
fair guard, all to hell. This policy is calculated to let frustrations
out, draw the team together. Calculated. For he has no stomach for
it. McGuire has seen all he would ever want of fighting.

It was an old Irish thing. His father, John, Sr., delighted in it. What
more could a man want than to sip a beer and watch his boys mix
it up? If not large for a basketball player — 6′ 3″ — McGuire was a
big kid in a saloon, and he worked behind the bar from an early
age. It was the bartender's job to break up fights. If you hired a
bouncer, the trouble was he was liable to start fights himself; otherwise, he couldn't justify his job. So, fight started, the barkeep had
to come over the bar. Feet first. Always come feet first. Or, if the
action was slack, a slow Tuesday or whatnot, old John McGuire
might drum up a fight for one of his own boys, and they would "go
outside" to settle things.

Al McGuire played ball the same way. His older brother Dick,
now a Knick scout, was the consummate Noo Yawk player for St.
John's and the Knicks — a slick ball handler and passer. Al was what
he himself calls a dance-hall player. He was good enough to star as
a college player, at St. John's, but as a pro could only hang on as an
enforcer for three seasons with the Knicks. Once he grabbed Sid
Borgia, the famous official, in what was described by horrified ob-
servers as "a boa constrictor grip." Counting two technicals, he got

eight fouls in less than a quarter in one game. He boasted that he could "stop" Bob Cousy in his heyday, which he could, after a fashion, halting the action by fouling Cousy or the guy who set picks for him. It was McGuire's big mouth that first sold out the Boston Garden for the Celtics. They paid to see the brash Irishman try to stop their Celtic. In the off-season McGuire would go back to Rockaway, tend bar, and go outside when his father asked for such divertissement.

"We all thought it was so romantic," he says, "so exciting, but, Frank, looking back, it wasn't, Frank." Not long ago McGuire was in a joint in Greenwich Village. A few tables over, there was an argument. The guy took off his watch. It took six, seven guys to subdue him. McGuire turned to the businessman he was with. "He'll be back," he said. He had seen it so many times. Sure enough, in a little while the guy was back, and there was another mess. The next morning, at breakfast, McGuire began thinking about the previous night's incident, and just like that, he threw up. "Maybe it was the orange juice," he says, "but I don't think so. It was what that fight made me remember. It scared me. I don't want those memories."

One time, when he was about 24 or 25, his father got him to go outside with a guy. "I was handling him, but I couldn't put him away," McGuire says, "and I knew I couldn't get away with this." He was very relieved when the cops came and broke it up. Al went back into the bar and told his father, "Dad, that's it, Dad. I'm never gonna go outside again." And he never did. His father sulked for a month or more. It was not long after that that Al decided all of a sudden he could be very successful in life at large.

But money, or the lack of it, has influenced Al McGuire more than taking guys outside. Some people who grew up in the Depression are that way. The McGuires had food on the table; they weren't on the dole. Still, money was a concern. Of the sons, John, now 52, was considered the clever one. And he was, except for the gambling. He has adapted well; he runs a gay bar now. Dick, 50, was considered the bright one. At an early age he could do the *New York Times* crossword. Al, the youngest, was dismissed as a glib scuffler. Everybody, himself included, figured he would become an Irish cop, an FBI man if he got lucky. He was scheduled to take an FBI physical one day but played golf instead. He thought he had blown a great chance in life and, remorseful, on his way home he stopped his car on the Cross Bay Bridge, got out, and chucked his clubs, the cart, the whole business, in the water. It was a little while later, when he was an assistant coach at Dartmouth, that he decided he could be a success, he could make money.

You see, even when nobody figured Al for anything, the family let him handle the books. The kid was at home with the numbers. And then one day at Dartmouth, where it snowed a lot, he was alone, and had time to think, and he figured out he had more talent with the numbers than with the baskets. "Since then I've never had any trouble making money," he says. "All I have to do is sit down and think. I believe I can do anything in that area."

Since then, while he has coached every year, while it is his profession, coaching has never been the ultimate. As a consequence, he is not vulnerable there. McGuire often says (indeed, he doth protest too much), "I've never blown a whistle, looked at a film, worked at a blackboard or organized a practice in my life." Which is true, and which drives other coaches up the wall. But McGuire, the anti-coach, regularly discusses land mortgages, Medalist shoulder-pad marketing, and his theories on the short-range future of municipal bonds. Intellectually, temperamentally, what is the difference between a fascination with a high-post back door and a short-term bond yield?

And yet, McGuire is only hung up on the numbers in the abstract. *The numbers:* It is a euphemism, like the Victorians using "limbs" for legs. Real money doesn't mean anything to him. He carries it all scrunched up in his pocket: bills, credit cards, notes, gum wrappers, identification cards, all loose together. He takes out the whole mess and plops it on the counter. "Take what you want," he says. A credit card? Two dollars and sixty-three cents for breakfast? My driver's license? Take whatever you want. The Depression baby just wants to know that the money in the bank is solid and permanent. *Never undress until you die.*

"I must be the highest-paid coach in the country," he says. "I wanted it. I thought it would be a goose for basketball. I don't mean just what I get from Marquette. I mean all the numbers. If anybody put all the numbers together it would amaze people. But understand: It hasn't changed me. I've always lived the same. My friends are still hit-and-run types. I eat the same as ever, drink the same, clown around the same. My wife still wears Treasure Island dresses."

He is not friendly with many coaches. Hank Raymonds has been beside him on the bench all twelve years at Marquette and has never had a meal at the McGuires'. Raymonds and young Rick Majerus do the Xs and Os, the trench work. McGuire believes in "complementary" coaches, as he does in complementary players, units that support each other's efforts, not duplicate them. "I can drink enough cocktails for the whole staff," McGuire says. "I don't need another me."

His assistants (McGuire, out of respect and guilt, has taken to calling them "co-coaches") understand his soft-shoe. One asks Majerus: What is it above all about McGuire? We are so used to hearing about the originality, the insouciance, the motorcycle flake, the ability to get along with black players — what is it really with McGuire? "The one main thing," Majerus answers, "is this insecurity Al has about money. Still. I guess he'll always be that way."

There was a group with McGuire a couple of winters ago after a road game. As always, he wouldn't countenance any talk about basketball, but soon enough he brought up the subject of the numbers. Typically, it was the woman in the gathering that he turned to, confided in. Speaking softly, as he does on these occasions, he told her he thought he had things worked out OK for his three kids, for Pat. They were going to have enough. For a Depression baby this made him feel good, he said. But what if he accumulated more money, the woman asked him, what would he do with that?

McGuire was not prepared for the question. He thought for a moment. "A park," he said then. "With what's left, I'd like to see them build a park for poor people."

To most everybody in the business, McGuire is a nagging aberration. Listening to him lecture 500 coaches at a Medalist clinic, Chuck Daly of Penn whispers, "If the rest of us operated his way, we'd be out of business." That is the conventional wisdom. But before he said that, Daly made another observation: "Al's logic is on a different level, above everybody else's." And that is the conventional wisdom, too. So wait a minute. If McGuire wins twenty-five a year and he has the logic, he obviously has the right way. That is logical. Nonetheless, he remains the only coach who waits in the bar, and he stays frustrated that coaches have such low esteem and little security.

"Coaches are so scared," he says. "Every day, practice starts: gimme three lines, gimme three lines. You come out and say gimme two lines, everybody will look at you like you just split the atom.

Me, whether it's business or coaching, I'm so pleased when I look like a fool. When I don't do foolish things, make foolish new suggestions, I'm not doing my job. I'm just another shiny-pants bookkeeper.

"The trouble with coaching, the prevailing image, is that coaching is like what you had in high school, because that is the last place where most people were involved with coaching. But coaching college is not pizza parties and getting the team together down at the A and W stand. People can't understand my players screaming back at me, but it's healthy. Also, I notice that the screaming always comes when we're fifteen, twenty ahead. When it's tied, then they're all listening very carefully to what I have to say."

Many adult coaches demand unquestioning loyalty from 20-year-old kids. As McGuire points out, some of the most successful coaches even refuse to accept kids with different philosophies, conflicting egos. "Dealing with problems, with differences — that is what coaching is," he says. "Running pattuns is not coaching." He does not believe that character can be "built" with haircuts and Marine routines and by coaches so insecure that their players can never challenge them.

Off the court, McGuire sees his players only when they come to him in distress. He would be suspicious of any college kid who wanted to be buddy-buddy with a middle-aged man, and vice versa. "I don't pamper," he says. "These guys are celebrities in their own sphere of influence — top shelf, top liquor. Everybody around them touches them with clammy hands. That's the only word: clammy. Well, they don't get that from me." Often, he doesn't even bother to learn their names. For much of last season the starting center, Jerome Whitehead, was called Chapman. Sometimes McGuire has stood up to scream at a player and then had to sink back down because he couldn't remember the kid's name.

"Look, if you're into coaching heavy, into the blackboard, if you're gonna charge up the hill into the machine guns, then you might as well stay at St. Ann's in the fifth grade," he says. "Because coaching up here is something else. You're gonna have to deal with the fifth column, the memos and pipes. And you're gonna get fired. The trouble is, every coach thinks he has the new wrinkle and is gonna last forever. Coaching is a mistress, is what it is. If a job opened up in Alaska tomorrow, two hundred fifty guys from Florida would apply, and they wouldn't even ask about the numbers, and they wouldn't ask their wife, either, like they wouldn't about any mistress.

"But to the players you ain't a love affair. You're just a passing fancy to them. It's pitiful, too, because about every coach who leaves makes better numbers on the outside."

Everyone assumes McGuire gets along with his players — especially the inner-city blacks — because of his unique personality. It counts, to be sure; every charmer is an overlay. But look past the French pastry and his calculation surfaces again — just as he promises. No con works unless the conned party figures he is the one really getting the edge. McGuire settles for a push. "They get and I get," he says. While the players don't get an uncle-coach, they get, as McGuire calls it, "a post-recruiter." He virtually forces them to get a diploma, and he hustles them up the richest pro contracts or good jobs in business. It is surely not just a coincidence that McGuire has thrived during the years when the big-money pro war was on. He has been a cash coach in a cash-and-carry era. On one occasion the Marquette provost had to personally intercede to stop McGuire from pressuring the sports PR man about withholding unfavorable statistics that might harm a player's pro chances.

Shamelessly, McGuire promotes his seniors, a ploy that keeps a kid hustling, playing defense, giving up the ball for his first three seasons, so he will get the ball and the shots (and maybe then the big numbers) his final year. Already, in anticipation of this season, McGuire has begun to protest that Butch Lee, a junior guard, got too much publicity as the star of the Puerto Rico Olympic team. Bo Ellis, a senior, is scheduled to get the ink this time around.

The McGuire Arrangement is, basically, us against them — "The only two things blacks have ever dominated are basketball and poverty" — and it works because he tends bar for everybody. Nobody ever fussed with McGuire more than last year's ball handler, Lloyd Walton. "Sit down!" he would scream at his coach all through games. Says Walton, "He figures your problems are his problems. Hey, I've had a black coach in summer ball, but I never had the rapport with him I had with Al."

When McGuire learned one November night back in 1968 that revolutionaries on campus were pressuring the black players to quit because they were being "exploited," he met with the players in a motel room sometime after 2 A.M. He didn't go long on philosophy. He told them he would support their decision if they left and gave up their scholarships, but he also reminded them that there were more where they came from — maybe not so good, but they weren't Marquette basketball. He was.

Then he faced down the radicals. The smooth-talking theorists he screamed at. The tough guys he ridiculed. He suggested to an idealistic white coed that she should take one of the black players home to her suburb for Thanksgiving. To a priest, he snarled, "Don't come after these kids from the Jesuit house. You never bought a pound of butter in your life, and you're asking them to be kamikaze pilots." By 4:30 A.M. when Pat came to the doorbell to let him in, the revolution was dead.

The relationship between Marquette and McGuire is a curious one and, it seems, a push. Marquette is one of the few Catholic schools left that compete, year after year, with the huge state institutions. For that matter, Marquette is the only private school of any stripe that is always right there at the top. The Warriors not only sell out for the season, they do it head to head, in the same building, against the Milwaukee Bucks, a first-class pro team.

Never mind the ratings: Basketball pays a lot of bills at Marquette. It retired the oppressive old football debt. And McGuire must be reckoned with; for several years now he has been athletic director as well as coach. Of course, there are certain Marquette elements leery of the image of the school being filtered through the McGuire prism.

What the nation sees of Marquette University is a self-proclaimed hustler, ranting and raving at the establishment, running a team of ghetto blacks dressed in wild uniforms. What is this, some kind of desperado vocational school? In fact, Marquette is a relatively subdued place, Jesuit, stocked for the most part by white middle-class midwestern Catholics who end up as schoolteachers. Typically, McGuire — who sent all three of his children there — guarantees that it must be good academically or it couldn't get by charging such high tuition numbers.

While the coach and the school do share the same religion, McGuire does not get faith confused with the pattuns or the players who execute them. His only public concession to Catholicism, such as it is, is his pregame exhortation, which went like this last season, all in one breath: "All-right-let's-show-them-we're-the-number - two - team - in - the - country - and - beat - the - shit - out - of - them-Queen-of-Victory-pray-for-us."

Mostly the Jesuit fathers confine themselves to second-guessing the coach's substitutions rather than the morality of his antics. Says Father William Kelly, an associate professor of theology, "Al does use a few cultural expressions that some might find flippant — 'Hail Mary shot,' that sort of thing — but he is not sacrilegious in the traditional faith context. He has just found congeniality in colloquialism. In fact, in terms of his ideals and his faith, he is very much a man of the Church. He is really a very conservative Catholic, if not necessarily a very good one. But Al is loyal and deep in his faith. He is competitive, but when he loses there is no blame. And he always points toward other, more important things."

Ay, there's the rub. The man has never really relished coaching, and with each succeeding season has cared for it less. When the call came, out of the blue, to interview for the Marquette opening ("They were desperate, obviously; otherwise they would have taken a First Communion guy"), he was drifting into real estate and other ventures, coaching with his left hand at little Belmont Abbey College in North Carolina. He went 6–19 and 6–18 his last two years there and was preparing to leave coaching altogether.

He appears to be approaching that estate again. In many ways, as he is the first to admit, Marquette basketball survives on his reputation and the hard work of Raymonds and Majerus. McGuire deigns to make only one recruiting visit a year ("The kids know more about me now than I know about them, but even though I don't work at it, I'm the best recruiter in the world"), and, invariably — eleven years out of thirteen — he gets his ace with his one-shot road show. He is often late for practice; sometimes he doesn't even know where the team is practicing. He gets older and smarter, but for a coach time stands still. The kids are always 19 going on 20, and most coaches and fans are one-track zombies; the Germans have the best word for them: *Fachidioten* — specialty idiots. McGuire would rather talk about how his new uniforms will televise than about his player prospects. When he gets to the Arena floor, the first things he checks are the four most distant corner seats — the worst ones in the house. If they are sold, he figures he has done it again. Then, only then, does he come to life as a coach. For two hours.

"I hate everything about this job except the games," McGuire says. "Everything. I don't even get affected anymore by the winning, by the ratings, those things. The trouble is, it will sound like an excuse because we've never won the national championship, but winning just isn't all that important to me. I don't know why exactly. Maybe it's the fear, the fear of then having to repeat. You win once, then they expect you to win again. On the other hand, I found out when I got those two technicals in the NCAA finals that people sympathized with me for making an ass out of myself. I get thirty-five million people looking at me, I can't help it, I immediately become an ass. People relate to that.

"But, Frank, I'm not doing the job anymore, Frank. I never liked coaching, but at least I should be available more. I should be more courteous to my staff. I should have a more orderly process with the university. Maybe it's the repetition. You take the clinics we do for Medalist. They're almost a success, but now, just when they're getting to be that, I don't have no thrill anymore. I wonder about myself. Can I be a success in anything permanently? Anything permanent?

"I figure I'm wrong eighty percent of the time, but it takes too much time to be right. I won't pay that price with my life. I'm jealous of guys like Dean Smith, Bobby Knight. I'm jealous of their dedication. I wish I had it. I admire the way their teams are dressed, the way their kids handle themselves. At the regionals last year one of our kids came down to lunch barefoot. But I just don't like coaching that much to put the time in on a thing like that. It's not my world. I run my team the only way I can run it and still keep my life.

"I'm ready to get out. It's just the numbers. So many of my numbers depend on me coaching. I'm scared to get out. Fear there, too. So maybe it's time I concentrated on coaching just for one year. It's been long enough I haven't concentrated. Frank, we could have a destructive machine if I worked at it. A destructive machine, Frank."

Is he acting now? It certainly doesn't seem so. The green eyes are neither twinkling nor blazing theatrically, the way they do when they signal routines. By happenstance, McGuire has been momentarily distracted. He came to an out-of-town place under the impression it was a greasy-spoon Mexican joint, but it has turned out, instead, to be a fancy-Dan supper club. With floor show. With table linen, yet. McGuire, in his sneakers and sport shirt, wasn't figuring on this — and place, setting the stage, is very important to him.

He wants to recruit around the kitchen table. Depression babies are kitchen guys, not parlor people. When a player comes to talk to him, get him out of the office, out of Marquette; get him down into some back-alley saloon. Welcome to my world. Visitors are escorted to an oil-cloth-covered dining-room table in the back of a rundown Mexican bodega for a home-cooked meal. Or he just walks with people. Nobody anymore walks along and talks except for Al McGuire. Right away, the other guy is off stride, in the minus pool. You know what it must come from? From the going outside to fight guys. The meanness is out of it, but it's the same principle, same game. OK, let's you and me go outside. Let's go in here. Let's drive out to this lake I know. Let's go to this guy's apartment. Let's go to this little Chinese place. Let's take a walk.

Everybody makes such a to-do about Al McGuire's exotic travels. Big deal: New Zealand. What is that? Anybody can go to New Zealand. That is the diversion, his escape, the smoke screen. Look at his world. That is the truly exotic one. How could a guy so Noo Yawk fit in so well in Milwaukee, or in Carolina before that? It's easy. Wherever McGuire is, he constructs a whole universe out of selected bars and restaurants, places to walk, acquaintances, teddy bears and zanies, places to drive, back rooms and penthouses, motorcycles and country music jukeboxes. Tall guys with broken noses are also a part of this community. There is a cast and there are sets — everything but a zip code.

Nobody else is permitted to see it all. He tells his secretaries when he hires them: two years. After two years, no matter how good you are — especially if you're good — out. *It's 3 A.M., where have you been? Pat, any calls for me, Pat?* The only person who lives in Al McGuireland is Al McGuire. Cynics and the jealous take a look at the characters who pass through, and they check out his con and whisper that he is really an ice-cold man who surrounds himself with bootlickers and sycophants. But that is not true. On the contrary. Sure, they all play up to McGuire — remember now, charmers are an overlay — but he has a need for them, too. Not just the players and the coaches, but all the people and places in Al McGuireland are complementary. Like his players, all retain their individuality and integrity. That's the whole point: Otherwise they're no good to him. Lloyd Walton screaming back is the Lloyd Walton that McGuire wants, in the same way that sometimes he selects a fleabag hotel precisely because he wants a fleabag hotel.

The one permanent thing is the numbers. They are distant and bland, to be sure, but they provide permanency. The other things — the people and the places and the basketball games — are vivid and dear, but they consume too much of him to be sustained. And critics say it is all an act. McGuire wonders himself. But, no, he is not acting. He is directing all the time. Al, you're a director, Al. You're always running pattuns.

* * *

As might not be surprising from his remarks, McGuire decided to give up coaching shortly after this article appeared in the fall of 1976. His last team peaked at the right time, and, in his final game, Al won his first national championship. Doing it this way made it so that he didn't have to worry about the pressure of repeating.

After retiring from coaching, Al became even more famous as a basketball commentator on NBC and general all-around credit-card-wise sage.

This next article was suggested to me by Milton Lewis, a Methodist minister who had once lived in Pineville, Kentucky, where the story takes place. I had just written a story about a coach, and so I put this idea away for a couple of years before I went back to it. I welcome suggestions from readers, but the trouble is, in most cases, they're like generals fighting the last war. If I write a piece about a left-handed Chinese javelin thrower from Alabama, I'll get a letter telling me there's a much better story about a left-handed Chinese javelin thrower in Montana.

Every Little Town Has Somebody

THE Bishops, Fred and Inez, of Pineville, Kentucky, possess all the best American graces — faith and diligence, loyalty, sacrifice, and hard work. For most of their lives the Bishops were dirt poor, but there was bounty in what they bred: seven magnificent children, all of whom earned honors, scholarships, and college degrees. The Bishop children were bright and popular and so healthy that, in the aggregate, they didn't miss so much as a month of school days. This was a family blessed.

The three sons were all extraordinary athletes, though Fred and Inez never cared much about sports and certainly never pushed the boys to participate. Indeed, when Fred, Jr., the middle son, scored fifty-four points for Pineville High in a basketball game, Inez told the coach it was "ridiculous" that any boy should get so many points at the expense of his teammates. Fred, Jr., may have been the best of the sons, excelling at both football and basketball. Athletics came the most naturally to him, but his baby brother, Eddie, was nearly as good — some folks in Pineville would even say better. The first time Eddie ever batted in a baseball game, he hit the longest home run anyone in the county had ever seen.

Anyway, indisputably, Eddie came across as the most natural person among the sons. He was always the happiest child, laughing, beloved, well balanced — until one sweet green evening in April 1981 when, without warning, all the pressures of sport that we place upon our best boys suddenly swelled within his lithe young body and the dam burst, and Eddie Bishop went suddenly berserk, utterly mad. He tore away from his family and friends, and with that same facility he'd shown Pineville upon the playing fields, he dashed away as fast as he could, outdistancing them all, charging down the road, broken-field, gliding into the lingering twilight.

It was two years earlier that Eddie had decided to return to Pineville. He'd graduated from Morehead State the spring before and he was studying for his master's degree in health and physical education, but he had a wife and a son, and he was tired of schoolwork, and if he took the job teaching at Pineville High, he could make some money. There were a lot of people who had misgivings. Lee, the oldest brother, was against it, and he best realized the special pressures because, when he'd started teaching and coaching, that's exactly what he'd done: gone back to Pineville High for a year. But then Lee had left quickly for Fort Knox, across the state. Still, he says, "How could I tell Eddie not to do what I'd done myself?"

Jerry Woolum, a doctor at Pineville Community Hospital, knew the Bishops well, and he knew football. Woolum had been a starting quarterback in 1962 at the University of Kentucky. He was a member of the Pineville school board that hired Eddie to become the football coach a few months after Eddie had joined the high school faculty. "It's obvious now we made a mistake," Woolum says. "But it was an honest mistake."

Even up at Morehead, Eddie had been warned before he left. The Morehead coaches came down to Pineville after what everybody in town still calls "the accident." They dropped by Flocoe Drugstore, and Mason Combs, the pharmacist, remembers that one of the assistants repeated what he'd told Eddie: that he shouldn't go back to his hometown.

Even at that time, some people probably quoted Thomas Wolfe. They certainly do now.

But Eddie wasn't just another guy named Joe going home again. He was a bona fide, certified hero going home again. "Pineville's Star of Stars" is what the local weekly, the *Sun-Courier,* called him. You see, in situations like this, folks think: If we can only bring the old hero back, it's going to be jake again; he'll get it back for us. Pineville isn't alone in such thinking. Just look over at Cincinnati, where a few months ago they brought Pete Rose back. Same thing. Remember when they gave Bart Starr the job in Green Bay? Or when they brought Willis Reed home to New York? New York or

Green Bay, the Big Apple or Podunk: same thing. Of course, it almost never works, but people keep trying.

As D. C. Cloud, one of Eddie's best friends, says: "I was even awed myself. And Pineville . . . everyone was thinking: We're bringing one of the Bishop boys back, and so all our kids are going to be good, too. You've got to understand that for years, whenever the Pineville team came to a town, the people actually thought 'Bishop.'"

All over the state, whenever Retha, Eddie's wife, was introduced, someone would say: "You any kin to the Pineville Bishops?" And, she says, "The people in Pineville were telling Eddie: 'You're going to come back and make our town good because you were so good.'"

And boy, was he, too. All of the Bishops. Eddie after Fred, Fred after Lee. They all won athletic scholarships. They weren't just recruited; they were what we call *pursued*. Lee went to Cumberland College, Fred to Kentucky, Eddie to Morehead. Lee is the tallest, 6'6", and was primarily a basketball specialist, but Fred, Jr., and Eddie starred in both basketball and football, winning various and sundry all-state and All-America honors — and, more important for a town the size of Pineville, population 2,599, winning what's commonly known as "immortality." Jimmy Roan, who's retired now, the father of Robert Roan, the quarterback when Eddie starred for Pineville, jabs a plug of snuff into his left cheek and says it best: "Every small town has a great athlete everybody remembers. Every town has somebody. And sometime around here, thirty, forty years from now, some kid will come along, and he'll be real good. And people will start to say he must be the best ever, and somebody will say, 'Yeah, he's good all right — he's almost as good as Fred or Eddie Bishop was.'"

At 6'3", Fred knew he would have to make a transition from frontcourt to back if he chose to play basketball in college, so he very coolly chose football for his scholarship. But he thinks Eddie should have opted to play basketball in college. At 6'1", he was the shortest of the three brothers, a natural guard, but he chose football and went up to Morehead as a wide receiver, catching spirals from a quarterback named Phil Simms, who was good enough to go on and make a name for himself with the New York Giants.

Then, too, Pineville is just plain a football town. You say Kentucky, you think basketball, but that has never been the case in

Pineville, the Gem City of the Cumberlands. Pineville High has long been the smallest school in the state to play football, and through the years it has raised up some hellacious teams. In the old days, when they could slip in some of the coal miners as ringers, Pineville High could take on anyone in the Commonwealth; the Mountain Lions went all the way to Louisville to play the big city boys, and to Lexington, where they took on the UK freshmen. At the Baptist Church in Pineville, which is much the biggest parish in a "well-churched" town, the Reverend Charles Jones says: "It's just been an accepted fact that a healthy boy in Pineville played football." And two of his own did, too — including Johnny, who played with Eddie Bishop.

Over at Flocoe's Drugstore the other morning, some of the old-timers were having coffee and cigarettes with the mayor and the head of the school board and whoever else happened to come by. "The football team always gave us something to be proud of, and every little town *needs* that," one old fellow said. "Every little town needs something."

"I tell you what," said another, "every boy who only played in the band was a sissy."

"Well now," another graybeard said, "don't forget the ones that played on the team and then marched in the band at halftime."

Bobby Madon, the mayor, recalled that in glory times — like Coach Bill Adams's heyday, the late fifties and sixties — when the Mountain Lions played a big road game, there'd be bonfires on the courthouse lawn, all the stores would close, and the people in Pineville would nudge each other and say, "Last one to leave, please, you turn out the lights." At the Friday night home games, the stands would be packed, and the fans would ring the rest of the field four and five deep.

The '67 team was touted as being as good as any in the state. Adams had the team make trips in gray slacks and maroon jackets, with team bags, before a lot of college teams were doing that sort of thing. And the Pineville Athletic Boosters Club — "the finest boosters club in the state of Kentucky," many people said — even presented Adams with a brand-new automobile one year. "This is just a football-crazy town," says Wayne Knuckles, the editor of the *Sun-Courier.*

The best football of all was played by the Bishops: Fred, number 81 in the maroon and gold, and Eddie, number 14, holding on to the glory for Pineville, even as the coal played out and the number of good athletes dwindled. Then, after his older brother had gone to college, Eddie kept things going by himself, a one-man team, darting about in that pigeon-toed manner so many great athletes have, slashing down the field, bouncing back to the huddle. His greatest game may have been when he led Pineville past Twigg County High, state champion and twenty-eight-point favorite. Even better was beating Middlesboro. That's the town down the road, Route 25E — five times larger than Pineville, the one everybody in Pineville wants most to beat. "The man who did that magic is now the head coach. Maybe Coach Eddie Bishop can come up with another magic trick," the *Sun-Courier* wrote, years later, still savoring the 6–2 victory over Middlesboro in 1973.

Retha was there that night. She'd been the girl down the street all Eddie's life, but it was only when he was the football hero in town and she was one of the cheerleaders that they fell in love, she in her maroon-and-gold sweater and her pleated skirt, he in his maroon-and-gold uniform and his gladiator's helmet. All the folks in Pineville cheered off her cues, as she cheered for him, both of them in love, and neither of them knowing that it never gets any better than in high school, in the autumn, when it's the cheerleader and the one-man team.

Robert Roan was the quarterback that night, handing the ball to Eddie, or tossing it to him. "I'm happily married now, and we're having a baby, and I've been successful in business," Robert said one night recently, sitting over at Eddie's parents' house, out on the porch with the bugs and the memories. "But I'll tell you, still, the greatest thrill of my life was when we beat Middlesboro. That game. Isn't it funny the way a high school football game can stay with you?" He sighed. "But then, every memory of high school, and a lot of college, too, is of Eddie."

Now, Pineville happens to rest in the hills, where the Cumberland River cuts toward the Gap below, but it wouldn't matter if Pineville were in the hollows of Kentucky or on the plains of Texas, or in the mountains of Colorado or in the suburbs somewhere or down by the shore. It's all the same where Friday nights matter only for football, and the boys are made heroes before they are men.

On July 19, 1956, Edward Anthony Bishop was born at home in Pineville, the fifth of seven children. Inez (pronounced EYE-nez), the remarkable woman giving birth, remembers how curiously the father reacted this one time. "Why, Fred started chilling," she says. "And pretty soon he had that heater cherry red. The middle of the summer! And me burning up just from the hurting."

Fred, Jr., had been born barely a year before, and the last two children, Jennifer and Jan, would follow in such quick succession that Inez would bear four children, all single births, in a forty-two-month period. But there were no more pregnancies after Jan was born. Life was very difficult. Years before, Fred had come up from Alabama, a railroad man with a grade-school education, and now the L&N had laid him off for the last time, with seven children to support. Inez is as garrulous and irrepressible as Fred is quiet and reserved. She's a Dyer and has always lived in Pineville. Her father, a colossus of a man, reputed to have gone 450 pounds, had been killed in a mine accident when she was an infant, and she'd grown up a resourceful woman.

But when Fred was laid off for the final time, he and Inez faced a more desperate kind of nothing. They were bereft of all save "the milk in my breasts," Inez says. But the Bishops would not even consider going on welfare. Instead, they had bus tickets mailed to them and shipped out to Kingsport, Tennessee, seventy miles away, where they served as live-in domestics for three years. Inez's mother, Alice Dyer, tended the brood in Pineville. It would break Fred's and Inez's hearts when they returned home for a weekend every now and then, and their babies wouldn't even recognize them.

But the family center held. Lee, the eldest, set the pattern for the others, and Fred and Inez were able to put aside a few dollars. Finally, Fred got a job back in Pineville as a maintenance worker with what everybody calls "the K.U." — the state electric utility, the largest employer in Pineville. He still works there; Inez runs a day-care center in their house.

It's their house, too. The banks would go an extra mile for the Bishops; people would co-sign for Fred and Inez. Still, it was always a struggle, and Inez remembers one spring night when there was absolutely no money or food in the house when they went to sleep. Inez prayed to Jesus for help.

It snowed that night, and when the Bishops awoke, Pineville lay still under a freak wet spring storm. Fred and the three boys were able to shovel driveways. There was breakfast, after all. "The Lord had answered us," Inez says.

And then, one by one, the Bishop children graduated from

Pineville High and began to follow Lee to college. Eventually, they all got bachelor's degrees. Some went beyond that. Lee is a teacher and coach; Marie, the oldest daughter, is a policewoman in Memphis; Elaine is a hospital social worker in Lexington; Fred runs an urban-renewal agency in Frankfort; Jennifer, an attorney, works for Legal Aid in Cincinnati; and Jan is a social worker. Even if Lee and Fred, Jr., and Eddie had never picked up a ball, the Bishops would have been an admired family.

The fact that the Bishop children have left Pineville isn't surprising, though. There are very few opportunities for educated blacks in the area. Possibly because there aren't many blacks around, though, the whites don't seem to feel threatened, and race relations appear remarkably placid in Pineville. Indeed, Eddie's predecessor, Teddy Taylor, was a black man, and as the *Sun-Courier* wrote glowingly when Taylor left: "For many years to come residents of Pineville will be talking of the man with the bald head and that great team he had in 1978."

Of course, it didn't damage race relations that Taylor went 9–3 and took his team to the district finals.

For years, the few black families in Pineville encamped by themselves in the most vulnerable part of town, along Cumberland Avenue, where floodwaters periodically swept up from the river below. There is a floodwall there, and normally, too, the Cumberland is an agreeable stream, so much so that it was right there, in what became Pineville, that Daniel Boone led his pioneers west, over an easy ford. However:

When the rains come and the mountain creeks fill and rush into the Cumberland, it can become a wrathful weapon in God's hand, and at its worst, such as back in April of '77, the river crests above its banks, above the floodwall, and inundates the little town, the water eighteen or twenty feet deep around the courthouse where on warm, dry mornings old men whittle and nod at small lies.

The Noah-like flood of '77 even undermined the foundation of the old elementary school, which led to talk that the town would be well advised to give up the ghost and consolidate its few students into the Bell County system. But if Pineville was to lose its schools, then Pineville would lose its football team, too. So the townspeople approved a bond issue and had their taxes raised in order to build a new elementary school.

This is not a profligate people, either, and the mountain folk around the Gap — be they in Kentucky, Virginia, or Tennessee —

have always been a cussedly independent lot. Even now, just a few miles outside Pineville, in one of the deeper hollows, there's a good old-fashioned family feud taking place, with burnings and shootings and goings-on that not even the neighbors understand. Just up Straight Creek, over the mountain, there weren't any access roads in till after the war, and, right into the latter half of the twentieth century, the denizens spoke an authentic Shakespearean English. The towns around Pineville carry such names as Flat Lick, Salt Gum, Mary Alice, Field, Sunshine, Ogle, and Black Snake, and the people have always lived either off the land or of it, cutting timber or digging coal. Football was Pineville's game. Let those bluegrass pantywaists have their hoops.

Of course, like a lot of small-town kids, Eddie did some of everything there was to do. Because Fred was barely a year older and they were both outstanding athletes, they had a lot in common and shared a lot of friends. Still, everybody who knew the Bishop boys recognized the differences between them. Fred was more contained, less demonstrative, while Eddie, unlike most top athletes, was full of fun, never self-conscious, both a leader and a comic. The word *clown* is regularly summoned up to describe him, but always in a complimentary way.

Beaver Combs, who played center for the Mountain Lions, was one of Eddie's best friends, and he retains two visions of his old pal. The second one is of Eddie dashing about the field, the one-man team. But first, there was a Christmastime when a bunch of the guys went up to Lexington to go shopping, and Eddie decked himself out in black-and-orange shoes, green pants, and a red shirt. When he got separated from his friends, all the others went about laughing and asking strangers, "Have you seen a Christmas tree walking around?"

"Eddie just had a way of laughing everything off," Knuckles says. And he was carrying a lot: the fifth child in a proud family of achievers, the smallest brother after two distinguished athletes, a black in a predominantly white society. But he kept passing every test. He could charm anyone. Jennifer, his younger sister, even straight out asked her mother once, "Why do you favor Eddie so?"

Only Fred, Jr., looking back, sees him differently. "Eddie had a more serious attitude toward his relationship with people," he says. "I learned at an early age not to take people seriously. But, you see, most people didn't realize this because when they saw Eddie play, he was the one who always had a smile on his face. And I didn't.

But, in reality, Eddie was the serious one." Eddie always felt a responsibility to whatever he was part of — his family, his team, his town. Eddie was the sort of guy who was in the middle of everything, but he was out front, too, and that was a hard way to be, for a coach or for a hero.

It was in April of '79, after he'd been back at Pineville High for three months, teaching health and physical education, serving as an assistant coach for the basketball team, that Eddie was named head football coach in his hometown. He was just short of his twenty-third birthday.

Eddie had been reluctant at first to apply for the job, but once he was appointed, he threw himself into it. He went over to the school by himself and painted the lockers and lined the field. Nobody expected much from this edition of the Mountain Lions. There were only four seniors on the slim twenty-two-man squad. Even the *Sun-Courier,* which would become Eddie's most conspicuous critic, acknowledged that "the team is small and thin in numbers."

And so, everybody was perfectly delighted when Pineville beat Ewarts 6–2 in the Laurel Bowl, Coach Bishop's inaugural, on August 18, 1979. The accident was only twenty months distant, but there wasn't a soul in Pineville, or all of Bell County, who could have imagined what would happen to Eddie. He won his second game, too, 22–8 over Lone Jack, and if Pineville then got whipped 27–0 by Corbin, the winners were a larger, Class AA school. Next, hated Middlesboro also beat the Mountain Lions, but the score was only 9–8, the closest that Pineville had come since the classic victory of '73, when Eddie himself had run wild in the maroon and gold. Then, in the season finale, Pineville beat Bell County, another arch-rival, 20–19, and the team finished up with a 5–6 record. That certainly seemed, on paper, to be as much as anyone could have expected.

But behind Eddie's back, in certain precincts, there was criticism. The code word was *discipline.* Had Eddie had control of the team? The issue was of particular concern because drugs had finally reached Pineville. Adams, the former football coach and the Pineville High principal since 1977, agrees that the problem had begun to surface about the time Eddie took over. "It takes about ten years for something to get here . . . even a fad," he says.

During Adams's tenure as the coach, he could lay down the law. He wouldn't let players ride in cars during the season, except on weekends, and parents would call him up in the summer to ask him when the car rule would start. But now there was gossip that some Mountain Lions were messing around with *dope*. And while everybody would acknowledge that the times had changed, a lot of folks in Pineville, like a lot of folks everywhere, somehow wanted to believe that football coaches, and football coaches' authority, were exempt from the tides of change. Football coaches are supposed to be able to hand out backbones and gumption with the shoulder pads.

Inez can see it now: "There were some parents who couldn't control their children the way it used to be. So they wanted Eddie — they wanted the football coach — to do what they couldn't."

The 1980 squad was larger, with thirty-one players, but only half a dozen were seniors, and privately Eddie told friends that there were only two or three real athletes on the squad. Still, for whatever reasons, much more was expected of this team, especially by the *Sun-Courier.*

The general manager of the newspaper was the same Bobby Madon who was, and is, the mayor of Pineville. Madon is a one-man town. At the time, he wrote not only the weekly editorial column (entitled "Like It Is") but also the opinion column on the sports page ("Sports Slants"), and he broadcast the Pineville games on the local radio station. Moreover, his son was co-captain of the 1980 Mountain Lions, and the father expected a great deal of the lad. Very soon, Madon was describing the previous so-so season as "disastrous." And in a town used to fighting for survival from rampaging floodwaters, he raised the ante, declaring: "A losing football season is the most difficult thing to swallow in Pineville." And: "I remind you, when football dies at Pineville, so does the school."

In retrospect, Eddie's fate was all but sealed in the first game of the season, when Pineville was shut out 28–0 by Fleming-Neon High in the Laurel Bowl. Madon wrote, "This Laurel Bowl has been discussed over every cup of coffee in town . . . and no one can figure what's wrong with the 'Lions.' . . . This is certainly no criticism of anyone . . . but never have I seen a group with so much give so little. . . . We let a disciplined ball club control the ball all night."

Pineville fell to 1–4 and then 2–6. Worse, Middlesboro creamed

Pineville 30—0, so that the final 34—22 victory over Bell County was bitter consolation, and the season ended 4—7, 9—13 for Eddie's two years. Disgraced and disgruntled, Pineville cried for a new coach, one who could discipline its youth, the way it used to be. D. C. Cloud says, "I honestly think everybody knew how mediocre the material was that Eddie had. And they knew about the drugs when he came in. But people around here expect miracles in football."

The winter was long for Coach Bishop. The handwriting was on the wall. He wasn't allowed to return as basketball assistant. Public meetings at the school about the drug problem only generated more talk about how Eddie's team had been infected by drugs.

As was his nature, Eddie maintained a happy, hero's face. When alone with his friends and family, he did complain sometimes that the Boosters and old supporters — like Adams and Woolum — hadn't given him the backing he'd expected, but he never dwelt on the subject. He kept almost everything to himself.

Woolum went out of his way to try to counsel Eddie. As a member of the school board he was aware that Eddie was in trouble. "But as far as I know, right up to the accident, no one ever actually asked Eddie to resign," Woolum says. "I felt as responsible as anyone about what was happening, and the gist of what I said was: 'Eddie, I'm not sure your future is at Pineville.' What I thought he should do — and I told him — was to get a fresh start somewhere out of this town, where he was only remembered as a little boy. He agreed with me in some ways, too. But he didn't want to admit that he had been a failure in something he wanted to do."

Still, nobody had any idea how deeply that failure was wounding Eddie. "If I had to pick someone who did what Eddie did," Lee Bishop says, "Eddie would be the last one I'd pick."

After all, Eddie knew the American way, that coaches aren't hired to coach, they're hired to win. "Eddie understood his position," Woolum says. "That's the nature of the business, be it pro, college or high school. If you don't win. . . ."

Yet no one appreciated the depths of his agony, even when he went out and bought a punching bag and began to flail away at it, bang, bang, rat-a-tat-tat, or the day when he went over to his parents' house, which was just down from where he and Retha and Toby (as Eddie, Jr., is known) lived, and went into their bedroom, where his mother found him.

"Momma, I just wanted to lie down on your bed," he told her.

"Do you want to pray with me?" Inez asked.

"Yes ma'am," he said, and he got down beside her, on his knees, and when she prayed, Eddie cried, and he said, "Oh, Momma, the problems I've got. God's either going to take care of them or take me out of them." He stood 9–13, careerwise.

It was Wednesday morning, April 22, when, without consulting anyone, Eddie burst into the office of School Superintendent Ronald Jones. "I've got something that will make it easier for you," he said, and with that, he tossed a sheet of paper onto the superintendent's desk.

Jones read the note, puzzled all the more. It read:

"Mr. Jones: I think it is best for me and my family that I do teach in the Pineville school system next fall." Eddie was resigning, but, subconsciously, he had not allowed himself to put in the operative word. Helpfully, gently, Jones handed the paper back and indicated where he might have left something out. Eddie nodded, inserted a caret, and added the word *not:* "I do not teach. . . ." It was over. If he wasn't a teacher, he couldn't be the football coach.

Jones saw Eddie that afternoon, sat with him at the high school baseball game, and Eddie seemed perfectly composed. But when he went over to his mother's, Inez could sense his distress. "Momma," he told her, "they gave me the hatchet today. But I've told Toby all about it." The boy was six then. "He knows his father won't be a teacher here anymore."

The next morning, Thursday, Eddie cleaned his locker out and left school without teaching his classes. He went home and brooded, punching the bag, fretting, his mind unraveling — although not enough for anyone to see for sure. He went over to his parents' and Inez gave him some lunch, "but it was just like foaming in his mouth, so at last he just raked it out for the dogs."

Around quarter to five, he called up D. C. Cloud, who, by chance, had come home early from work. His conversation rambled. "Don't worry about it, Deke," Eddie reassured him at one point. "I've talked to the Lord, and I've got it all worked out."

When Eddie rang off, Cloud could only shake his head. "That was the weirdest conversation," he said to a friend. But Cloud soon forgot about it. It was just Eddie, Eddie Bishop, Pineville's Star of Stars, the easiest-going hero this side of Gary Cooper. Besides, even if

Cloud had gone over to Eddie's, he would have just found his old friend casually watching TV, which he did for a while until he told Retha he was going over to see his parents for a few minutes.

His mother and father had endured, even thrived in the face of ongoing adversities others can only imagine. Maybe that crossed his mind. Maybe they could help. His mother wasn't in, though; she was "second door" down the street at a birthday party. But Elaine and Jan were there, and so was Fred, Sr. He went into the bedroom with his father and sat in the rocking chair.

Soon, at last, it began to tumble out. "Those people did me wrong, Dad," Eddie said. "I know I can do the job — if only they'll give me the chance." His voice rose. "That's all I want, Dad — just give me another chance."

His father consoled him, commiserated, and suddenly Eddie was himself again. And soon the two men were happily chatting about events reported on the sports pages, like fathers and sons all over this shining land. The insanity was stilled again, and there was another of those soft, misleading lulls when Eddie was perfectly normal and happy and lucid, when he was himself. Only, the madness had the upper hand now. It had pursued him, and now it had momentum, and only for shorter and shorter intervals could he hold it off. Again! Now: "These people did me wrong!" he screamed. "I know I can do the job! That's all I want, Daddy, another chance . . . another chance."

No man is calmer than Fred Bishop, Sr. Nobody in discomfort could have ordered up a more reassuring presence. "Son," he said, "we know you did your job, and your mom and me and the rest of the family are proud of you."

Eddie spoke more softly this time. "I'll tell you, Dad, what I'm going to do tonight will cause embarrassment to you and Mom and the rest of the family. I'm sorry, but I have to do this."

Fred was again ready with support. "Son, there is nothing you can do to embarrass me or the family. You know that we'll always stand behind you."

"All I want is another chance. I know I can do the job. The people did me wrong!" Eddie said, his voice beginning to rise, louder, louder, as he brought himself out of his chair, screaming now: "Stand back, world, here I come! Stand back, world, here I come! Don't nobody try to stop me! I want the world to know how they mistreated me!"

Elaine was scared now. She heard her father's voice tremble a little when he said, "Son, don't let those people upset you like that. It ain't worth it." Quietly, she left to go fetch her mother. Eddie grew wilder. He began to lash out physically. He broke a mirror, he turned over the Bible stand, and then, in the living room, in one final, mad outburst, he struck out at the picture window, and it shattered, the shards gashing his wrist, slashing it horribly.

However, minutes later, by the time Elaine arrived back at the house, Jan had wrapped the bloody hand, and the bizarre tranquillity had returned to Eddie. It was like the studied violence of the scrimmage followed by the peacefully dispassionate huddle. Retha was called for and came over and remembers that everybody was talking mostly about going down to give blood. A squad car pulled up then, in answer to a call someone had made, and Eddie was not only rational, but also thoughtful. "I'm sorry, officer," he said politely, "but I just got a little upset and broke my mom's window. I'll talk to her about the window. I'm getting ready to go to the hospital now."

"Well, OK," the policeman said, and when he left, Elaine and Jan drove Eddie through town, out Tennessee Avenue, which is what 25E is called as it passes through Pineville, west, past the Bethel Baptist Church, the black parish where the family worshipped, past the Chevron station, around the big sweeping bend in the road, to the hospital.

Only Inez Bishop wasn't so sure. "A mother can look into her child's eyes and tell a lot someone else can't see," she says. "Eddie's eyes were so red, like he was straining for something." She pauses. "I think he was just straining to be Eddie, but the pressure was getting too great." Inez decided she'd better go down to the police station and get a warrant, because she feared that Eddie was going to need much more help if he was ever going to be Eddie again.

Down at the hospital, Eddie kept shifting back and forth between extremes. First he was very calm, but then he grew unsettled and began to run about, and then Elaine helped soothe him, and when the doctor found Eddie in the treatment room, he was sitting there, so peacefully. But that was the final lull. The strain to be Eddie any longer was now too great. He jumped off the table, hollering that he wouldn't accept any treatment. Elaine and the doctor pleaded with him, but Eddie backed away, until suddenly he stopped, and he said, "I saw the light, and I'm getting out of here."

And, with that, he broke past them, burst out the door and down the hall. Elaine chased after him, calling to him, but Eddie tore out the emergency room and down the incline that leads to Route 25E.

It's funny how we use the football field as a way to measure things. We never say, "Oh, that's about as far from here as it is to first base." Or, "That's about four basketball courts long." But we count by football fields. So, it was about three football fields down the road to where 25E turned, and maybe two more to Eddie's church, the Bethel Baptist.

The road widens to three lanes in front of the hospital, and for some reason, Eddie cut across all three lanes to get to the other side, the far side. It would have made more sense for him just to stay on the hospital side, on the town side; there's even a sidewalk on that side. But, instead, he darted across the road and began to run back into town from the far side, on the shoulder, against traffic.

It was dusk, and it was hard to see him. Elaine didn't see him, and the truck driver saw him only at the last instant, as he brought his rig around the bend and glimpsed, before him, the form that veered from the side of the road, ducking directly into the path of his truck. Eddie had decided to run right into the truck, as you would a tackler, and they met head on in the twilight.

The funeral was the largest Pineville had ever seen. After all, as the *Sun-Courier* wrote, "Regardless of his record as a coach, Bishop was loved and well respected by the community." Regardless. Nine and thirteen. The mayor himself drove the lead police car in the funeral procession. The outpouring was extraordinary, and the tears rent the church. "Well," says the Reverend Jones, who presided, "he was *our* coach."

"Praise the Lord, God's in control," Inez Bishop says. Fred, Sr., still finds it difficult to talk about any of it.

Bill Adams was prevailed upon to return as coach, but only sixteen boys came out for the team that fall, and it was a real struggle. Just to scrimmage, Adams had to work one side of the line against the other. But, still, football survived in Pineville, and with it the school. This autumn, three years after "the accident," Adams stepped aside for a new coach, and the Mountain Lions had a 9–3 record. "At last," says Bobby Madon, "we have a whip snapper who demands respect."

And someday, too, there will be another great player in Pineville, a regular one-man team, and the recruiters will pour down 25E and pursue him, and the stands will be packed, and the roars for him will roll up to the mountains and down to the river, and someone will say, "Why, that kid must be the greatest ever to play for Pineville." And some old-timer will say, "Yes, indeed, he's good all right. Why, he's almost as good as the last Bishop boy was."

"I Don't Date Any Woman Under Forty-eight"

1977

THE old warrior fights his battles from a desk now, but he is there all day every weekday and half a day Saturday, the way everybody in America worked when the warrior was in his prime. And not puttering around, you understand — working. Dressed in a snappy shirt and a flashy tie, with a short zippered coat we used to call an Eisenhower jacket (one thinks of skycaps now), he means business. His eyes are clear, his jaw juts, and his memory is unimpaired, which is the euphemism employed in print to mean he still has all his marbles. George S. Halas still has all his marbles.

Of course, as we know, it's a young man's game, sports. And Papa Bear is 82, going on 83. Eighty-two, for Pete's sake. Eighty-two and still at it. George Halas is even older than George Burns, and George Burns is the oldest man in the world. "First of all," says Papa Bear, "I wouldn't know about old, because I'm not old. I have only one rule: I don't date any woman under forty-eight." He actually said "date." He has outlived a loving wife and then a steady girl, and he has outlasted all the other ancient symbols of sports.

Sports used to abound with grand old men who grew with their games: Mr. Mack, Colonel Matt, Amos Alonzo Stagg. Sunny Fitz and Old Case are gone, too; the Masters' maestro, Clifford Roberts, blew his brains out the other day. Tom Yawkey, Phil Wrigley, and Tony Hulman of the Indy 500 have left us. They pulled the Baron, Adolph Rupp, kicking and screaming, from his bench, and they shot Jack Dempsey's restaurant out from under him. It's a young man's game. It has been ten seasons now since Papa Bear stopped coaching, but he is the only grand old man left at his desk, working every weekday and half a day Saturday.

To be sure, a couple of youngsters, Jim Finks and Jack Pardee, actually run the Bears, and Halas's son and son-in-law head up the office. But the old man is on top of things. He is still heard from. For the purposes of this account, just so there wouldn't be any misconceptions, he prepared a detailed account of his quotidian activities. It is entitled "Outline of Typical Day — Geo. S. Halas," and it runs to four typewritten pages. It lists all the things Papa Bear does as chairman of the board of the Chicago Bears, as president of the National Conference of the NFL, and in his numerous civic and charitable capacities. From time to time he provides helpful commentary. Listen, not everybody's a quick study, like Sid Luckman. "Why, I used to call Sid up at eleven-thirty Monday night with all the plays for the next game," says Papa Bear, "and the next morning he could rattle them all off to me. And you know why? Because he worked hard and he was sharp as a tack."

Here are some samples from "Typical Day":

Financial Matters
Responsible for investing all club monies — Therefore, each morning get current financial picture — Bankers, Brokers, Publications. . . .

Interviews
In Person
Telephone — These are taped — Calls are from coast to coast. All calls are logged. Each day is heavy. . . .

Correspondence
Every day is heavy. Runs the gamut of all subjects. Other than letters pertaining to business, my correspondence is from all ages. From people in all walks of life — some from inmates of penal institutions — people with problems, etc. etc. . . .
Try to keep current with reading material.
Attempting to write my autobiography.

Apropos of the last, it all seems like only yesterday. Events of, say, 1909 or 1932 are recalled as clearly as those of Tuesday past. References to the present Bears, whoever they are, are trotted out in the same tone employed for the tales of Red Grange or Bronko Nagurski. Moreover, because Papa Bear has an extraordinary ability to recall all street addresses he has ever visited in "Ellanoy" (the state Chicago is located in), his discourse has a distinct tour-guide ring. It is distracting, in the same way the Old Testament would be if it were studded with such workaday postal minutiae: 84 North Pharaoh Court, Horeb; 2163 Tabernacle Boulevard, Jericho; and so on.

Also, whatever Papa Bear thinks of Chicago sports journalism, he has been reading it for so long that his speech has taken on the properties thereof. In Halasian argot, people of all ages really do hail from all walks of life; America, a football hotbed, is that part of God's green earth which stretches from coast to coast; one's heart goes out to the less fortunate; athletics formulate character, as they have produced the stars of yesteryear, and have also given us the stars of today (the Bears themselves are coming of age under Finks, who is as sharp as a tack). Then, too, Halas can communicate in other subcultures when that is required, e.g., "Forget the rollovers. I'm just interested in the Double A, with a minimum of eight and a quarter." Not for nothing was Papa Bear also known as the Bland Bohemian. Maybe this is how you get to 82, memory unimpaired.

It is easy to forget that this man across the desk is a certified institution. Papa Bear was tackled by Jim Thorpe and struck out by Walter Johnson. He played six games in right field for the Yankees in 1919 (the Babe settled in that very realty the next season), and Halas was also there in Canton, Ohio, sitting on a running board in a Hupmobile showroom on September 17, 1920, when pro football was created. It was a Friday, one of the last things to be created in just one day. And this fellow across the desk was right there, live. Then Papa Bear won 326 games, 12 more than Stagg, more than anyone in the history of the pros or the colleges. He is the only man Vince Lombardi would embrace and one of the few he would call Coach.

Coach, what makes a good coach?

"Complete dedication," Papa Bear declares straightaway. And another surprise: "He must know football." Hmmm. "And he must apply himself. And he must have the right temperament."

Which is what?

"I don't know. I just knew my own."

Which was what?

"I liked to win and I fought for everything in the book. Nothing else mattered." Pause. "That's all."

Autographing

Cards, pictures, magazine articles, books, old programs — these are sent in. Then the usual requests for autographed pictures and footballs. (These requests, again, come from people of all ages, in all walks of life.) . . .

Unless I have an appointment for lunch, my lunch is brought in. At this time, I read *The Wall Street Journal,* Kiplinger and Janeway.

Coach Halas has lived virtually all his days in Chicago, starting at 1850 South Ashland Avenue. He was born in 1895, when Grover Cleveland was president. It is hoary journalistic custom to certify American antiquity by citing the president in office at the subject's moment of birth. This tradition is exceeded in uselessness only by the one wherein the size of a distant patch of earth is identified as being equivalent to the size of a couple of disparate states. Thus, for example, Yemen is equal to Nebraska and Virginia put together, which they are not. Well, George Halas is the age of Senator Joseph Biden, Tatum O'Neal, and Billie Jean King put together. Think about it that way.

His birth date is February 2, which is Groundhog Day or, on the Roman Catholic calendar, Candlemas; in either case, February 2 is the first official day for looking ahead to spring planting — surely, a felicitous day to be born.

Halas's father was an immigrant tailor, from Pilsen, in what is now Czechoslovakia, but in Halas's Chicago pretty near everybody was an immigrant, and he recalls no discrimination. Of his childhood, Halas volunteers these three things, in order: 1) the addresses where he lived, 2) the observation "That's where I learned to work," and 3) detailed recollections of playing games and attending them — most especially watching Tinker to Evers to Chance at the old Cub Park, which was located at the corner of Polk and Wood ("Very few people remember that").

Then there was college — he lettered in football, baseball, and basketball at the University of Ellanoy — followed by the Great War and the season of baseball. The rest is pro football. And for a fact, the early years of Halas and his Bears are the early history of the game itself. Halas, 6' and 170 pounds, played end and was known for his toughness and skill, as well as for his eloquence in the illegal use of the hands. He was coach from the team's inception — the first year as the Decatur Staleys, the second as the Chicago Staleys, then the Bears in 1922, and soon, in legend, the Monsters of the Midway. *Papa Bear and the Monsters of the Midway!*

In 1925, in league with the storied promoter Cash and Carry Pyle, Halas signed Red Grange and toured the land, coast to coast, eighteen games in two months. It did not make pro football in the United States, but at least it dented some consciousnesses. Some. "I always enjoy animal acts," President Coolidge said when he was introduced to Messrs. Halas and Grange of the Chicago Bears.

It was Halas who brought the T formation to the pros. Also daily practices, assistant coaches, press-box spotters, training camps, films, the first pro marching band, and the first pro fight song, "Bear Down, Chicago Bears." With George Preston Marshall, the truculent chief of the Redskins, Halas usually fought tooth and nail, but in rare moments of concord they worked to introduce a championship game to the NFL; they produced a more exciting passing game, too; and they had the goalposts advanced to the goal line to boost the offense.

Papa Bear was occasionally out of tune. In the '34 championship, on a frozen field, the Giants donned sneakers at halftime and slipped away from the exasperated Bears. A few years later Halas perceived unlimited substitution as a potential evil, and he warned the brethren that it would "take all the fun out of the game." Luckily, this time the other owners did not heed the admonitions of the old sixty-minute man, and thus were platoons platooned and money coined.

But Papa Bear sees no flies on the game today. Oh, sure, if pressed he agrees that here and there you might chance upon an owner who is a tad selfish, but otherwise, hear this: "Football! First, you've got competition! You've got to be alert to play it! You've got to be sharp! The stars of yesteryear had a great desire to play, and they set the pace for modern-day football, that fine brand of football that you see on the field today! And we know it's got appeal! Why, it's the greatest game there is! You've got action! And it's a spectacular! It's — "

Maybe just a wee bit violent? Is it really necessary for quarterbacks to be maimed at the rate of Ugandan cabinet ministers? (This unseemly intrusion from a captious and ill-bred caller.)

"It's a violent game, sure," Halas goes on, suffering fools, "*but it's just that kind of game!* It's always been violent! But it's not dirty! No, football's not a dirty game! We haven't come anywhere near to its zenith!"

Papa Bear sits back for the moment, spent from delivering this encomium for his game, his love. The office is a fair representation of what football has been in his life. It is done largely in gridiron green. Save for two volumes of *Who's Who* and another testifying to *The Joys of Wine,* every book — 200 or more — appears to be about football. On a shelf there is one framed exhortation — "Never Go to Bed a Loser," it says. George S. Halas said that and lives by it.

And across the way there is a long sofa where he naps every afternoon. This is no concession to the years. Papa Bear has always napped every day. Not for him three-martini lunches, or rich, starchy foods. "All those younger coaches always wondered where I got my energy," he chuckles, relishing the memory. Eleven, twelve o'clock midnight, they'd be yawning and bleary-eyed, while Papa Bear, fresh as a daisy, would be ready to dial Luckman with the plays.

What was your greatest satisfaction, Coach?

"The seventy-three-to-nothing," he replies directly, sure that no elaboration is required. The numbers are sufficient. It is probably the most famous score in American sports. When you think about it, very few scores are remembered. What was the score of Don Larsen's perfect game? Of the Super Bowl just last January? Name any basketball score in history; surely, not even Jerry Lucas can pull that off. But everybody knows 73–0, the Bears conquering the hated Redskins in the 1940 NFL championship game 73–0. The Monsters of the Midway! Incarnate.

The Bears won the title again the next year, in Pearl Harbor month, and in '43 when Halas was Commander Papa Bear, and in '46 when he was back from the war, 51 years old. But thereafter, the Bears declined, drifting most years in the horse latitudes of mediocrity. Halas took his third respite from coaching in 1956–57, but he returned by personal demand. The Chicago press always remained in his corner, but this time he was scarred by whispers and innuendo: He was too old; it had passed him by; he was a miser, too patronizing of the players; he was blindly loyal to the family and old cronies who rattled about the Bear payroll.

Some of this was all too true, but probably these grumblings dog anyone who stays in one place for so long. As consistency is the hobgoblin of little minds, so, too, does it sustain the steadfast soul. And loyalty. What would we expect of someone who spent his whole life at the same stand — the migratory qualities of Elizabeth Taylor?

Then, too, there is something about Halas's hometown that nurtures — or countenances — these virtues. Chicago is, after all, the second largest city in the United States, but for all its size it is curiously contained. It never makes waves across the land, as New York and Los Angeles do. In a way, Chicago is not an end in itself but only a huge crossroads, which, throughout history, Indians, cattle, gangsters, conventioneers, trains, and airplanes soon enough have stumbled upon. Merely because of its convenient central location, all sorts of national publications, such as this one, are printed in Chicago. The *New Yorker,* of all things, is printed in Chicago. Type is set there. But these magazines are not conceived in Chicago, not written there, not affected by the place, any more than are America's networks or fashions or mores.

Hence, local figures can grow to large proportions in Chicago while rarely casting long shadows nationally. The sagas of such diverse creatures as Mayor Daley, Colonel McCormick of the *Tribune,* and George S. Halas are not that dissimilar.

So Chicago was just the ticket for Papa Bear and, save for the odd world war, he has never really been away from the Windy City, nor it from him. After he came back from the Navy in 1945, he did not age so much as he fell out of joint with the times. There was nothing in the immigrant tailor's son to prepare him for the relaxed days of peace and prosperity. Here was a fellow who had played a football game with a broken jaw, who had threatened to slug affable Art Rooney of the Steelers over a lousy $500 dispute, who, a friend once said, "believes that if you haven't got anything to do, you ought to be at your office doing it."

He still thought it a point of honor to fight for everything in the book, but now it was a world of easy credit, cigarette-smoking women, and Saturdays off, and nobody else wanted to put their dukes up. "He succeeded in rewarding all the wrong people," says an old colleague. "The more intelligent, sensitive players wouldn't fight him, so they got screwed." No indeed, Papa Bear never did grow old, but he did grow old-fashioned, and it really was incidental whether that happened when he was 60 years of age, or 40 or 25. He was a man of the times, and the times had changed.

He suffered most for his parsimony. Mike Ditka's celebrated gibe — "He throws nickels around like manhole covers" — cemented his reputation for all time as a Scrooge. It did not matter that his family always knew him as a benevolent patriarch, that he was an easy touch for friends and good causes, that he had made a fortune in oil and real estate and several other endeavors. The Bears' ledger was frozen in time, back when Halas's office was a hotel lobby, when he sold tickets himself on the street, when Bronko and the Galloping Ghost had to take IOUs.

Maybe it is easy to throw nickels around like soybean futures if you are from money — Lamar Hunt, Clint Murchison, that crowd. And it is easy to spend rashly if you are nouveau, if you make it wheeling and dealing — Ray Kroc, Gene Autry, fellows like that. It is seldom how much money we have that indicates how we will spend it. No, it is how we obtained the money. And what Halas made from oil and land doesn't count, not with the Bears it doesn't. Here are three stories that will tell you something or other about this.

Story one: Brian Piccolo used to shake his head and laugh about it, even as he neared his death. In Piccolo's last season, he fought Halas for three weeks to get an extra $500. Then when Piccolo became ill with cancer, Halas paid all his bills, thousands of dollars' worth, right to the end. And never a word.

Story two, told by Mike Pyle, the center on the '63 team, the only Bear champions since '46: "The two years before, Green Bay had won and Lombardi had given fur coats and TV sets to the wives and girlfriends. So we win, and the old man gives some charms — worth maybe fifty dollars, tops — and only to the wives. The single guys don't get a thing. I mentioned this to Mugs [Halas's only son, a team executive] and he said, 'Now, Mike, of course I'm not talking about you, but we just can't take the chance of having any Bears jewelry end up on some Playboy bunny or some Rush Street floozy.'"

Story three: George Allen ran the team defense and the college draft in Halas's last years of coaching. The '63 club won because of its defense, Allen's defense. When Allen got a chance to take over the Rams a couple of years later, Halas refused to let him out of his assistant's contract and took him to court over it. As soon as it was routinely established in court that Allen and the Bears did have a contract, Halas rose and withdrew his objections. Then, all he asked of Allen was that he hand over his Bear playbook.

George Allen says now, "Grudge? I understand completely what he was doing. George Halas is a great man, and every day I appreciate him more and more. Just a great, great man."

Probably it has never had anything to do with money. It was just that Papa Bear valued the Bears more than anyone else, and no one was going to take a piece without his extracting fair payment. Buying jewelry, giving Jim Finks his authority, parceling out a $500 raise — it is all the same when you are the guardian of an institution and/or you are the institution itself.

So, Coach, do you have any regrets? Any at all?

"Well, I'd be glad to do it all over except for two things."

Yes?

"First would be the goddamn rubber-shoe game."

And the other thing?

"It was the Depression, and I decided to buy out my partner, Dutch Sternaman. But to get his half of the team for thirty-two thousand dollars, I had to pledge everything, including my half. You understand? If I couldn't get all the thirty-two thousand in time, Sternaman got the Bears. And I couldn't find the last five thousand. It was the Depression, and I couldn't raise it anywhere.

"Luckily, a few years before, in 'twenty-eight, I had invested in a development in Antioch, Ellanoy, and so I knew Mr. C. K. Anderson, who was the president of the First National Bank of Antioch, and so I went to see him at his office at One Thirty-four South LaSalle Street, and I explained my predicament, and he gave me the five thousand dollars, and I got the money to Sternaman five minutes before I would have lost the Bears. Now, that is the other thing I would not like to go through again."

You mean you wouldn't try and buy the other half of the team?

"No, I mean I wouldn't ever want to come so close to losing the Bears."

Appointments

Several each day — some days are entirely devoted to appointments; many people — authors, press from out of the city — just drop in and my schedule must be such to accommodate them.

Appearances

Civic (Mayor's functions, etc.)
Educational Programs

Benefit Functions
Award Ceremonies — Now booked through April 1, 1978
(Most recent — the "I" Award and the M.S. Award. Coming up:
Mother Cabrini Award — Dec. 3)

The lobby of the Bears' offices is pretty much filled exclusively with Halas's memorabilia, awards, and trophies. Strangely, the one picture of Papa Bear in the lobby shows him on the sidelines with George Blanda, who spent his most depressing seasons in Chicago, subsequently testifying that Halas "took my ten best years in pro football and all he gave me in return was a dead sparrow and a piece of string."

But inside the offices, on the wall leading to Papa Bear's office, there are several photographs of the more convivial stars of yesteryear, most of whom — Grange, Luckman, George McAfee, Gale Sayers — are also registered as "men of character, then and now." Every year, Halas holds an Alumni Day, and this year the proceedings were highlighted by a duet sung by Papa Bear and Ed Healy, a tackle on the 1922 team. They warbled "Hail to the Orange," the University of Ellanoy fight song. A fine time was had by all, although here and there some of the old-timers wondered out loud when the Bears would growl again. The newspapers and television stations are now doing nostalgia features on the '63 Bears, who played when Lyndon Johnson was president and George S. Halas was a kid of 68.

Just about everybody but a few surviving contemporaries calls him Coach. Last year, as much of the family gathered for the holidays, an interview with Papa Bear and Phyllis George was aired. For some reason, Miss George's usually impeccable Miss America manners deserted her, and throughout the interview she referred to the gentleman octogenarian as "George." The family watched, aghast and bemused at such sassiness, but Papa Bear himself did not appear to be distressed at this untoward familiarity. What the heck, Phyllis was single at the time, some dish, and in another twenty or twenty-five years she is going to be 48.

The coach is quite well behaved, except perhaps at games. He would not permit an observer to accompany him to see the Bears play, lest he appear too coarse and obstreperous. At all times his life is well ordered. In his six-room apartment at Edgewater Beach, he begins each day with exercises — riding a stationary bike, lifting dumbbells, and jogging in place. For breakfast, he fixes himself grapefruit, bran flakes, sliced bananas ("That keeps up the potassium levels in my body"), coffee, and a sweet roll. Then he drives himself to the office and gets down to business. For lunch, he partakes of soup and crackers at his desk, or a fruit plate and salad with Thousand Island dressing. Then he takes his nap, getting an edge on all those dissolute whippersnappers.

The day's work done, he returns home for a dinner of veal, chicken, or fish ("Stay away from animal fats") and more salad ("I'm a firm believer in roughage"). He exercises again ("Never go to bed a loser"), and before he turns out the light he makes sure that a notepad and pen are arrayed at his bedside in case he has any inspirations in the middle of the night.

Papa Bear is on the move. He is first on the dance floor; he legged out a triple in a recent family whiffle-ball game; and now that his arthritic hips have been repaired, he is preparing to take up golf again when the Bears season is over and he holidays in Arizona. He has no intention whatsoever of retiring; his brother Frank labored contentedly for the Bears until he died several years ago at age 89. "I see some of these old people mooning around who have given up," says Papa Bear, "and I try to give them a little goose." He is older than the Pope and Sam Ervin, if not quite so old as George Meany and Norman Rockwell. Papa Bear is just about as old as the states of New Mexico and Alaska put together. Think about it that way.

And largely because of the Monsters of the Midway, it has been one great life, booked up now through April 1, 1978. Here is why, Papa Bear explains: "Look, you can have a session with your girlfriend. What's that last you? Twenty minutes, half an hour? Or you can go out and get stiff with the boys. A few hours, right? But to win a game in the National Football League! That lasts a whole week!" A pause. (A savoring pause.) "Whatta thrill!" He said that: "Whatta thrill!"

> Review my calendar for the next day.
> Leave the office between 6:30 and 7:00 p.m.
> I have no need to search for hobbies or outside interests — I have them all.
> Each day is most interesting and rewarding — As I leave the office, I look forward to tomorrow.

*   *   *

George S. Halas lived another six vigorous years after I wrote this piece. He died on October 31, 1983, at the age of eighty-eight. The Bears are still owned by his family, and, in 1986, when Ronald Reagan was president, they won their first Super Bowl.

Tender Cheers for the Prospect

1977

The Arm

The man born to money expects riches for a lifetime, just as the man born with good looks assumes they will always get him by. But if the gold or good looks disappear, most such men learn to accept it. Even the vainest of men succumb at last to the reality that their physical gifts are gone. But perhaps no man is so haunted as the one who was once stunned by instant success, for he lives thereafter with the illusion that tomorrow is bound to bring one more bolt of good fortune.

Once upon a time Jim Bouton was an ugly duckling: scrawny, pimples on his face, braces on his teeth, a pitching arm so ordinary that he was known as Warm-up Bouton for the position he customarily filled. Then, overnight, he had an arm. Oh, but he could smoke it. He was 21–7 with the American League champion Yankees in 1963, 18–13 and twice a winner in the World Series the next year. And, just like that, his arm was gone. Dust to dust. No vehicle to overnight success can be more fragile than an arm. Not swords, not cleavage, not wit, not fraud, not nothing. Just like that: 4–15. Long relief. Sent down: 2–8 in the minors. Traded. Given up on. Quit.

Usually *forgotten* follows that, but in Bouton's case, with his best-seller, *Ball Four,* he traded simple fame for notoriety. He became a TV sports announcer in New York and proved to be so naturally His Glibness that soon he sat on the *What's My Line* panel, cheek by jowl with Arlene Francis and Bill Cullen themselves. Jim Bouton was a name.

But all the dumb sonofabitch ever wanted was to be an arm again.

This is why, in the middle of his life, when all the children he grew up with have turned in their mitts and marbles, Bouton plays the boy again in the Class AA Southern League, starting every fifth day for the Savannah nine, throwing against the bats of certified prospects who can tell the correct time of life. One motive for this mad indulgence is, surely, a search for vanished youth — Bouton will be 40 years old next March 8. Also, there is the fantasy of playing Peter Pan, and the real escape from the responsibility that a wife and three children press upon a man. But mostly, it seems, the dream of being an arm, only briefly fulfilled, has never left Bouton.

"It's all face value," says Vic Ziegel, Bouton's old friend and writing partner. "Jim was simply never better as a human being than when he had a uniform on." Bouton subscribes to that. Someday, he says, it will be time to move on again from baseball, but do not ask exactly when. Bouton is honest enough to sense what Oscar Wilde divined, that "the only difference between a caprice and a lifelong passion is that the caprice lasts a little longer."

The Old Man

Savannah is but the latest way station. Bouton has been there since mid-May, and his knuckleball (mixed with a palm ball and cut fastball — "cut" apparently being a euphemism for "slow") has brought him a 4–4 record, with a 3.46 ERA. But in the last year or so, Bouton has hired out for whoever would take him on to pitch, in whatever backwater on the North American continent. He even had a deal set for the Netherlands, if no team in the New World wanted him. His comeback has been so painfully extended that no one can any longer seriously suggest that Bouton has been tramping through the bush leagues merely to research another book. One might as well say that Richard Nixon orchestrated Watergate merely to obtain anecdotal best-seller material.

"Someday I may want to do a book," Bouton says, "but I have absolutely no intention of doing so now. I wouldn't want a book as a saving thing. I'd lose the fun of the experience if I had that to fall back on. If with each setback I could say, 'Well, it really doesn't matter because it's another good chapter,' then the experience itself would be devalued.

"People have got to understand — I want to get to the highest level of competition I possibly can, but I swear I am not *trying* to get to the majors. It's sort of like Zen. I don't want to aim for the target. The way to hit it is not to aim for it. All I know is that this experience has been satisfying in every respect. It was even satisfying last year when I couldn't win a game. So I know I've made the right decision whether or not I ever get any higher. I've been happy most of my life, but never more than now. Of course, the minors are not as good as the majors, but the question to me is whether the minors are better than much of the rest of life. And to me, they are.

"I remember when I first quit TV to go back and everybody said I was crazy. There was a producer at CBS named Eric Ober, and he said, 'Hey, I know why you're doing this.' I said, 'Yes?' and he said, 'Because when you die, you're dead for a long time.'

"Dead for a long time. That's the truth. And they say I'm old now. That's funny, because when I really am old, I'm going to have a lot of fun. I'm going to have some stories to tell. All the kids on the block are going to want to come over and listen to strange old Jim as he sits in his rocker and talks about the old days. And professionally, when I get to be an old man, I'm going to be a terrific actor. I know that. All this stuff is just getting me ready to be an old man. I am going to be one great old man."

In fact, at this juncture, Bouton is a very youthful middle-aged man, towheaded and shiny-faced, with a countenance and form belying his four decades. He is not quite 6′ tall. When he starred with the Yankees in a previous generation he weighed 185 and threw with such velocity that unseemly grunts — backfires — emanated from his throat, and the force of his delivery kept knocking off his cap. He appeared stocky and blurred, whereas now he is lithe and defined, with pectorals and biceps bulging out of a 165-pound body that never, never knows the backslider's joy of tasting refined sugar. As a young Savannah teammate said in the dugout one evening, "There's no fat on him except in his head." Or, as Bouton's wife says, "Have you seen those thighs? Aren't they something?"

Yes, besides the mistress baseball, there is indeed a wife — Barbara Bouton, usually known as Bobby. Her husband identifies her as a good scout, inasmuch as she tabbed him as a husband prospect when he was still a homely and insecure little fellow who was hoping to make the freshman squad at Western Michigan University. Bobby is pretty, sweet, and fun, and not so very long ago she had a husband in the 50 percent bracket who came home nights and did fine handiwork on weekends about their twenty-room mansion, which stood upon a choice acre of land with a kempt lawn, flourishing trees, and a swimming pool. Now her husband resides in an efficiency in Georgia, and her days in New Jersey have been filled with trying to fix up a turn-of-the-century house that they picked up from a widow, because they sold their estate to pay the food bills while Daddy pursues his search for temporary happiness. To put up with this, Bobby Bouton is obviously either a saint or as nutty as a fruitcake. Notwithstanding, she explains quite evenly, "I'd feel terrible if we held him back. I agreed he needed a break at this point in his life. Of course it's been tough on me. I miss him very much. It's hard. But whether or not what Jim is doing is fair to me or the children doesn't matter, because for now he's doing what *I* want him to do."

The Knuckleball

Bouton is not merely indulging some quixotic daydream. He is a 39-year-old athlete with a knuckleball; Phil Niekro, of Savannah's parent team, the Atlanta Braves, is a 39-year-old knuckleballer who leads the big leagues in innings pitched. Hoyt Wilhelm labored successfully in the majors till age 49. A knuckleball (in fact, it is thrown with the fingertips digging into the ball, so the knuckles loom over it like a parapet) is shoved plateward with little stress on the arm, and even the most cursory inspection of the American League's premier knuckleballer, the corpulent 36-year-old Wilbur Wood of the White Sox, shows that the knuckler does not require a well-honed body. Sexy thighs are quite optional. Moreover, Bouton first tamed the pitch at age 12, and although he shelved it when he got his arm, he actually won a handful of games with it in the major leagues after he lost the arm. So, theoretically, Bouton certainly can make a comeback at 39.

In fact, the Zen business and the testimonials to inner happiness in Double A are probably delivered as verbal waste pitches. It is difficult to believe that Bouton, who in his Yankee days was called the Bulldog, is not striving to go back up, even if he knows that the odds are against him — geriatrically and culturally. Of the latter: For having written *Ball Four,* he remains a pariah to many of the higher-ups in the national pastime. Though Bouton volunteered to pay all his own expenses, only two major league teams would so much as agree to cast eyes on him. Seattle, which has a team ERA of 4.41, tendered the most thoughtful turndown: "If we gave you a chance, *we'd have to do it for everybody*" — and thereby handed Bouton a title, even if he doesn't have a book.

It is instructive that the only ones who would permit Bouton, at his own cost, to soil their practice diamonds were those two prize eccentrics, Bill Veeck and Ted Turner. Veeck's White Sox organization released Bouton last year, and Turner's farm director, one Henry Aaron, released him earlier this season. Bouton survived only because Turner in a gesture of noblesse oblige ordered his underlings to take Bouton back. "I already had a thirty-nine-year-old knuckleballer [Niekro] and, besides, Bouton's entertaining just to have around," Turner says with a chuckle, just as the lord of the manor might explain why he had added another dwarf or concubine to the castle manifest.

But Bouton is undeterred. Despite the fact that the Netherlands is only an owner's whim away, he possesses an unholy belief in his ability to thrive by rising to the occasion. "I can pitch with my stomach," he declares proudly. *Is i magen,* the Swedes call it — ice in the belly. While Bouton believes that he has always had this super quality, now he knows he is almost impregnable to failure: win, he goes up to major league baseball; lose, he goes up to major league television.

Make no mistake — he is deadly earnest in what he is attempting. He is risking embarrassment and the financial and emotional well-being of his family. But it does not tarnish the sincerity of the endeavor to say that it remains, most of all, enchanting.

Bouton's whole career has been so. Unlike most successful athletes, whose skills were so apparent that they had endorsement contracts in the sixth grade, Bouton had no expectations of sporting achievement. He was just a fan who borrowed a uniform. Even when he got his pinstripes, he kept number 56 — his original minor-leaguer's temporary number — and he kept the locker nearest the door as if he didn't want to be any trouble when he was asked to leave because there had been some mistake.

Talking to Bouton and to those close to him, there is even the odd sensation that they still do not believe that the big leagues really happened. Bobby Bouton kept scrapbooks during those years, but no more diligently than she did when, a couple of years back, her husband pitched indifferently in the Jersey semipros. It is all of a piece, all just some fun pitching Jim did. Some husbands bowl, some have a darkroom in the basement.

Bob Bouton, one of Jim's brothers, called up Bobby the other day to check on his brother's progress in Savannah, and when he learned of another good outing, he said, "You know, Bobby, if Jim makes it again, this time we'll be able to really enjoy it. The first time was such a surprise, it happened so quickly, and then it was over so fast. This time we'll be prepared, and we can really savor it."

No, Bobby Bouton is probably neither a saint nor a screwball. She just loves her husband and appreciates that he is possessed and that only patience or glory can exorcise the commanding spirits. What a chance he has! All those pitchers in the Hall of Fame — Cy Young, Walter Johnson, Bobby Feller, that whole crowd — they only made it up once. But Jim Bouton with his magic knuckleball, he might be able to do it twice! He'd be the one and only! Bobby Bouton a good scout? Hey, good isn't the word! She picked out this century's Faust. Only he's a lot better than Faust. Faust had to make a deal. Jim Bouton is the first free-agent Faust! Oh, that Marvin Miller!

The Mound

Bouton's unlikely ascension from teenage obscurity to the world champions in less than four years was propelled by a succession of fluke chances, each of which he met by triumphing with the ice in his belly. This power, as we shall see, appears to have returned to him, reinforcing an assurance already brimming past flood levels. Ziegel, who in 1976 was one of Bouton's collaborators when *Ball Four* was made into a TV sitcom, recalls in fond exasperation, "I could never win an argument with Jim because he is unshakable in his beliefs. I'm human. I have doubts. Jim doesn't have doubts. He believes: I think it, therefore it must be true."

This supreme self-confidence has been nurtured by the course of events, in which every time Bouton has been set back, he has rebounded higher. He left the majors, not as a failed pitcher but as a celebrity author with a handsome job waiting at a New York television station. Fired from that (for refusing to be a shill), he was instantly hired by a more prestigious and sympathetic channel. And given a raise. The televising of *Ball Four* followed in time, and while the show was a disaster, a searing episode devolving ridicule upon Bouton, he was personally rewarded with offers to go to Hollywood and write TV shows or to return to TV news as a sportscaster.

Instead, he decided to escape back to the diamond, a notion he had been flirting with almost from the day he left the sport eight years ago and discovered that he literally itched whenever he was obliged to attend games as a reporter. He kept pitching semipro, he hauled his family off on pitching vacations to Canada and Oregon, and once he and some friends seriously considered buying their own minor league club so that Bouton would be assured a spot in the pitching rotation.

Unlike television (or almost anything else, for that matter), baseball offers consummate order, plus control for the man on the mound. Bouton was pilloried as an author, fired as an announcer, and then had his work perverted by network groupthink, even though he was himself a main writer and star of *Ball Four.* "From the very beginning I told CBS that we should deal with real people in real situations," he says, "but all they wanted were forced laughs. None of the writers knew about sports. Sports is one of the most pervasive elements in our society, but no one in television knew about them. But they knew about *Gilligan's Island,* so they made *Ball Four* into a *Gilligan's Island* in baseball suits. Then they would send it out to Hollywood, to the laugh room. It's called 'sweetening.' Once I counted; they put in two hundred thirty laughs in twenty-three minutes. Oh, it could have been so good. But after what they did to it, I was actually relieved when it was canceled."

It was while he was in this dejected spirit that Bouton decided to return to a familiar haven. Baseball does, after all, appeal to the more introspective side of an athlete. Young sports stars discover early that high school football and basketball games are occasions for hero-worshipping that are woven into the emotional fabric of the community. By contrast, high school baseball games — and even college and minor league games — are attended for the most part by a coterie of kind relatives and connoisseurs. Football and basketball players tend to be sensitive to their team and the crowd, baseball players to their game and the experience.

But even beyond that, Bouton was a pitcher, the most independent figure in a team game that with every pitch is played one-on-one. When Bouton sighs how he loves baseball, he means the green gardens, a slide into third, the laughing and spitting in the dugout. When he says he loves pitching, he is talking more about destiny. "From the time I was a kid, I had to be out there determining what happens in the game," he says. "In pitching, you are initiating the action, you are in full control. Pitching is the thinkingest of all positions in sport. Pitching most challenges your ability to put mind and body together. At this age, I couldn't be coming back as a right-fielder. I'd be bored."

Certainly one of the most telling terms in the game concerns the pitcher's *responsibility* — "Bouton leaves, but the runner on second remains his responsibility." Seldom elsewhere in life is responsibility clearer than in pitching. In the real world of flux and situational ethics, responsibility is blurred and shifted. The very command and initiative that Bouton has exhibited to his advantage on the mound are precisely the qualities that have left him a cropper in other endeavors. But pitching is neat, doubtless, perfect for Bouton. There are just outs and runs, and if another fellow makes a mistake, it isn't tabulated into your earned run average. Ultimately, it seems, the mound is just a well-lighted sanctuary that Jim Bouton has returned to for some peace.

The Busher

Bouton is something of an odd duck, certainly, but he isn't the only guy who has sacrificed for the love of baseball. It might be easier to understand Bouton if you also consider the life of Bobby Dews of Edison, Georgia, who was born (this is a little eerie) on March 23, 1939, only fifteen days after Bouton. Probably you have never heard of Bobby Dews, unless you grew up in the Peach State and remember him from twenty years ago as the bowlegged basketball guard who played at Georgia Tech alongside Roger Kaiser, the All-America. Dews had to play defense against the opposition's better guards, so Kaiser might be spared for scoring points.

But Dews took it in stride. He was all the things Jim Bouton wasn't; he was a natural athlete, the son of a baseball pro, and basketball was merely a recreation he had mastered on the side. Baseball was his game, and the Cards signed him out of Tech for $10,000. It has been eighteen years since then, and Dews has never left baseball, to make fifty grand on TV or to do anything else. He has never gone anywhere, either; he just stayed in the bushes. He has his college degree and he could do a lot of things, but he scuffles by on $15,000 a year, helping prospects. He has never gotten a cent of hospitalization, life insurance, pension funding, or profit sharing. His first wife left him when he wouldn't give the game up. And for what? He knew fourteen years ago he didn't have a chance.

That was 1964, the year Dews made it to Tulsa, Double A, the year Bouton beat the Cards twice in the Series. "I hit two-seventy-seven and stole thirty bases," he says. "I was the MVP — the team MVP. Joe Morgan was the league MVP. And I played everywhere they needed me, fielded everything. I knew somebody in the majors had seen me, the kind of year I had, and they'd draft me. I knew. And they didn't. Nobody did. I played another five years, but I knew it was all over then. I knew it.

"My grandfather was a lawyer. When I signed, he said, 'Give it five years, and if you don't make it, get out. I'll get you into a good law school, give you my books.' These kids now, they try it three or four years, and if they don't make it, they phase themselves out. A few years ago, when I was managing Modesto for the Cards, I had a kid named Bobby Corcoran. He had signed for a fifteen-hundred-dollar bonus out of Harvard or Yale, one of them. He was with me two weeks, and he called me up and asked if he could meet me at three. When we met, he said, 'Look, I got a problem. This is not for me.' And so he left — went to law school, as a matter of fact. The next day I opened the paper and saw that a reporter had asked the kid why he wanted out. The kid had said, 'Because I don't want to end up like Bobby Dews.'"

Somehow, Dews laughed. He is remarried, happily, and after managing eight years in Class A, at last he got promoted a notch this year. When he pitches batting practice he works without a glove, so he can get to the balls more expeditiously, save a few precious seconds, give everybody a few more swings. "It's a small thing," he says. "You pitch hours of extra batting practice, a kid's average goes up, and they say he's a natural. He stays at two-fifty, then I can't coach. All the kids who have gone up that I've had, I've never heard one of them mention my name. Wouldn't you think?

"Sometimes I think I ought to take stock. There's a lot of things I could do for fifteen thousand dollars. But you see, I'm obsessed with this game. My God, but I love it. There've been times I've been with a team fifteen, twenty games out in August, but the minute I get to the park I'm completely in the game. Win, we're fourteen out. Right? I come home in November after working in the instructional league, and I'm exhausted. And my friends say, Bobby, will you give it up? We can put you in real estate. We can get you into this or that business. But I'm obsessed. February, I'm back for spring training. I don't know why I love it so, but I do."

One day last month, Bobby Dews, 39, got a call from Atlanta that Jim Bouton, 39, was being assigned to his team. Dews would have to cut a player and bump the last starter to the bullpen so that Bouton could work in rotation. The funny thing is that Dews, who has given up his whole damn life for the love of baseball, could not understand how Bouton could give up fifty-grand TV work to come back to his love. Mostly Dews was concerned for Al Pratt, who was sent to the bullpen. "Al's a prospect." Dews says. "He was eleven-and-eight for me at Greenwood last year." But then, love is blind.

The Comeback

Bouton's full-time comeback began last spring in Veeck's White Sox system. It was not immediately auspicious: 0–6 at Knoxville, Double A, released; 1–4 at Durango, Mexico, Triple A, released; at last, 5–1 at Portland in the depths of Class A. But Bouton contends that it takes years to perfect the knuckler. Niekro and Wilhelm put all their effort into it, because they never woke up with an arm one morning and were diverted to fastball orthodoxy. Bouton would need more time. He cashed in his children's college savings, sold his house and his lakeside vacation home, and worked out all winter in a college gym — at midnight, so he could be alone. With Turner as his angel — Turner, like everybody else in this saga, happens to be 39 — Bouton eventually ended up pitching batting practice for meal money at Atlanta's Triple A farm in Richmond.

Then the Braves came to town for an exhibition, and Turner had two ideas: He would umpire third and Bouton would pitch. The park was packed with 13,000 witnesses, including Bobby Bouton, who drove down from Jersey with Michael, 14, and David, 13. (Laurie, 12, had a gymnastics meet.) Bouton trotted out his stomach to do the pitching. As he recalls:

"It was my greatest day in a baseball uniform. I never had more pressure, because if I didn't come through, I was gone. You lose in a World Series, you'll still be a starter next spring. I hadn't pitched in competition for a month, and nobody would let me throw my knuckler in batting practice. And I walked out on that mound cold, and I stuck it to the Atlanta Braves before thirteen thousand people. They got one run off me in six innings, and I struck out seven of them.

"And those kid pitchers who had thought I was some kind of pathetic old man, when they saw me control that game from the first, I know that every one of them would have liked to have been able to do what I did with my stomach." He sighed. "That night I was magic. I've had other great moments, but that night I felt I was omnipotent, and once you've done that you've got to think that you can be magic again."

His two sons watched, enthralled and disbelieving. If nothing else, it eased the pain of having to give up their pool so their old man could follow his dream. Past a certain age, comebacks are group efforts.

"Look," Bouton snaps rather testily, well prepared for this defense, "it's not like I sold a twenty-thousand-dollar house and put my family in a shack. We went from a hundred-and-twenty-five-thousand-dollar house to a seventy-five-thousand-dollar house, and as I keep telling the kids, there's still food in the refrigerator. [As a flanking action, Bouton follows this with a long outtake on the tyranny of the American banking community, which refused to spring for his advanced knuckleball education.] Anyway, I can spend my own money the way I want to."

Bouton also advances the proposition that the relative deprivation and the unsettling experience that have been forced on his children are for their own good. "Ideally," he says, "if you could program this kind of controlled crisis into a kid's life, you would. I think it is going to be better for them that they've seen their old man struggling."

While all this may sound calculated — pure rationalization — in Bouton's case it is consistent with the rest of his life. He is, perhaps, too sure of himself, occasionally smug and the zealot, but he is honest in his actions and sincere in conceding that he does act. It is not just that he passes up sugar, thank you. A fervent McGovern supporter in 1972, he became one of the senator's delegates to the Democratic convention, though he knew his direct participation in politics would require him to absent himself temporarily from the public air waves. He and Bobby planned a large family, but after they had a boy and girl, Jim got a vasectomy and they adopted David, a Korean orphan. The Boutons reside in Englewood, New Jersey, a once-elegant suburb that has suffered many inner-city problems. The high school is 60 percent black, and while many liberals have moved or transferred their kids to private schools, the Bouton children not only remain in the public schools, but the parents also go out of their way to celebrate the diversity of their town.

Yet the flip side is that there seems to be something of the flagellant in Bouton. It is as if the fame and easy success he unexpectedly found have left him feeling guilty. It's good to see their old man struggle? Yeah, but it's even better for the old man *to* struggle. He remembers the month in Durango last summer as an ennobling family experience in which all of them were forced to cope in an isolated mountain city in a foreign land. Bobby Bouton remembers it differently, recounting with horror the awful night when Laurie ran a frightful fever — it was strep throat — while Jim was away on a road trip. She and the kids were stranded without telephone, without car, without friends, and without the ability to speak the language.

So far the Boutons have not even discussed how much longer the provider might go on coming back. The Netherlands is still on hold, and there must be area codes for Italy, for Japan, for Finleyland. For Bouton, the knuckleball is a timeless challenge, an enigma like the cure for the common cold or the itinerary of Leon Spinks.

"All right, I will admit that the person who suffers in all of this is Bobby," Bouton says. "For whatever benefit this may be for the kids, she's the one left alone to take care of them. But I feel a need to be away from my family for a while right now. I need to be by myself at this point in my life. Look, I'm in my mid-life crisis. This is all part of that. It's more than just wanting to pitch. It's wanting to prepare myself for the rest of my life. When *Ball Four* was canceled, I had a lot of good options, but my body told me to play ball again. My body knows more about me than my conscious mind. On the mound, my instincts have often determined for me what pitch I should throw. It was those feelings that told me to pitch again."

The Prospect

His body, sweating, suggested to Bouton's mind that he move his chair out of the midday summer sun. The chair rested by a swimming pool at the Hilton Inn in Orlando, Florida. You see, minorleaguers stay at the same places as tourists and salesmen and weekend lovers. Bouton has not gone to Coventry. As Bobby Dews says, "It's really not all that hard to take. You can sleep in and read the sports pages." Players only get $7.50 a day to eat on, which is impossible unless you think French fries are the staff of life, and the locker rooms are too crowded, but the parks are generally clean and the uniforms fit. Of course, travel is by bus, and everybody in the national media who hears that — buses! — swoons and screams, "Get shots of the bus!" But, for goodness' sake, it is a nice modern bus with rubber tires and air conditioning, and the Apaches haven't attacked it once all season. There are worse environments than the minor leagues in which to endure mid-life crisis.

Although no one else on the Savannah Braves has seen the dawn of 25, Bouton, in his dotage, fits in as well, if not better, with this crew as he ever did with his teammates in his first incarnation. Then he was viewed as a peculiar fellow because he read books without pictures, made jewelry, and roomed with Latin players so he could help them and improve his Spanish. Today's players, those who read *Ball Four* in their formative years, are more apt to accept his individuality. Besides, they discover that Bouton is a likable chap who works hard and demands no favors.

For that matter, just about everybody but the hidebound baseball traditionalists has been rooting for Bouton wherever he has pitched and regardless of how well. Generally his record has been marred only by slow starts; like most knuckleballers, Bouton gets better as the game goes along. In the wake of the Richmond resuscitation, he opened in Savannah in a blaze of national publicity before an unusually large crowd — an imaginative management let a fan in for free if he brought along a copy of *Ball Four.* Responding to this pressure, Bouton struck out eight and won 5–3. In Orlando in his next start, the inscrutable knuckler failed him at the outset; he fell behind and was yanked in the sixth. Bouton came off running, and the crowd, swelled to double the usual for his appearance, applauded so generously for him, an opponent in a garden-variety defeat, that he doffed his cap and waved it to the good people. Some stood for him, and all of the applause was warm and telling.

At sporting events there are three kinds of ovations. The first is the most common, the spontaneous happy roar for the home team. Number 2 is the studied courtesy cheer reserved for beloved opponents, coaches who field foul grounders, uninvited dogs, and umpires who either fall down or retrieve errant paper napkins. The third is a special, generous cheer, filled with rare, warm appreciation.

None of these cheers may be distinguished simply by decibel count; the identifying characteristics are much more subtle. For example, when John Havlicek was trooping the NBA in his farewell tour this spring, he received standing ovations — all prolonged and loud — at each stop, but they were strictly Number 2 courtesies. What the hell, he was getting a Cuisinart and a leisure suit at half-time, and a tape deck and a ten-speed bike in Detroit tomorrow night. On the other hand, when Havlicek was playing on the road and he did something singular, diving for a loose ball after sprinting forty-three minutes straight, opposing fans often could not help crowning him with Number 3, that cheer of affection, which was not so long and loud . . . but was so much nicer.

This third type of cheer can be detected by the fact that it swells with no pattern. Instead it grows in choppy bursts. Hollering is out of place, and people pause from clapping to exchange happy talk with their neighbors: "Isn't that great?" or "Good for him." Stuff like that. Then they clap a little more and pause and smile. It's a tender cheer.

And that is the sort of cheer Bouton has been getting good nights and not so good. People seem to respond to his obsession, even if they don't necessarily comprehend it. "Hell, if he's a prospect, then I'm a prospect, too" is what Dews said late one night. "He makes me think somebody is going to take me up there." Prospects are not just kids with arms that scouts want or customers with orders that salesmen want. Bouton evokes the thought that a prospect can be anybody who wants to go up, wherever up may be.

"I told him last year, 'The odds are with you because it's never been done before,'" Bobby Bouton says. "And sometimes now it's easy to dream that it will happen." The next time out after she said this, Bouton came back to Knoxville, where he was 0–6 last year, and pitched a 1–0 two-hitter. He had told them at Knoxville that it would take a while to get the knuckleball to behave. And here it was, falling off the table. Falling off the proverbial table! Now, per-haps, everybody will get a chance in Seattle.

*   *   *

Bouton compiled a 12–9 record at Savannah, with a 2.77 earned run average, and, in September, was called up to the majors. He performed creditably for Atlanta, winning one game (his sixty-second lifetime victory in the majors), but after the season, he abruptly quit for good. Jim had found that the satis-faction was in proving that he could come back; once he had accomplished that, the experience itself was something of a letdown.

He returned to New Jersey, where he became an entrepreneur. His most successful endeavor was the creation of Big League Chew, a bubble gum which comes in a package that resembles chewing tobacco. He is also in considerable demand as a motivational speaker. Unfortunately, the mid-life crisis that took him back to professional baseball had one more lasting effect: It rent the marriage with Bobby, and the couple was soon divorced. Jim has remarried, to a psychologist.

Bouton's obsession turned out to be another man's great, good fortune. Bobby Dews had languished in the minors all those years, doing his job as a good soldier, unnoticed, but when Bouton showed up in Savannah, it brought some reflected attention to Dews. It was largely because of this article (Dews told me) that Ted Turner plucked Bobby out of the minors and made him a coach with the Braves. Given his chance, Bobby was subsequently promoted again, to the front office, and now he serves as assistant to the director of player development.

The Toughest Coach
There Ever Was

1984

Robert Victor Sullivan, whom you've surely never heard of, was the toughest coach of them all. He was so tough he had to have two tough nicknames, Bull and Cyclone, and his name was usually recorded this way: Coach Bob "Bull" "Cyclone" Sullivan or Coach Bob (Bull) (Cyclone) Sullivan. Also, at times he was known as Big Bob or Shotgun. He was the most unique of men, and yet he remains utterly representative of a time that has vanished, from the gridiron and from these United States.

Coach Bob "Bull" (Cyclone) Sullivan was a legend in his place. That place was Scooba, Mississippi, in Kemper County, hard by the Alabama line, hard to the rear of everywhere else. He was the football coach there, for East Mississippi Junior College, ruling this, his dominion, for most of the fifties and sixties with a passing attack that was a quarter century ahead of its time and a kind of discipline that was on its last legs. He was the very paradigm of that singular American figure, the coach — *corch,* as they say in backwater Dixie — who loved his boys as he dominated them, drove off the weak and molded the survivors, making the game of football an equivalency test for life.

Bull Cyclone had spent his own years struggling through a hungry country childhood, getting wounded and killing in close combat as a Marine and then coming home to raise a family and till a tiny plot of American soil he had fought for. Once that would have meant working forty acres with a mule and a plow. What Bull Cyclone turned was a parcel of earth 100 yards long and about half as wide, scratching out boys as his crop. "There are two reasons people play football," Bull Cyclone was heard to declare. "One is love of the game. The other is out of fear. I like the second reason a helluva lot better."

Randall Bradberry, who is now the football coach at East Mississippi — most people just call it Scooba — was a quarterback there in 1967. One day a Buckeye jet trainer from the nearby Meridian Naval Auxiliary Air Station went out of control. The pilot bailed out, and the empty plane winged in dead over the campus, missing the boys' dorm by forty feet before plowing into the ground, miraculously doing no damage to edifice or person, except for muddying N. J. Smith, an agriculture teacher, whose outdoor laboratory — "Mr. Smith's pasture" — abutted the football practice field. But what a God-awful noise! Bradberry heard the jet skim over and then explode. "The only thing that crossed through my mind was that the Russians were attacking us," he recalls, "and that they had decided they had to go after Corch Sullivan first. I mean that."

Except possibly for the story about how he made his team scrimmage in a pond full of man-eating alligators, none of the tales about Sullivan have been exaggerated. "I mean, everything you hear is true," says Joe Bradshaw, who played guard for him in the early fifties. Bull Cyclone did sometimes run scrimmages in the pond, except the only gator certified to have been in it was an itty-bitty one the coach's family had brought back from Florida as a souvenir. And maybe it did grow up.

Few of the stories were written down. Instead, as if from some other age, an oral history of the coach developed, and whenever old players or other Scooba minstrels gathered, they would share Bull Cyclone stories, telling the same ones over and over, word for word, liturgically, as the wives drifted to the corners and shook their heads. Nobody even knows how many games Bull Cyclone won, although the best detective efforts puts his record at 97–62–3. That was over sixteen seasons, his life's work. However, he never had any real fame outside of Scooba and environs, he never won a national championship, never even won a Mississippi Junior College Association title, and he was too ornery, too cussed independent, for any big school to take a chance on him.

A lot of folks recall that Bear Bryant himself was on record, way back when, as saying he wasn't near so tough as Bull Cyclone. As early as 1959, Jim Minter, now the editor of the *Atlanta Consti-*

tution and the *Atlanta Journal,* wrote in fascination about the growing Scooba fable. Minter had heard some coaches talking about tough. Their opinion, wrote Minter, was that Wally Butts, "the Little Spartan . . . was left at the gate. . . . Bear Bryant failed to win, place or show. . . . General Bob Neyland was not even mentioned." Instead, when it came to old-fashioned tough, "without dissent. . . . Shotgun Sullivan." And Minter's story went on: "'I can tell you one thing,' offered one college coach who has seen Shotgun Sullivan in action. 'If you get a boy who has survived him for two years, I can guarantee he will make your team.'"

Though many football people acclaimed him as a genius, and everyone accepted him as a man of integrity, no one would dare hire him in the big time, because Bull Cyclone sure as shooting wasn't going to be a football *assistant* for any mother's son. It's apparently true that Norm Van Brocklin, an old pal of his, did once ask him to take over the Atlanta Falcons' offense when Van Brocklin was head coach, but Bull Cyclone declined, saying, "Now, Norm, why should I come up there and work for you when I already know more football than you do?" So he stayed in Scooba, eking out a living for his family, hunting and fishing, developing offenses that big-city coaches would make fashionable a generation later, and driving his players, whom he tricked out in skull-and-crossbones helmets and short-sleeved jerseys he designed himself. The shirts were known as star jerseys because below the black shoulder trim and above the numerals, there across the chest, were arrayed five stars. As far as anybody knew, no one, not even his wife and children, had any idea what the stars signified, and, of course, no one dared ask Bull Cyclone prying questions such as that. He was some coach. Curiously, as you shall see, he was also beloved.

He was 32 years old, a veteran, husband, and father, when he returned to the Deep South in 1950 to assume his first head coaching job. East Mississippi had gone winless the autumn before and, for that matter, had seldom ever won a game. Even as the years wore on, as he produced thirty-one J.C. All-Americas, Bull Cyclone would tell his players they were suiting up for the smallest football-playing college in America. That might well have been true. Scooba had only about 250 to 300 kids then, a third of them girls. So in any given year, a substantial proportion of the male enrollment was playing football for Coach Sullivan.

The hamlet of Scooba (Choctaw for "reed brake") then boasted 734 souls, which made it a metropolis in Kemper County. The county must look exactly the same now, only less so; when Bull Cyclone arrived in Kemper in 1950, the population was 16,000; today only 10,000 remain, planting a little cotton or soybeans, cutting pulpwood — "pu'pwood," as everybody says. Even into the sixties Scooba's main street had hitching posts, and it still has a big faded sign that reads "Serve Coke at Home." For more substantial spirits, the folks would go out to what were known as "jig joints," illegal roadhouses in a state of Baptists and bootleggers that nevertheless winked at Prohibition, which remained the law in Mississippi until 1966. More than that, of course, Appomattox had yet to be acknowledged anywhere in Mississippi, especially not in Kemper, its most antediluvian, impoverished outpost.

Bull Cyclone had been reared nearby — "So far out in the country you could still smell pu'pwood on his breath," according to his old friend Carlton Fleming. Sullivan moved his wife, Virginia, and two daughters — another daughter and a son would come later — onto campus into what was known as the Alamo, a broken-down dormitory that housed the football players. It was reputed to be the only three-story public building in the county. The old place was so ramshackle that the Sullivans had to practice "leak drills." But it was home, and Christmastime they'd set up the tree out where the boys on the team could share it.

Getting those quarters in the Alamo was crucial because all Bull Cyclone was paid for being the football coach — and the baseball coach and athletic director — was $3,600 a year, plus $75 for every game he won. Most of the latter went for gas so he could go on recruiting trips. Bull Cyclone couldn't do much work over the phone inasmuch as there were only three in all of Scooba, one at the drugstore, and one each at the president's house and the president's office.

What Scooba had above all was homogeneity. The students were all the same, bound together in a way that most of today's diverse student bodies couldn't conceive. The girls were only allowed out one night a week, and on the Sabbath girls and boys alike were "urged" to attend both Sunday school and church and then, for good measure, to observe a "quiet hour" from two to three in the afternoon. "At this time," the school catalog explained, "students are to be in their rooms. It is suggested that they write their parents

during quiet hour and that they spend some of this time in medi-
tation." The college library had only 4,500 volumes. A football
coach could be a gigantic personage in that sort of place.

And he was. For amusement Scooba had jig joints and bad girls,
hunting and fishing, and, in season, football. It has always been Dixie's game. Bradberry, who was raised close by in the little town of
Sturgis, says, "If you were a boy and grew up in Sturgis, Mississippi,
and didn't play football for the high school, your daddy didn't get
credit at the grocery store."

Said the East Mississippi catalog the year that Bull Cyclone arrived, "Athletics may be justified as part of the physical culture program, as a recreational feature and as disciplinary measure. . . .
We also teach good sportsmanship and self-denial in habits and attitudes."

Armed with that mandate, Bull Cyclone got in his old station
wagon and, like some preacher or salesman, hit the highways
and byways in search of football players. He had only one returning from the winless '49 season. Sullivan ranged far and wide
and, brandishing the GI Bill, even induced some soldiers at various posts to abandon service for their country to play for Scooba.
Tales of such outlanders arriving on motorsickles can still be
heard. "They'd put 'em in jail for tearing up, and then they'd tear
up the jail," Fleming recalls with a guffaw. But on his field, Bull
Cyclone, who peaked out at around 6' 5" and 285 pounds,
brooked no backtalk.

His first team assembled, Coach Sullivan called up and got a
game with Little Rock J.C. to open the season. And what was Little
Rock J.C.? Only the '49 winner of the Junior Rose Bowl, the junior
college champion of America. Bull Cyclone was scared of no one,
and he would prove it.

When the Scooba team arrived in Little Rock, it was told to practice at the stadium itself. Bull Cyclone, who was especially attuned
to spies, suspected that some would be hidden in the stands, so he
had his players run all sorts of goofy plays. After a while, Bull Cyclone called over his manager. Managers were very important to
Bull Cyclone, and he expected almost as much of them as he did
of his quarterbacks. "The trouble with being a manager for my father," recalls Bobbie, his oldest daughter, "is that he assumed a manager would know what he wanted before he asked." Bull Cyclone
instructed this first manager to play dumb and to go over to the

Little Rock J.C. locker room and tell the coach that Scooba had forgotten to bring kicking tees. He then was to ask whether he could borrow some. Sure enough, the manager saw that the Little Rock coach was drawing all the ridiculous East Mississippi plays on a blackboard for his players.

Bull Cyclone was pretty sure, then, that his first game as a head coach would be "like taking candy from a baby." One of his major tenets was to strike fast with surprise. He knew Little Rock wouldn't know what hit it.

Back in Scooba that night, the postmistress, who had a good radio, picked up the game all the way from Little Rock. Bull Cyclone had promised that he would call in the outcome to the phone at the president's house, but during the game the lady with the radio started going around town giving everybody updates. Pretty soon a lot of townspeople were congregated around her radio in the Sullivans' apartment at the Alamo, listening to the game. This was the biggest thing that had ever happened to Scooba, and Bull Cyclone had only just come to town.

He beat the defending national champions 34–14, and his legend was in the making in that grateful little crossroads. As best we can tell, Bull Cyclone went 8–3 that first season, and 21–9 for three years, which was more victories than Scooba had enjoyed in its entire previous history since the college had been chartered in 1927, a step up from a county agricultural school.

However, in 1953 Bull Cyclone departed Scooba, taking his family up to Nashville, where he wanted to finish up work for his bachelor's degree in physical education at Peabody College. Once he had his degree in hand, though, he planned to return to Scooba. And he did — for the '56 season.

East Mississippi had taken on a new president in the interim, a local man familiar with Bull Cyclone's exploits, and he hired him back. The president was a little red-haired fellow named R. A. Harbour. He always went by his initials, hoping that no one would remember that his square name was Ritzi Algeine. Unfortunately, behind his back he was called Stumpy, for he was as small a man as Bull Cyclone was big.

Like the coach, though, the president was married to a smart woman, one who was every bit his partner. Edna Harbour joined the faculty at Scooba, and she eventually became its public relations director. Edna was a beautiful woman, taller than her husband, and she constantly pushed Stumpy, regularly correcting him and embarrassing him in front of his colleagues.

Still, it's fair to say that Stumpy wanted as much for the college he ran as Bull Cyclone did for the football team, and the new president was delighted to get Sullivan back in '56. The team had again fallen on hard times, and the fans had grown resentful, as all fans do, at the lack of success. When Stumpy hired Bull Cyclone, the *Kemper County Messenger* ("This is the only newspaper in the world whose sole interest is in Kemper County") exulted: "He is considered one of the best offensive coaches in existence, including senior college. . . . Sullivan's teams didn't always win, but they always put on a show for the spectators. When you saw Sullivan's boys play, you saw a jam-up scoring, razzle-dazzle game that left you breathless and sometimes mad also. But you saw a football game."

But it was just like 1950 all over again. Scooba had only two players back from the '55 squad, so Bull Cyclone had to scour the territory for live bodies. The way it worked then, at Scooba and at a lot of other places, a coach would rope in so many players, weed out the losers during summer practice, and then "dress out" the survivors. Bull Cyclone didn't disguise what he was doing. Just the opposite. A candidate he was recruiting would ask, "Corch, are you giving me a scholarship?"

"Yeah," Bull Cyclone would grumble, "I'm giving you a scholarship *if* you don't quit or *if* I don't run you off." It was customary for a Scooba player — freshman or sophomore — to sign his scholarship form as he boarded the team bus to go to the first game.

Understand, "running off" was a fairly common gridiron practice in those days. It was, for example, what cemented Bryant's reputation as a martinet when he started coaching at Texas A&M in '54. You didn't get cut, you got run off the team. Or perhaps, more often, you chose to run yourself off. "Bull ran off more All-Americans than he kept," says Don Edwards, who played quarterback at Scooba in the late fifties. Players can remember hearing suitcases banging down the stairs of the Alamo just before dawn as boys decided not to go through another two-a-day. Others would leave surreptitiously in the black of night. They'd sneak down the stairs and then push their cars out of earshot before starting them up, lest Bull Cyclone wake up and come after them and make them stay on the team.

When Sullivan's old players get together, they often wonder about the ones that quit. It wasn't exactly dishonorable to get run off. After all, a lot did, and damn near everybody *almost* did. Edwards, for example, left six times before ultimately deciding to stay. Still, the survivors wonder what ever happened to the others. Well, here's one report, from C. R. Gilliam of Carrollton, Alabama: "We'd practice four hours in the morning and then four more hours in the afternoon. I was playing defensive guard and got my nose broken. It was bleeding real bad and pushed around to the side, but Bull just kicked my butt and told me to get back in there.

"That night, I'm laying on that pillow, my nose is aching, I'm feeling real sorry for myself, and I'm thinking, 'I don't have to take this.' I got up and met Bull in the hall the next morning and told him I was going home. 'How?' Bull asked me. 'Walkin',' I told him. I started out and must have gotten four or five miles, to near Geiger, when here come that red Pontiac station wagon of his. He picked me up and took me on home to Carrollton. I never did go to the doctor about that nose."

Something like 200 of Bull Cyclone's players became coaches, and he'd tell them, "Son, don't never worry about a player who leaves. The only thing for you to do is find out why he left and work on it for the next one comes along like that."

Coaching, at least as it was practiced then, in the good old days, wasn't exactly like the ministry. The idea wasn't to save all the souls. The ones that got run off were on their own, but the ones who stayed would be affected far out of proportion. Bull Cyclone, like a lot of coaches, especially football coaches, had more impact on many boys' lives than did their fathers. It was all very basic, really. "You either loved him or you didn't stay," says Bill Buckner, Scooba's best quarterback, who is now the coach at Hinds J.C. "He pushed everyone to the point where they either left him or they gave him what they were capable of."

Edwards remembers the year he was captain and a big lineman complained that Sullivan was slugging him. "Nobody hits me, not even my daddy," the lineman said. But Edwards wasn't about to get involved. "Besides, Bull wasn't really hitting the boy," he says. "Just in the solar plexus."

"Yeah," says Bill (Sweet William) Gore, a retired postman who was Bull Cyclone's good friend. "They'd think he was killing a boy out there when all he was doin' was gettin' his attention."

Bull Cyclone's attention-getting took varied forms. One of his favorite tactics was to have his players practice hitting one-on-one, head on, right before a game or, when he was especially irritated, at halftime, or even during time-outs. More often than not, this was very disconcerting to the wide-eyed opposition, not to mention what it did to the bodies of the Scooba players. Often in these drills Bull Cyclone wouldn't tell his players who was supposed to be the ballcarrier and who was supposed to be the tackler. So, starting twenty yards apart, a pair of players would tear into one another. Before such drills, Bull Cyclone also had the habit of saying, "Now, I don't want to see any of you bastards standing up, and I don't want to see any of you bastards on the ground."

L. C. Jeffries, who played on one of Bull Cyclone's early teams after having seen combat with the Second Infantry in Korea, says, "Sure, we broke some ribs and noses going one-on-one with ourselves at halftime, but understand that what Bull did didn't come out of cruel rural ignorance. He was a smart man and he was playing on the psyche."

Although Bull Cyclone would line up all his players in their star jerseys for the pregame head-ons, he often made sure that his best ones, especially the quarterbacks, who were inviolate in his scheme, never took a lick. When they neared the front of the line, one of the eight or nine scrubs would jump ahead and replace them in the rotation. These unfortunates Sullivan called the "gook squad." Hence when the opposition looked over to see Scooba banging heads, what it unknowingly saw for the most part was the gook-squadders repeatedly laying into each other.

Bull Cyclone made sure, though, that no one on the team felt safe. Sometimes he would advise his players, "I've killed more men than I can *stack* on this football field." That usually got their attention. One time, when he was mad at Bradberry, he said, "Bradberry, I killed seven gooks with a foxhole shovel. One more sonofabitch like you won't matter."

If these remarks were hyperbolic, their substance was real enough. Sergeant Sullivan had fought the last battles of the Pacific with the First Marines, ending up on Okinawa, where he was wounded on June 16, 1945. Maybe that's why he thought he could demand so much of his players, whose sacrifices couldn't compare with those of the good Americans he had fought alongside, and left behind — and finally, as we shall see, honored. He never quite separated war and football. Flipping through what seems to be a scrapbook dedicated entirely to football, one suddenly comes to a long clipping about Okinawa, with a huge headline: BLOODIEST BATTLE OF THE PACIFIC. Once at halftime Bull Cyclone spread his players along the fifty-yard line — "Team! A-ten-shun!" — and marched them to the end zone, military style, to reacquaint them with that foreign terrain.

Bull Cyclone didn't always need a whistle to get his players' attention. He just hollered "Whoaaa!" and everything screeched to a halt. His language, especially in the earlier years, could wilt the blossoms in Mr. Smith's pasture. Grown men listened in awe when he cursed — "Unbelievably vile," says Charlie Box, who was a fullback and no prude. One time, Dick Potter, a referee, felt obliged to penalize Scooba fifteen yards for unsportsman-like conduct because of how grossly Bull Cyclone had yelled at one of his *own* players.

But more frightening was his mere presence. He was big all over — ham-like arms, huge feet, a melon head so large that when he decided to change his game ensemble, switching from a ten-gallon hat to a baseball cap, he had to split the cap in back to get it comfortably on his head. Virginia, a lovely woman, his second wife, who was at his side all the years in Scooba, remembers a player telling her, "Miz Sullivan, we're not afraid of Corch. Why, we reckon ten or twelve of us together could whip him." Players commonly took off their shoes as they passed his room, fearful that they might awaken him from a nap. A lot of times he would tear off his coat in the middle of a game, throw it down, stomp on it, and then sort of hurl it back to the bench. Whatever player got in front of it would quickly pass it along, because nobody wanted to be holding it when Bull Cyclone started looking for his coat again. And, to be sure, nobody dared put it on the ground. So the coat would go up and down the bench like a hot potato.

Lester Smith, a quarterback from Foley, Alabama, recalls one game at Southwest during which the fans were "giving him fits." When the game was over and the fans were threatening his players, Bull Cyclone told them, "OK now, if I say 'sic 'em,' I mean *sic 'em!*" But he became the point man and went and stood in the stadium gate and glared at the fans until one by one they all melted away, and Bull Cyclone's team filed out, unmolested.

To spice up practices Bull Cyclone would sometimes have the

managers wrap old mattresses around pine trees to make blocking targets. The idea was to see if anybody could slam into a tree hard enough to knock off a pinecone. Try it. Or, if he thought things were slack during a scrimmage, he would scream, "Get after it!" and the linemen were automatically obliged to choose up and start fighting one another.

From his Parris Island days, Bull Cyclone borrowed the idea of an obstacle course, adding a wrinkle of his own — a trip wire in the tall grass that the managers yanked as the weary players came through. From another part of the course, Bull Cyclone would hurl bricks at the players as they tried to regain their balance after clambering over a wall. He would miss, but barely. He did, however, get their attention.

Probably his most famous gambit was to hold scrimmages at the edge of the pond, which is located at the bottom of a gentle slope, down from where Mr. Smith's pasture used to be. Bull Cyclone came up with the scheme in order to test goal-line defenses. He took his defensive unit and lined it up in the shallow water, which came up to about the players' knees.' Then Bull Cyclone had the offense storm down the hill. It "scored" if the running back could make it into the water.

Gerald Poole, who's still on the faculty at Scooba, was Bull Cyclone's defensive assistant the day he dreamed up the pond scrimmage. "You think your fucking defense is tough?" Bull Cyclone roared, and then had Coach Poole station his players in the water. The first two goal-line plays, off-tackle, failed to get a splashdown. On the third and last shot, Poole told his middle linebacker that he thought the ballcarrier would come right over the middle on the next assault. "If he does, I'm gonna shoot him like an old dove," the linebacker said. Sure enough, the runner took the handoff and tried to leap into the pond over center. The linebacker popped up, met him at the height of his dive, and the two players crashed into the muck, headfirst. It wasn't uncommon for the defenders to lose their cleats in the Mississippi mud.

The reference to dove shooting wasn't unusual, either. Most Scooba players were country boys who had, like the coach, grown up with guns. Because Bull Cyclone was almost paranoid about opponents spying, he outfitted his managers with rifles. On at least two occasions it's documented that Bull Cyclone grabbed a rifle from a manager and fired at a private airplane that had strayed into his practice airspace. Another time he bade the manager to open fire on a plane, but the boy panicked, threw down the gun and, so the story goes, ran off the field, never to show his face again in Scooba. On another occasion, a succession of shots was heard from where a manager was stationed — with a shotgun and orders to shoot to kill any suspected spies.

"Oh my Lord!" Bull Cyclone screamed. "Who did he shoot?"

Mercifully, no one. The manager was just another old country boy, and when he saw a covey of quail nearby, he had blasted away.

Scooba boys were the last in the country to eschew leather helmets, because Bull Cyclone believed that the hard modern helmets caused more injuries than they prevented. He thought his players would be better off with the nice, soft leather helmets — especially if they were decked out with skull and crossbones. No sooner had he thought of the skull-and-crossbones idea than he dispatched a manager with a bunch of helmets for Mrs. Sullivan to start painting. "Bob thought the skull and crossbones would kind of rattle the other team," she says. "He told the players, 'Now, you don't have to make faces. But don't smile.'"

Traditionally, when the Scooba players came out before a game, they didn't make a sound. Most teams scream and shout and carry on to prove they're *ready to play,* but Bull Cyclone thought that was a waste of good energy. His charges came out as silent as the fog. Imagine being a player on the other team, and here comes the bunch you're going to play, togged out in star jerseys — and now in skull-and-bones helmets — quiet as mice, and then on the sideline they start going one-on-one. That was likely to get your attention.

Bull Cyclone had some kind of temper. Because he was a man of his word, remarks he made while in a rage were not disregarded. He often drove the team bus, a rattly, broken-down vehicle that was known as Night Train because it seemed to function better after the sun went down. After one defeat, Bull Cyclone climbed behind the wheel and announced that he was so mad he was going to run the bus off the road and kill the whole team. Box, who was aboard, says, "I don't know how many of us believed him — most of us believed everything he ever said — but the manager sure did, because he started crying, 'Well, let me off first, Corch, because I'm just the manager, and I didn't have a thing to do with us losing this game.'"

Bull Cyclone's tempestuous hijinks didn't go unnoticed. People would come out just to watch him carry on, throw his coat down, stomp on his hat. One time at Holmes the crowd got so abusive that Bull Cyclone called time and had his players pick up their benches and march to the other side of the field. Robert McGraw, now an assistant at Ole Miss, recalls seeing Bull Cyclone storm onto the field because a wide receiver had run the wrong route. He picked up the player by his jersey and sort of flung him aside. The boy scurried to the bench and hid under it, quaking, while the coach stormed back, the fans all the while chanting, "Give 'em hell, Bull!"

At his maddest, he could really kick a ball. Langston Rogers, who served as Bull Cyclone's aide-de-camp and is now the sports information director at Ole Miss, swears that on one occasion when the coach got mad at the officials, he blustered onto the field between plays, right up to the line of scrimmage, and booted the ball thirty yards, soccer style, dead through the uprights. Another time he went out and kicked the game ball into the stands. As a result the Mississippi Junior College Association required him to spend the whole next game in a chair on the sideline. Stumpy Harbour was infuriated. He acted as if Bull Cyclone had embarrassed him in front of the other presidents. None of them had a football coach kicking game balls into the stands, did they?

A lot of people thought Bull Cyclone would never be able to sit still in the chair the entire game, so there was no telling what Stumpy would do. But, wouldn't you know it, Bull Cyclone stayed put, barely even rising from his seat. That might have made Stumpy even madder. Bull Cyclone could control himself when he had to. Why, to this day, you'd have a hard time finding a lady in Kemper County who ever heard Coach Bob (Bull) (Cyclone) Sullivan utter a curse word.

For that matter, although he constantly fought with officials, he never argued just to dispute a call. Bull Cyclone only let the officials have it when he thought they had misinterpreted a rule. "You stink, Billbo!" he screamed when Billbo Mitchell made a call that Sullivan didn't agree with. Mitchell stepped off fifteen before saying, "Can you still smell me, Bull?" Bull Cyclone was a stickler about the rules. He knew the book so well and cared so passionately for it that General Neyland, the revered Tennessee coach, eventually got Bull Cyclone from Scooba appointed to the NCAA rules committee, even though his unknown little school wasn't even a member of that august national body.

This isn't to say that Bull Cyclone was above taking the rules as far as they could go. At least one time, in the rain, he taped thumbtacks to his quarterbacks' fingers so they could get a better grip on the ball. That worked just fine until the tacks started scratching up the pigskin better than a Don Sutton belt buckle. Another time, Bull Cyclone got to thinking about how his linemen pulled out to block. He was using the split T then, and most of the plays came off the quarterback rolling right. So Coach thought, "Well now, if my guard and tackle are going to pull on just about every play and everybody figures this, I might as well get them headed in the right direction to start with." So he had them come up to the line of scrimmage and take their three-point stances facing the other way, with their rear ends staring the opposing linemen in the face.

And on a most memorable occasion, just as Scooba was about to score against Southwest, the officials called a holding penalty, citing the number of a player who wasn't in the game. Enraged by this breach, Bull Cyclone ran onto the field to get his point across better. That's an automatic fifteen on top of the fifteen for holding. First-and-forty. Potter, the referee, said, "You gotta go back, Corch," but Bull Cyclone kept on coming. Another fifteen. First-and-fifty-five. "C'mon, Bull," Potter pleaded. He liked him. "Go on back, or I gotta give you fifteen more."

"I don't give a damn!" Bull Cyclone thundered. "You're wrong!" Potter stepped off fifteen more. First-and-seventy. Then, as soon as Potter placed the ball down once again, Bull Cyclone went into his patented kicking phase. He booted the bejesus out of the ball. By the time they retrieved it, it was first-and-eighty-five.

Because they had nearly run out of acreage and he had made his point, Bull Cyclone returned to the sideline, pausing only to tell his quarterback to call a Z-out, Z-in. This was one play, mind you. Southwest was still laughing and, needless to say, wasn't looking for Bull Cyclone to try to get the whole eighty-five back on one play. But he was. Z-out, Z-in, TD.

"Wooo, that did it," Poole says.

Bull Cyclone enjoyed matching wits with other coaches. Dobie Holden down at Pearl River was his favorite rival. Pearl River was often the top team in the conference. It was a much larger school than Scooba and always well coached. One year Pearl River was an overwhelming favorite against Scooba and was at home, to boot. This brought out the best in Bull Cyclone. He really put on his thinking cap. Scooba would normally arrive for a Saturday night game around 4 P.M., after stopping along the way for a typical training meal that the players referred to as "the four Ts": tea, taters, toast, and tough meat. This time, however, as old Night Train rattled through Hattiesburg on the way to Pearl River, Bull Cyclone had the bus pull up to one of the fanciest restaurants in all of Mississippi and treated the boys to the finest of repasts. Then, as Night Train rolled into the Poplarville area, where Pearl River is located, Bull Cyclone diverted it to a roadside park. Everybody in Pearl River was wondering what was up as game time approached. Where were Bull Cyclone and the Scooba team? Finally, just in time for the players to dress, Night Train arrived.

In the locker room, Bull Cyclone told them not to utter a sound until right before the kickoff, whereupon they were to "go crazy." Pearl River, already discombobulated by the late arrival, was put off even more by these antics, and the home team left the field at halftime down 3–0. Unfortunately, Bull Cyclone didn't have any more psychological tricks up his sleeve, and Pearl River won something like 42–3. Edwards, who was a sophomore, remembers saying to Bull Cyclone afterward, "Well, that kinda backfired."

"Oh, we got a half out of 'em," said Bull Cyclone, with equanimity. He never had any difficulty accepting defeat — or even losing seasons — as long as he thought he was outmanned and everybody had done his best.

Most of Bull Cyclone's players still maintain that the public never really saw him at his best — at halftime. Even with one-on-ones awaiting them, Scooba players were wont to say, "It's safer on the field than in the locker room." As Poole remembers, chuckling, the players would "draw up" during halftime. Among other things, Bull Cyclone threw a lot of objects, from salt tablets up to and including a huge axle-grease drum. To give the devil his due, Sullivan thought the drum was empty. It wasn't. It had been used as a trash container, and when he flung it at a post, the top flew off and the garbage poured over the poor lad who had chosen to sit against the post. Petrified, the player never budged, just letting the trash spill on him and his star jersey, while the coach raved on. Other times, Bull Cyclone destroyed a chair by smashing it against a table, kicked any number of things, drove his fist clear through a blackboard and, to use the singular Mississippi expression, "forearmed" a variety of stationary objects.

But halftimes weren't just pyrotechnic displays. Indeed, to add to the air of uncertainty, Sullivan would always leave his boys alone at first, letting them unwind with Cokes and Hershey bars. Because he favored wing-tip brogues that always seemed to squeak, everyone could hear him approaching. The first game Bradberry played for Scooba, Bull Cyclone came in and squatted on the floor in front of the quarterback. Bull didn't say a word until it was time to go back onto the field. Then, staring straight through poor Bradberry, he snarled, "Come on, young lady," and got up and departed. The performance so unnerved some of the veteran sophomores that a couple of them threw Bradberry against a wall and advised him he damn well better not screw up and get the coach down on the whole team. Terrified, Bradberry brought Scooba home 29–3.

During another memorable halftime, Bull Cyclone suddenly materialized in the locker room on his hands and knees, with his overcoat collar pulled up around his ears. He gave no explanation for this bizarre posture but merely crawled from player to player, stopping before each one, staring him dead in the face, like a mad dog. This caught their attention.

Bull Cyclone usually started at halftime by walking the length of the locker room. Then he'd shorten the span until eventually he wasn't taking steps, but just sort of doing an about-face. It was mesmerizing. Next he would talk. To hear him was a hypnotic experience, for he would blink a lot — an aftereffect of his war experiences — or his eyes would sort of roll back up in his head. When he spoke with emphasis, which he invariably did, his jaw would shake, so that his gruff voice resonated all the more. Edwards recalls one halftime when Bull Cyclone went through this routine, never saying a word, until, at the last, he spun on his heels and screamed, "I was on an island with five thousand Japs! Now, get out of here!" The players all but stampeded in an effort to escape him, and then destroyed an unsuspecting opponent.

Box remembers when Bull Cyclone gave his finest Knute Rockne oration. He spoke very softly, recounting how he was in a foxhole with a buddy who had just been hit by shrapnel. Blood was pouring out of the Marine, and he obviously wasn't going to make it. "Anything I can do for you?" Bull Cyclone whispered. The locker room was still and reverent.

"Yeah, Big Bob, just win one for me sometime." Well, this was the sometime. And Scooba won, too. Apparently, that was the only time Bull Cyclone invoked his friend's dying wish. But he always wanted to do something for the ones he left back in the Pacific. Sometimes, when he was really furious, out of the blue he would holler, "You cocksuckers, you're out here playin', breathin' this fuckin' free air because a heap of people died for you."

If he cared, he would never let up. That was the way men were made then. Maybe it was the wrong way, but it was the way back then. "He'd ride you to just before he got you to the ground, and only then he'd let you up . . . some," Bradberry says. "Then he had you in his hip pocket."

"Yeah, he was tough," Edwards says. "But I loved him like a father. And I'll tell you: Any player who ever stayed with him will say that."

That was the way it was. That was the way people let it be. The players were all the same sorts, they were in it together, and football and Okinawa were very much the same. "Football doesn't mean near as much as it used to," Bradberry says. And no, he goes on, there's no way in the world that he — or anybody else — could coach Scooba the way Coach Sullivan did. "The ones playing now look at football differently," says Bradberry. "They've got more to do. There's nowhere near as many dedicated people."

Bull Cyclone's family remembers the first time he saw the Beatles, and, recalls Royce Tucker, one of his daughters, "he thought the world had come to an end." Still, everybody could see that at least he made some accommodations as the sixties came to an end and a new type of player evolved. Nonetheless, as Royce says, "Yeah, he changed some. He changed, but he liked the old ways best. You could see he was under some stress."

One time he told Royce flat out, "You can't coach in the same way."

"Why?" she asked.

"Because it doesn't work anymore." And that was all there was to that.

At a very early age the boy who would become Bull Cyclone realized that the best chance he had on this earth was with football. That doesn't mean he was dumb. Mrs. Elizabeth Cunningham, one of his high school teachers, remembers that he was an "excellent" student, and all through his life he loved such un-pigskin things as

writing and anthropology. But the Sullivans were the poorest of
poor whites in the poorest of times in the poorest part of the country. Mrs. Sullivan had to support six children by herself because her
husband, Wild Bill, dropped dead one day, down at the creek, fishing for dinner. Mrs. Sullivan barely got by, working at the cotton
mill in Aliceville. That's just up from Scooba, only on the Alabama
side.

Bull Cyclone was born in Echola, in Tuscaloosa County, Alabama,
in 1918, and the family moved to Aliceville when he was 10. Mrs.
Sullivan moved the family again when young Bob was 16. She went
down to Mobile, hoping to find a better paycheck in the big city.
But Bob stayed behind to play football for Aliceville High. He got a
room in back of a store by the cotton mill, paying for it by sweeping
out the place. Years later, as a coach, no matter how badly Bull
Cyclone would embarrass a player, he'd never let a boy be embarrassed by his clothes. Whenever possible, he'd try to get the youngster some better duds.

He also learned to abide almost any sort of person except someone who put on airs. It especially irritated Bull Cyclone that
Stumpy Harbour had come to be more interested in the trappings
of his office than in the substance. According to Bull Cyclone,
Stumpy would rather gussy up the president's expanding mansion
than improve the curriculum. Bull Cyclone never could tolerate
Kemper County's self-proclaimed social elite, which dismissed the
Sullivans as boorish newcomers even after they'd lived in Scooba
for fifteen years.

One spring Sunday, Bull Cyclone took his family out to lunch
over at the old Five Points Restaurant. It had a fine reputation, although its owners closed down with the onset of integration
rather than serve the colored on white tablecloths. But on this particular Sunday, one of the pillars of Scooba society was also dining
there, and she kept casting sideways looks at the Sullivans. Bull
Cyclone stared back at the dowager, and out of the corner of his
mouth, to his family, he whispered, "Don't anyone dare laugh."
Then, while smiling at the matron, he reached over, picked up one
of the daffodils that decorated the table and, most conspicuously,
ate it, stem and all.

Staying alone back in Aliceville paid off for Bull Cyclone. He cap-
tained the football team in '37 and was its biggest and best player,
a barreling fullback in the old short punt formation. On defense he
was a linebacker. His play gained him passage to Union University

up in Jackson, Tennessee. By then Bull Cyclone had married a hometown girl named Thelma. The marriage didn't work, except for the three children it produced. One of the two sons was named Vic. Later on, when Bull Cyclone married Virginia, they named *their* only son Vic, too. The two half brothers are known as Big Vic and Little Vic. Few people knew that the father's middle name was Victor, and if you ask anyone why Bull Cyclone gave two sons the same name, he'll say, "Corch always wanted to have a victory around." That isn't as farfetched as it seems; he and Virginia named their third daughter Gael because he wanted to have a Little Cyclone.

In 1942 Union was a football powerhouse, going undefeated and outscoring the opposition 211–75 behind a fabled back known as Casey Jones. Sullivan, big number 41, was settled at center by then and was good enough to get an offer from the Detroit Lions. But he joined the Marines instead.

Bull Cyclone probably decided to be a coach while in the service. Certainly, his experience at Parris Island, where he became a DI, relates to Scooba. "The recruits hated you so much it was hard to take," he once told Virginia. "But by the end of the training cycle they had come to love you. They'd even buy you a little something, and then they'd leave, and the awful part of it was, there was a whole new group in there the next day, hating you all over again."

The members of that great '42 Union team had vowed to come back and finish school together. But when Bull Cyclone returned late in '45, shrapnel in his right leg, blinking nervously from all the gunfire, jumping at unexpected noises, he discovered that the Union administration had eliminated football. For one of the few times in his life he was bitter. In the college paper he wrote this in his sports-page column, which was entitled

by **S**ullivan
on **S**ports:

"Then the matter of a war came along and the boys left the football field for the battle field only [to] return and find what they fought for [had been] taken from them by people who slept between clean sheets while the boys made themselves cozy in a muddy foxhole."

Before departing Union at the end of the school year, Bull Cyclone got his first real coaching experience and crowned it by marrying one of his players. His marriage to Thelma had been dissolved by now, and when Bull Cyclone took over a girls' softball team on campus, he took a shine to the shortstop. He named the team the Terrapins because he thought the players were so slow. He shifted the shortstop, Virginia Dale, to first (and later tabbed her All-League in his column) and led the club to an undefeated season. The first big game he ever coached was a showdown between the Terrapins and their main rival, which boasted the league's fastest pitcher. To prepare his girls Bull Cyclone brought in his roommate, a softball pitcher, to throw batting practice. The first two days, they didn't get a bat on the ball, but by the time they had to face the female fireballer, her vaunted offerings looked like change-ups, and she was quickly driven out of the box. Not long afterward, Sullivan married his first-sacker, and they headed to Reno so he could play football at the University of Nevada, where a coach named Whistlin' Jim Aiken was assembling a postwar juggernaut.

Nevada set national offensive records that stood for years, and Bull Cyclone was a standout at center and linebacker, good enough to make the Shrine All-Star game in Honolulu, where he intercepted three passes. The Baltimore Colts of the old All-American Conference offered him a contract. But when Whistlin' Jim went north to take over as coach at the University of Oregon in 1947, he asked Bull Cyclone to come along as an assistant, and he did. Sullivan had decided it was time to stop playing and get on with his calling in life, which was to coach football.

When Bull Cyclone arrived in Scooba in '50, the split T, a grind-'em-out power offense, was in fashion, but he favored a wide-open passing game, so he operated from the I formation. Jimmy Jobe, who played and coached against Bull Cyclone, says, "Things you saw last Sunday for the first time on TV, well, I guarantee he was doing them twenty years ago. All that motion and then reverse — Bull was doing that in the late *fifties*."

"I had to laugh when Bill Walsh won the Super Bowl two years ago and everybody discovered a genius," says Bradberry. "Corch Walsh may be a genius, but Corch Sullivan was doing the same thing when I played for him in the sixties. I don't believe we ever ran a play that didn't have five receivers."

Adds Poole, "Every play was pass action. I don't know how anybody prepared for us. He'd make up at least six plays for every game."

He conjured them up at all waking hours. Around the house, plays would be sketched on newspapers, napkins, books, calendars; they were found on church programs and high school prom dance cards. One morning Bobbie discovered that her father had absentmindedly scribbled plays all over the margins of a term paper she was turning in that day.

Box remembers being awakened in his room in the Alamo at 3 A.M. by Little Vic. Instructing Box to follow, the boy took him downstairs to the Sullivan apartment and then right into his parents' bedroom. Virginia was sound asleep in her half of the bed. But Bull Cyclone was sitting up next to her, running a projector, staring at films on the far wall. He ran a play and asked Box if he thought a new variation involving him would work. Flabbergasted, Box said, "Yes sir, I don't see why not."

"OK," Bull Cyclone said. "Go back to bed." He promptly began to diagram the play on an index card. He usually had all his special plays for that week's game designed by Monday.

Bull Cyclone would take the basic stuff he planned to use and make a deck of plays that he flipped through on the sidelines. Says Bradberry, "I can see him now, wiping the blood off my face with one hand, shuffling through his deck with the other to find me the play he wanted." Purists maintain that one quarterback must be deputized to be in charge of a team, but if Bull Cyclone didn't believe he had an outstanding player, he'd use two or even three quarterbacks during a game, alternating these paragons of leadership after each play. And it worked just fine.

For example, as a freshman Bradberry alternated with a string bean named Ricky Garner. In one game, Bull Cyclone got furious with Bradberry for citing some wrong information about a linebacker and yanked him. "You little sonofabitch," he screamed, "don't you ever open your mouth again. The only way you'll ever take another snap for me is if Garner breaks both his legs." But, out of the blue, late in the first quarter, Bull Cyclone summoned Bradberry from the bench, riffled through the deck, and dispatched him to run one play. It wasn't exactly a vote of confidence, for the call was a rare halfback sweep, in which the quarterback was supposed to block. Bradberry ran the play and, on another possession midway through the second quarter, Bull Cyclone sent him back in to run the same punishing sweep.

Then, right before the half ended, the coach yelled for Bradberry again, shuffled through his deck and, like a magician, pulled out a card and showed it to the quarterback. "See this," Bull Cyclone said. "Hit the tight end, and it'll be a fuckin' touchdown."

Telling the story, Bradberry merely smiles, then shrugs and says, "And hey . . ." and raises his arms in the TD salute.

Defense bored Bull Cyclone, so he let his assistant handle that. Of course, from carefully studying the passing game, he became an expert at pass defense. Scooba played man-to-man and stunted constantly. "Forty-four red dog" was his favorite defensive alignment: four-man line, four others up close, blitz. Against running attacks, which were what he usually faced, Sullivan's basic concept — again presaging the future — was to have his linemen "mess things up" so that the linebackers could dash up and make jarring tackles. A wiry little demon of a linebacker named Bob Wilson is reputed to have made as many as 25 stops in a game, 150 in one season.

In practice, though, Bull Cyclone would spend almost all of his time working on passing — seven-on-eight — exiling the interior linemen to the sidelines, where they could get at it among themselves all day. Nowadays, major schools have so many assistants that a head football coach primarily has to be an administrator just to keep practices running effectively. But Bull Cyclone was always in the midst of things, and when he ran his beloved passing drills, he'd move right along with the team. Most coaches stand in one spot and shout "Bring it back." Bull Cyclone's players would practice up and down the field, simulating a real drive. No one was allowed to disturb this routine, and, of course, no outsiders were present, lest they be shot as spies.

One thing Bull Cyclone had going for him was that few other teams concentrated on the pass — and none in all of America as much as he — so that opponents weren't geared to stopping a promiscuous aerial game. On the other hand, Scooba was invariably the runt of the litter. The Mississippi Junior College Conference had fifteen teams then, and the rules limited recruiting to certain areas. Bull Cyclone, like Bradberry today, was left with slim pickings in his six backwoods counties. Big as he was himself, Bull Cyclone came to admire the tiny farmers' sons he had to make do with — "little itty-bitty boys," says Box, who played fullback at 160 pounds. Smith was a 150-pound quarterback, and Garner didn't weigh even that much. Wilson, the best linebacker Scooba ever had, barely went 135. You've heard of baseball players who can't hit their weight. The year Wilson supposedly made 150 tackles he might have been the only college football player in history to tackle more than his weight.

For all the great quarterbacks Bull Cyclone had — at one stretch four in a row went on to star at four-year colleges — the only uniform number he ever retired was 31. It belonged to a halfback named Clyde Pierce, who was always described as "Baby Doll Pierce, 124 pounds, soaking wet, from West Point, Mississippi." Bull Cyclone even had a reel of film made up just of Baby Doll to show the big guys what tough really was. One time Baby Doll got hurt, and as the call went out for a stretcher, Bull Cyclone just scooped up the limp little form and carried Baby Doll off the field in his massive arms.

Though quarterbacks enjoyed an exalted status in Bull Cyclone's cosmos, they suffered much more for their sins than other players. Smith was brought to Scooba two weeks before school opened in 1962, and he moved in with the Sullivans. As he studied the offense with Bull Cyclone, he became a member of the family. But in the first quarter of his opening game, after he had marched Scooba to a touchdown, he muffed the two-point conversion pass attempt. Smith turned around to find Bull Cyclone running at him, screaming, "You traitor, Smith! You're a traitor!" Smith couldn't believe what had come over the man. "I was fixin' to go over the hill right then," he says.

Smith stayed, however, and Scooba went on to qualify for something known as the Magnolia Bowl. Shortly before that game, Bull Cyclone saw quarterback Billy Wade of the Chicago Bears play a game on TV with tiny shoulder pads, and he figured Smith would profit from the same gear. Only Sullivan didn't have any tiny pads, so he asked Smith if he'd go padless. Smith quickly agreed. "You must understand, he had enough effect on me that I wouldn't even question him when he asked me to play without shoulder pads," Smith says. Bull Cyclone didn't let the rest of the players know what was up until just before the game. "Fellows," he said. "Lester's not going to wear any shoulder pads tonight." Long pause to let that sink in. *"And . . . he . . . better . . . not . . . get . . . hit."* Smith didn't, either, except on two occasions when he lost his head, checked off the coach's plays, and ran the ball on sneaks.

Although Scooba won and Smith escaped the coach's wrath, Bull

Cyclone usually went berserk when a quarterback of his risked getting tackled. A perfect game wasn't a quarterback completing every pass. A perfect game was a quarterback not having his star jersey touched. The first thing Bull Cyclone taught any quarterback candidate wasn't how to throw a complete pass but how to throw an incomplete one. Bradberry well remembers the time Bull Cyclone ripped off his jersey and another time when he yanked off his helmet and chucked it clear into Mr. Smith's pasture, to illustrate how you threw a ball away with proficiency.

Once that art was mastered, Bull Cyclone's quarterbacks got down to completing passes. He required them to come out an hour before practice and half an hour before games and throw to each other "on a knee" — that is, kneeling — a drill that improves form and increases arm strength. Buckner threw so many passes that, for a while, he had to keep his arm in a sling when off the field. Over and over the quarterbacks would work on the same precise patterns, learning to release the ball before the receiver broke. And if a quarterback did anything incorrectly — or worse, stupidly — a terrible wrath was visited upon him. "Get out of my fuckin' huddle! Get out of my fuckin' life!" Sullivan would bellow. The quarterbacks were different, and everybody knew it. Even now, the quarterbacks talk about Bull Cyclone in a more intimate way than do the other players. The quarterbacks were really the only ones who were back with him, alone, on Okinawa.

Bradberry says the most memorable moment of his life came in the first game of his second season. To this point, he'd never been anything but a "fuckin' idiot" who did what he was told off the index cards. Suddenly, while standing on the sideline before one play, Bull Cyclone turned to him and said, "Well, what do you think?" Bradberry's knees turned to jelly. He had been ordained. The rest of the season he was a junior partner, and, afterward, Bull Cyclone highly recommended him to Delta State. He was awarded a scholarship, and he broke the records Buckner had set there.

But Buckner was undoubtedly Bull Cyclone's best quarterback. He was the one who almost got everything for Coach. With his little itty-bitty boys, only twice did Bull Cyclone have enough to win it all. The last time was in '69. Looking forward to that season, he told Virginia, "It's going to be like taking candy from a baby." To others, more worldly than she, he advised that he was "holding a royal flush." The other time he could have won a championship was in '64, Buckner's final season.

In '63, when Buckner was a freshman, Scooba went 10–1–1 and was ranked seventh in the national J.C. rankings although, wouldn't you know it, Pearl River still won the conference. But with Buckner back in '64, Scooba was even more formidable, winning its first eight games and climbing all the way to Number 3 in the country. Scooba was a lock to be invited to the Junior Rose Bowl if it kept winning. Scooba was going to come out of nowhere and show California football that Scooba was fifteen to twenty years ahead of its time. Buckner was already a J.C. All-America. He had thrown for thirty-nine touchdowns and almost 5,000 yards in twenty games. Further, he was Mr. Everything: president of the student body, head of the local branch of the Fellowship of Christian Athletes.

Scooba's ninth opponent was Jones Junior College, the top defensive team in the conference. With a 6–1 record, Jones had lost only to Pearl River, by 6–0. It was homecoming at Scooba, and the festive crowd of 4,000 overflowed the stands, whose normal capacity was 3,000. Buckner didn't disappoint anyone, either. On the game's first offensive series, second-and-one on his own forty, he called an audible and struck with a touchdown pass to George Belvin. Sixty yards, just like that, for his fortieth TD toss. Only 2:11 gone, and Scooba was up by seven. On to Pasadena!

Not only that, but Scooba held Jones and got the ball right back. Buckner had had such an outstanding career that all week Mississippi had been buzzing with rumors that Jones was out to get Buckner. However, Bull Cyclone had his charges ready. He put them through the toughest week of practices any of them had ever experienced. One day, Bull Cyclone even lashed out at Buckner, and pulled him from the starting lineup. Benching the greatest quarterback in junior college ball was ludicrous, of course, but Bull Cyclone was bringing everything to a boil. "That man had a gift to know," Buckner says now.

But at the time Buckner was simply distraught. That night he left his room in the Alamo and went outside, thinking he might keep right on going. A mattress was airing out on a fence, and Buckner lit into it, pummeling it, harder, harder, harder, all his anger and frustrations pouring out. A man has to wonder if Bull Cyclone might not have heard all the commotion and come to his window and watched, smiling, content.

The next day, Buckner was still second-string. Only, as soon as the other quarterback made an error, Bull Cyclone was all over

him — "Get out of my fuckin' huddle! Get out of my fuckin' life!" —
and Buckner was back in the saddle. They were getting ready for
Jones and then the Junior Rose Bowl. Coach Sullivan didn't have
much more to tell Buckner, except throw the ball and throw it
away if pressured.

So it was 7–0 Scooba. Buckner was back to pass again, and the
Jones defenders rushed in. Instead of lobbing the ball far away, he
thought he saw a way to salvage the play and scrambled. He
ducked this way and that, but two Jones linemen were still closing
in on him. "Throw it away!" Bull Cyclone hollered. "Throw the
sonofabitch away! Get rid of it!"

Buckner was trapped now; it was too late. He was hit low, and as
he went down, another defender caught him with his fist, solid,
square on the cheek. As he buckled, Buckner could feel his whole
face cave in as if it were papier-mâché. The man who took the game
films for Bull Cyclone told him he'd caught it all. But the films had
to be developed in Jackson, which is Jones territory. When they
came back that one play had been spliced out. Bull Cyclone didn't
care. He'd seen it all himself. He vowed never to play Jones again,
and he never did.

Buckner struggled to his feet and staggered to the sideline. He
didn't lose consciousness, but he knew his jaw was broken the instant the blow landed. Now he was bleeding so much he had difficulty talking. His face was all splintered. He went over to Bull Cyclone, and he mumbled, "Corch, I believe my jaw is broken."

Bull Cyclone just stared at Buckner, dead on, for the longest kind
of time. Finally, he balled his fists and screamed, "You damn idiot! I
told you not to run that fuckin' football!" Then he turned away
from Buckner and sent in the number-two quarterback. They
would retire Baby Doll's number, but not Buckner's. Jones won the
game.

Bull Cyclone's youngest daughter, Gael, Little Cyclone, was 12
then. She used to race her friends onto the field after games, all of
them trying to see who could get to her daddy first. This time Gael
won, but as soon as she reached him, she froze. "Right away, I knew
something terrible had happened," she says. "This time I could tell
he was sad, not angry."

Scooba was in shock and lost the next week, too, finishing 9–2.
Buckner never again wore his star jersey. Somebody else got invited to the Junior Rose Bowl. Somebody else was national cham-

pion. Scooba fell in the polls. It didn't even win the conference. Bull Cyclone never won it, and he wouldn't have another terrific shot for five more years, with the royal flush team of '69.

A few days after the Jones game, Sullivan went to the hospital in Meridian to visit Buckner. He was carrying flowers. A lot of times he would yank up some black-eyed Susans and have the managers take them over to Mrs. Sullivan, but now he was carrying a real bouquet. Buckner has never forgotten any of it. Bull Cyclone came in, laid down the flowers, and just stood there at the end of the bed. Buckner was waiting to say something after Bull Cyclone spoke, but Bull Cyclone never said a word. For ten minutes he just stood there, until, at last, bereft of voice and dreams, he turned and walked away, going back to Scooba.

Finally, in 1966, the Sullivans got their own house, a neat and sturdy red brick just beyond the end zone. President Harbour thought that respectable faculty housing was good for the campus. But that was the coach's only perquisite, and for his $5,600 salary, Bull Cyclone wasn't only football coach and athletic director but dean of men as well. A friend gave him a partnership in a little local franchise known as Chicken Chef, even though Bull Cyclone never had the cash to invest in the deal. "If Bull lived to be two hundred years old, he'd never have had any money," says his old buddy Fleming. Friends say letters would come in from his former players, down on their luck, between jobs, and old Coach Sullivan would pull out his last five-dollar bill and send it on.

The best way to sum up Bull Cyclone was what a boy named Bernard Rush heard from an old-timer after Rush quit the team and went back home, over in DeKalb. "Son," the old fellow said, "you ought to get yourself back over to Scooba. Corch Sullivan will do anything *to* you on the football field, but then he'll do anything *for* you once you left." Rush went back.

Then, too, some said he even mellowed a bit in the sixties. During each Religious Emphasis Week, it was Bull Cyclone, the toughest coach there ever was, that the girls wanted to come to their dorm and talk to them about boys and morals and sex. He was a Methodist, but the Baptists wanted him to address them. He began to take to religion seriously and to punish himself. If he let loose a "goddam" during practice, the whole team was permitted to go in early. Finally, says Gael, one night in '67 he went to the front of his church and fell to his knees "in unashamed prayer." Scooba had telephones now, and the cynics in town burned up the wires questioning Bull Cyclone's sincerity. However, it was real, and it was true.

A few months later, Bull Cyclone brought a black player onto the team. Nineteen sixty-eight: Now that may not sound especially progressive, but it was three more years before Bryant integrated his Alabama squad and a year before any of the major Mississippi teams welcomed blacks. And Kemper County was the deepest part of Dixie.

Sylvester Harris wasn't just the first black player on the Scooba team; he was the first black to attend the college. In fact, East Mississippi had lost a lot of federal funds because President Harbour hadn't let in blacks. Sullivan's action made a good many people around Scooba mad; Kemper wasn't called Bloody Kemper for nothing. Not long before, when a company bought some timberland and began enforcing no-hunting regulations, forest fires were set all through those lands. One day, one of the big shots in the county offered the coach $500 to run Harris off.

It would've been easy, too, because Harris wasn't all that good a player. But Bull Cyclone just told the man to clear out, and he went on treating Harris like any other player. Bull Cyclone once said to Tommy Atkins, a player who became a career Marine, "Tommy, there are two kinds of young men — those you have to kick in the pants to get their potential and those you have to pat on the back. If you, as a leader, make a mistake, you've done a great injustice. So be very careful and decide as accurately as you can whether to kick or to pat."

Away from the field Bull Cyclone could be a different character altogether. In his classroom, where he taught sociology and anthropology, he was, his students said, "like a Sunday school teacher." He got his master's in anthropology from Mississippi State in '66 and spent more and more time working in that discipline. He exchanged a lot of correspondence with Senator John Stennis, who came from down the road in DeKalb, about archeological work in Kemper. A 1968 photo shows Bull Cyclone with three of his students following a dig. In a caption he's quoted as saying, "The only significant find seemed to be a complex of single-shouldered projectile points, found in lower-strata kitter midden. The people who populated this site probably belonged to a Woodland Culture some 2,000 years ago."

Says Fleming, "Yeah, Bull had an old skeleton head and all." Otherwise, he devoted his spare time to studying the Good Book and watching football film. Praise the Lord, and pass the ammunition.

At home, for relaxation, he loved to listen to "Stardust." Bull Cyclone could never get enough of "Stardust." His favorite acquisition in all his life was an album he chanced upon that was entirely "Stardust" — fourteen versions of "Stardust." His other musical favorites included "Harbor Lights," "Somewhere My Love," and "Easter Parade," which he enjoyed twelve months a year. His daughters were musical, and often he would cry out, "You can be a second Lennon Sisters!" Then he would fall asleep while Bobbie played "Stardust" for him on the piano.

When he'd first get home from practice, "we'd just lay back for a while," Gael says. The family cat was used as litmus paper. If the cat spied Bull Cyclone and ducked away, the practice hadn't gone well. Sometimes he'd line the family up, as if he were back at Parris Island, and make them fall in and count off. But it was fun. Their favorite order was "Get in the car!" because nobody knew whether he was going to take them for a drive, flying off the bumps in the road, or just go around in little circles in the driveway. One time, when they came to a Howard Johnson's, he pulled in and ordered twenty-eight scoops of ice cream, one of each flavor. "We thought everybody had a family like ours," Bobbie says, laughing. His kids still refer to him as Bull.

Royce had to write this, because it was too emotional for her to say: "Bobbie spent her closeness with Bull at the piano. Gael would sing to him, and Vic was at the field house sharing his life there. My time with Bull was spent in nature and with animals. We would walk to ponds and put out fish traps (we always caught turtles). We would walk in the woods on Sundays. Bull would help me care for and learn all about my animals. This is where Bull taught me about God and the way of mankind and the world."

Still, no bigger school would touch Bull Cyclone. The word that traveled before him was that he was a thug, the meanest football coach that ever walked the land. Buckner remembers getting an offer to play quarterback at a major school "up north in Virginia." The backfield coaching job was vacant, and he said he'd come if Bull Cyclone was hired. Buckner tried to explain what a genius the man was. The head coach told him to save his breath. "Hey, I'm afraid of that man," he said.

Clois Cheatham, who is now the president of Scooba, shakes his head. "Off the field, no one was more compassionate," says Cheatham. "But the name was right. He was bullheaded, and he couldn't always make the right transition to others after dealing with players."

At Perkinston J.C., they used to fire a cannon right behind the visitors' bench to stir up the crowd. Bull Cyclone, who could still get nervous when he heard loud noises — "You didn't sneak up on Dad," Bobbie says — protested to the president of Perkinston, but the reply came back that the cannon was "tradition." Bull Cyclone then wrote that "my managers and I will bring double-barreled shotguns to Perkinston, and if there is one tradition I learned in the military it was to retaliate." The president agreed to silence the guns of Perkinston. And so the tales of rough, tough Bull Cyclone spread, and Stumpy Harbour simmered.

By now, too, Bull Cyclone had been pretty much his own football boss for a long time. Maybe he never could work well under someone else. Virginia recalls sitting in the press box with Bull when he was a lowly assistant at Oregon. Over the phone he kept imploring Whistlin' Jim Aiken to employ a certain strategy. After a while, when the head coach didn't, Bull Cyclone just sat back, folded his arms, and watched the game, refusing to answer the phone for the balance of the half.

Without question he would have delighted in a larger stage, for even his family agrees that he loved recognition. But he had to learn to take refuge in his pride. "He knew he was a great coach," Bobbie says, and that had to be enough for him. Besides, he had come to believe that Scooba was his destiny, that that little stretch of nothing on the one hand and pu'pwood on the other was his realm. That was where he would teach football players to be men, and everybody else he could to be patriots and Christians. If the world was changing, at least the gridiron was a rectangular verity.

Around campus he came to be an amalgam of Mr. Chips and Mr. Roberts. This image was heightened by his disputes with Stumpy. "If I agreed with Harbour on anything it was unintentional," Bull Cyclone later wrote. Once during a cold snap, many of the school's pipes burst. The campus had no water and the toilets didn't work, but Harbour wouldn't cancel school. Eventually Bull Cyclone persuaded him otherwise. Sullivan became even more of a hero. Some came to think that the roughest, toughest football coach in creation might make a terrific college president. Insecure little Stumpy, literally in the big man's shadow, envious of his esteem, now imagined a rival to his throne.

In 1967, *The Lion,* the Scooba yearbook, was dedicated to Bull Cyclone, with this inscription: "We respect your strong will, strength and spirit. We admire your nature, loyalty and competence. You are just, you are fair, you are great." The coach who had spent a lifetime hewing grown-ups out of pu'pwood had shaped himself into a whole man, too. This may be the best thing about the best coaches — not what they make of others in a couple of years but what, in the long run, they make of themselves.

Bull Cyclone was comfortable now. His family was growing up; two of the girls were already in college. He had his house by the end zone. He had completed his studies, and he was at peace with his God. The rest of the football world was even beginning to catch up to his wide-open style. All that eluded him was a championship, the one that had been wrenched from his grasp when Buckner ran with the damn ball in '64. And the '69 squad was going to give him that. Already, by that spring, Virginia says, he had so many index cards that he had "a whole new box of offense." It was a lock. It was, as we know, "going to be like taking candy from a baby."

School was out, so the players and students who loved Bull Cyclone were away from Scooba when Stumpy Harbour convened the board of trustees to fire him on June 29, 1969. Three of the coach's strongest supporters weren't on hand. Still, word of the meeting and what the president had in mind leaked out. Joe Bradshaw, one of Bull Cyclone's former players, distributed petitions in his support that were signed by every high school coach in the Scooba district. Stumpy refused to admit the petitions. Neither did he admit friends of Bull Cyclone's who gathered outside the meeting room.

Bull Cyclone couldn't speak in his own behalf, but he wrote a letter to the board. His desperation was obvious, his supplicant's tone almost pitiful: "I have heard through the grapevine that you have been called together to take up my contract as coach at East Mississippi Junior College. I beg you not to do this. This school is part of my life and I am a part of it; as a matter of fact, this school is my life."

He was dictating to Virginia. "If you put me out now it will be just like killing a man, for I know that I wouldn't live six weeks." When she finished typing the draft, she told him that that last sentence was overwrought. He took out his pen and scratched this instead: "If you put me out now I won't live long." But the letter went on, pleading — he had only four more years to retirement; he was working sixteen to twenty hours a day at a summer job to help put his kids through college. "I have given of myself to this school so diligently and so long and so completely that now I have nowhere to turn. . . . Thank you and God bless you."

Harbour and his cohorts weren't moved. Bull Cyclone was a disgrace to a respectable institution. He was a Neanderthal man, more backward than his Woodland Culture people. Why, he'd been forced to sit in a chair for a *whole game.* No, he was fired. All he got was a thirty-day eviction notice to clear his family off campus and a deal to keep his mouth shut or forfeit eighteen months' severance. "Our entire lives, value systems and hearts were ripped out and we were cast to an unknown destiny," recalls Royce. "Being young and having been raised to believe in justice, honor, patriotism and love made our pain and confusion undefinable."

The family found an old house up in Columbus, where the Chicken Chef franchise was. A radio station there hired Bull Cyclone to do some sports commentary, and he got a job selling insurance. All his friends bought a little, and that helped. That the situation was so desperate was good in a way, because he didn't have the time to dwell on football when the season started. "Still," Bobbie says, "you can't imagine what it did to him after the leaves started to fall, and he knew he was supposed to be on a football field, and everybody knew he was supposed to be on a football field, and he didn't have his field."

Under its new coach, Scooba had a fine year. He installed a conventional attack — you established the run before you dared pass — and he went 9–1. Nonetheless, Pearl River won the conference, and there wasn't any national championship. The 9–1 finish kept the pressure off Stumpy for a while, but he had signed his own notice when he got Bull Cyclone fired. The coach's friends began to mobilize, and on April 10, 1970, the board summarily fired Harbour. The school comptroller was ordered to change the lock on the school safe.

But all that was small beer for Bull Cyclone. "The firing of Harbour does not restore my wrecked life," he wrote shortly afterward. "I came to Scooba when I was 30 years old and left when I was 50. If ever a person gave his life for anything, I gave mine to EMJC."

His anguish increased as another football season approached. A few schools had talked to him about coaching positions, but when they asked Scooba for a reference, the academic dean, operating on orders from Harbour, responded with a scurrilous letter, defaming Bull Cyclone with false charges. The new president, Earl Stennis, fired the dean when he learned about the letter, but that was no consolation for Bull Cyclone. The first game in Mississippi that year was an NFL exhibition over in Jackson in early August. Bull Cyclone was given a couple of tickets, and he invited Gael to join him. He enjoyed the game, too, but driving home he told her that he prayed every day for Stumpy, and that she must do so as well.

Then it was September again, and the season was upon him in earnest. Some friends in the Lions Club invited him to speak the next Tuesday, the eighth. The subject was to be how best to watch football on television, and Bull Cyclone got some old blank index cards and made notes for his talk.

While he was getting dressed, Bobbie called from Tulsa, where she had moved a few days earlier to take a job as a junior high physical education teacher. He chatted with her and told her how much he missed and loved her, and then he handed the phone to Virginia and went to finish dressing for the Lions Club meeting. In the bathroom, Bull Cyclone had just slapped some cologne on his face when he dropped dead without a sound.

Nobody in the family, or any friends, or anybody who ever played for Coach Sullivan doubts that he died of a broken heart. Everyone who ever knew him says that unequivocally. It was football time again, and Bull Cyclone didn't have a field.

When they buried him, cradling a pigskin, Little Vic didn't want to leave his father. Finally, he snatched off his jacket, took a shovel from one of the workmen, and began to toss dirt on the casket. Without anyone saying anything, one by one, all the men there, so many of them Bull Cyclone's old players, removed their coats and took turns shoveling the grave full. A rose fell and someone tried to pluck it out of the dirt. Little Vic stopped him. "No," he said, "it's over his heart. That's where it belongs." So the rose wasn't moved.

A couple of years later Little Vic was on the varsity at New Hope High in Columbus, and he was playing a good game. The referee was old Billbo Mitchell — *Can you still smell me, Bull?* — and when he kept hearing the name Sullivan on the PA for making tackles, he came over and peered closely at the rangy boy. Little Vic thought maybe he was being assessed a penalty for something or other, but he couldn't figure out why. Finally, Billbo said, "You wouldn't be any kin of the late Bull Sullivan, would you?"

"He was my daddy," Vic said.

And then, right there, right in the middle of a game he was refereeing impartially, Billbo put the ball down and stuck out his hand and made Little Vic shake it. "I loved that man," he said.

Years before, Coach Poole had been sitting with Bull Cyclone in Bull's office in Scooba. Bull Cyclone put aside his index cards, pulled out a piece of paper, and started doodling. Before long, Poole could tell he was drawing football jerseys, because he could see their general form and the big numbers. Of course, he didn't say anything. He just watched.

Then Bull Cyclone started on about the war and about the time he was with five soldiers with whom he had grown close. But when the island was secure, Bull Cyclone was the only one of them who came home. "There must be a reason," he said.

Coach Poole nodded.

"I've been searching for a way to honor them," he said, and then he doodled some more. He passed the drawing to Poole. "There, Corch," he said. It was a rough draft of the star jersey, with the five stars across the breast for the five boys who didn't get out in '45.

Bull Cyclone would live another twenty-five years, changing the autumns and the lives of Scooba football players he didn't run off in the summers.

*   *   *

The story of how I found out about Bull Cyclone Sullivan is almost as fascinating as Bull Cyclone's story. It is a case of such coincidence and serendipity as to be fantastic. I stumbled onto a plane in Birmingham, Alabama, one morning in 1982, and because the plane had come through Jackson, there was a copy of the Jackson Clarion-Ledger *lying on the seat next to me. Idly, I picked it up and skimmed through it, and came across a wonderful feature piece on Bull done by a writer named Rick Cleveland. Instantly, I saw the potential in the story, although at that time I didn't know how poignant Bull's ending really was. Rick had devoted his piece almost entirely to Bull as a character and coach.*

The Sullivan family still looks upon me as some sort of instru-

ment of the Lord — and I'm not prepared to doubt them. The Rick Cleveland article seems to have been the only major story ever written about Bull, the only story of any sort done since his death, more than a decade previous; if I had not been on that plane that day, sat in that seat, and found someone's abandoned copy of that Jackson newspaper, I never would have heard of Bull — and neither would anyone else outside of Mississippi.

Because of the story, Bull was elected to the Mississippi Sports Hall of Fame, and I was honored to make the induction speech on his behalf. I also spent an evening drinking with even more of Corch's old players — who came out in hordes to salute him — and learned even more fantastic tales about the man.

PART OF THE GAME

Rhythms, Baseball, and Life

1978

OPENING DAY. There is only one, and it's in baseball. The theater has opening nights scattered here and there about the calendar, and there are various opening days of . . . the fishing season, the race meeting, the NFL season. But there is only one Opening Day, when grandmothers drop like flies and dreams are born anew.

Opening Day means spring. It means, literally, an opening: of buds spreading and jackets unbuttoning; of little birds' mouths gaping; of rubber bands being released from neat's-foot-oiled baseball mitts that have been held tight around a ball all winter. The Louisville Slugger sends painful jolts up your arms if you don't connect properly in the chill air. It will be better soon: warmer, and the wind will die down. But even now, if you keep the label up, you can knock that old horsehide clean and far and feel nothing but warmth.

The beginnings of the other major sports seasons have no connection with the natural rhythms of life. To be sure, they arrive according to an annual schedule, but so do subscription renewals and visits to the dentist. If anything, the starting dates for football, basketball, and hockey are reminders to look back. The beginning of football heralds the conclusion of summer; it goes hand-in-glove with — ugh! — back-to-school. And winter sports? If they're starting, then it must soon be — oh, no — winter. It is significant that of all the sports seasons, hockey and basketball most sneak up on us; if you are not attentive to the fellow with the blond teeth on the TV news, you will suddenly open the paper one day late in

October and discover that the Celtics have already played four games.

But baseball. Opening Day. To have picked up the newspaper one fine day in April and seen this:

	W	L	Pct.	GB
Washington	1	0	1.000	—
Boston	0	0	.000	½
New York	0	0	.000	½
Detroit	0	0	.000	½
Chicago	0	0	.000	½
Cleveland	0	0	.000	½
St. Louis	0	0	.000	½
Philadelphia	0	1	.000	1

Why, that told you better than anything that God had truly kissed the land again, that a whole life lay ahead. Play them one at a time? Ridiculous. There were 154 to play, a number that overwhelmed a child's mind. Where would we be when the season was done? In a new grade, for certain. And perhaps our team would win. That, too. Not believe in Opening Day? Why, you might as well have said you didn't believe in Tinker Bell.

So, if you cannot bury your poor grandmother one more time, here is an article for Opening Day. It is not really about baseball. There are no bunts and round-trippers and sliders and curves. We have a whole summer for that. No, this is about Opening Day, about baseball sensations, about throwing out the first ball, about Cracker Jack and Louisville Sluggers, and about *Who's on First?* Let's start off with a quiz. The answers will be found buried in the article. If you bat .300 — get five or more correct — you pass. You are also stamped as a strange person for knowing such foolishness.

1) Everybody knows that Taft was the first president to throw out a first ball. You think I'm going to ask a simple question like that? Who caught the first ball that Taft threw?
   a. Clark Griffith, the Senators' owner
   b. Gabby Street, the Senators' catcher
   c. Walter Johnson, the Senators' pitcher
   d. Vice-President Sherman

2) Cracker Jack was invented in Chi by:
   a. The Wrigley Gum Company
   b. The head concessionaire at Comiskey Park
   c. Two German immigrants with a sidewalk popcorn popper
   d. Pop Norworth, the older brother of Jack Norworth, who wrote "Take Me Out to the Ball Game"

3) Louisville Sluggers are now made in:
   a. Where else, dummy? Louisville
   b. Hong Kong and Haiti
   c. Slugger Park in Indiana
   d. North Louisville, U.S.A., which is in the great ash forests of Ontario

4) Only two real players are mentioned in *Who's on First?* They are:
   a. Joe DiMaggio and Ted Williams
   b. Mickey Owen and Ralph Branca
   c. Dizzy and Daffy Dean
   d. Babe Ruth and Ty Cobb

5) From 1910 through 1971, when the Senators left Washington for good, only two nongovernment officials threw out the first ball. They were:
   a. Perle Mesta, the famous hostess, and Clark Griffith, Sr.
   b. Mrs. Calvin Coolidge and Shirley Povich, *Washington Post* sports editor
   c. David Eisenhower and a returned Vietnam POW
   d. Duke Zeibert, the restaurateur, and Sammy Baugh

6) Every prize at Cracker Jack must pass:
   a. An esthetic test administered by the National Candy Coupon Council
   b. A screening by the baseball commissioner's office
   c. A simulated esophagus test conducted by Cracker Jack's "prize lady"
   d. Samplings personally undertaken by the chairman of the board and his grandchildren

7) The Old Gladiator was:
   a. Wilson R. Keeney, a fabled blind woodturner who made 162,000 Louisville Sluggers

b. Bud Hillerich, former president of Hillerich & Bradsby Company, who is said to have made the first Slugger

c. Pete Browning, star of the Louisville Eclipse, who reputedly used the first Slugger

d. The Slugger that Joe Sewell used for fourteen seasons

8) Lou Costello was only 5'4" and weighed 195 pounds, but he had many sporting interests. He:
a. Had fourteen professional prizefights
b. Was a movie stunt man
c. Owned a 2-year-old colt named Bold Bazooka that equaled the world record at five and a half furlongs
d. Spent $5,000 on a personal campaign to get the Dodgers moved to Los Angeles in 1953

9) Walter Johnson pitched twelve presidential openers, the first in 1910, when Taft started the tradition. The Big Train lost a no-hitter in that game because:
a. An easy grounder nicked a Philadelphia base runner, Ira Thomas, who had walked
b. While President Taft bellowed "Let it roll!" a bunt by the A's Rube Oldring stayed fair for a scratch single
c. Embarrassed for having unintentionally brushed back Home Run Baker, the easygoing Johnson grooved the next pitch and Baker, startled, poked an opposite-field triple
d. Washington rightfielder Doc Gessler tripped over a child who was sitting in front of the outfield ropes, and that allowed an easy fly to drop for a double

10) For sure, popcorn is this old:
a. 126 years
b. 360 years
c. 560 years
d. 5,600 years

11) When he hit number 715, Henry Aaron used this player's bat model:
a. Stan Musial
b. Eddie Mathews
c. Eddie Waitkus
d. Babe Ruth

12) The last player mentioned in *Who's on First?* is the shortstop.
    He's:
    a. Never Mind
    b. Because
    c. Why
    d. I Don't Care

13) In the past decade only three politicians have thrown out the
    first ball for two teams. They are:
    a. John Lindsay, Richard Nixon, Richard Daley
    b. Jimmy Carter, Spiro Agnew, Hubert Humphrey
    c. Nelson Rockefeller, John Connally, John Gilligan
    d. Gerald Ford, Ronald Reagan, Henry Jackson

14) The model for Sailor Jack, the little boy on the Cracker Jack
    package, is:
    a. R. W. (Boots) Rueckheim III, grandson of the company
       founder, who later became chairman of the board and is
       now retired in Lake Wales, Florida, where he lives next door
       to Red Grange
    b. An unknown street urchin who was paid his "fee" in
       Cracker Jack and was bitten by the mutt Bingo while posing
       for the artist
    c. A former minor league baseball player, Freddie Trail, who
       later gained brief notoriety when he was suspected of kid-
       napping the Lindbergh baby
    d. The Cracker Jack board chairman's grandson, who was a
       childhood pneumonia victim and whose gravestone bears a
       carving of the Sailor Jack–Bingo drawing

15) This Louisville Slugger model is the current best-seller:
    a. Johnny Bench
    b. Reggie Jackson
    c. Henry Aaron
    d. Jackie Robinson

16) When Abbott got the phone call telling him that Costello had
    died, he was:
    a. Packing to go to Cooperstown to present the *Who's on
       First?* script to the Hall of Fame
    b. In Walter O'Malley's box at a Dodger-Giant game
    c. Talking to his manager about performing *Who's on First?* at

the White House when President Eisenhower entertained
Canadian Prime Minister John Diefenbaker

d. Watching the *Who's on First?* routine in an old movie being
rerun on TV

EXTRA CREDIT: Name the rightfielder in *Who's on First?*

Opening Day seems to have attained a certain ceremonial status
long before presidents got into the act. Christmas found its arbitrary December slot on the calendar because there was already
cause for celebration: the lengthening of the days, which had been
the reason for the pagan festival of Saturnalia for centuries before
Jesus' birth. In the same way, Opening Day fit right in as a welcome
to spring. Of course, the vernal equinox always came before Opening Day, but in the northeastern quadrant of the country, where
major league baseball was contained until 1957, consistently mild
weather did not arrive until sometime in April. Moreover, it is
worth remembering that in those days people did not gambol on
indoor tennis courts all winter, or watch golf tournaments from the
desert on TV, or fly off to Barbados and the Yucatan. Baseball was
the only game in town, except maybe for some basketball over at
the Y, and its return was a true renaissance of life.

We do not know exactly when politicians began to exploit this
afternoon of goodwill, but it was surely by the Gay Nineties, perhaps earlier. When President Taft threw out the first ball on April
14, 1910, at National Park, a contemporary account noted that he
was usurping the "time-honored" role of the District of Columbia's
city commissioners.

But it has been the presence of presidents that has made Opening Day very special. No other private enterprise has ever been
accorded such cachet. Indeed, except for sporadic appearances at
the Army-Navy football game, incumbent presidents have rarely
gone to stadiums for sporting events and never to arenas. But
Opening Days have been treated by all presidents with an annual
deference given only two other nongovernmental functions, posing with the March of Dimes poster child and lighting the White
House Christmas tree.

From Taft in 1910 through 1971 (when the Senators left for
Texas), the eleven presidents went 45 for 62 on Opening Days.
Given wars, death, depression, Communists, and what-have-you,

this is an incredible record. When the chief executives could not make it, they invariably called in their top relievers, the vice-presidents. Only in the Senator's final two seasons did somebody other than a government official fire the first pitch. David Eisenhower did the honors in 1970, and in 1971 a released POW, Master Sergeant Daniel I. Pitzen, became the last man to throw out the first ball in the capital.

Most presidents quite enjoyed the task. Only Wilson (3 for 8) batted less than .500, but he attended other Senator games during the season, parking his limousine in deep right, where a substitute catcher was stationed by a fender to snare incoming line drives. Harding, Truman (7 for 7), and Kennedy never missed an Opening Day; Roosevelt made eight. Coolidge hated baseball. He had to be reminded every damn time why it was that everybody stood up in the seventh inning — something he remedied late in his term by leaving in the second inning. Still, Cal made four of his five Opening Days, and the missus was nuts about baseball. Grace Coolidge would not only pop up at Senator games during the season, but it is also on record that she kept score and stayed through rain delays.

Harding bet on the games to make them more interesting. Truman practiced surreptitiously on the White House lawn before his second opener in 1947 and then startled the photographers and everybody else by chucking the old apple southpaw. Ike was a good baseball fan, but shortly before his first Opening Day (1953) he announced that he would have to pass it up for a golfing vacation. All hell broke loose. The country club over the national pastime! Mercifully, old Jupiter Pluvius saved Ike; Opening Day was rained out, and he made it back from the links in time for the rain date. After that, Ike didn't mess around, boy; he made all Openers until 1959. Next question.

How did Taft come to start this great tradition?

Sorry, the folds of history have hidden that earthshaking story. When the Griffiths were running the Senators, the fable — in the best tradition of Parson Weems writing about Geo. Washington and the cherry tree — had it that old Clark Griffith dropped by to see Taft, presented him with a gold pass, and invited him to throw out the first ball. Because Taft had been a pitcher in his svelter, salad days, he leapt at this opportunity. This is a great story except that Taft first threw out the first ball in 1910. Griffith did not become an owner of the Senators until 1912.

In fact, there was no advance warning of Taft's appearance; "The opening will not be attended by any ceremony," reported the *Washington Post* that morning. It is quite possible that Taft just up and went to the game on the spur of the moment. He did very little as president except eat and fret that he could not be Chief Justice, so what follows would be consistent with history. One can visualize Taft, as he sat in the breakfast nook that morning, looking out of the window and saying, "Besides lunch, what are we gonna do today?"

It was a sweetheart of a day, "sun-kissed," according to eyewitnesses.

"Well," said a chum, General Clarence Edwards, spreading some marmalade, "it's Opening Day at the ball yard."

"Yeah, who are the Nationals playing?" asked the president, reaching for another apricot Danish.

"The Mackmen," piped up Secretary of State Philander Knox, polishing off the home fries.

"District Commissioner Rudolph will be chucking out the first ball," added Mrs. Taft.

"Hmmm," said the president, finishing his Western omelet. "That gives me an idea. Let's pack a picnic and pop over."

And thus, as the *Post* reported, did there come about "the auspicious union of official Washington and baseballistic Washington."

On the diamond the Big Train was mowing 'em down. All told, he was to start a dozen presidential openers, winning nine, with six shutouts, but he would never again pitch as well as he did in his first. He would have had the first Opening Day no-hitter (Bob Feller finally got one thirty years later) but for the overflow multitude that settled in the outfield grass. With two gone in the seventh, Baker lifted an easy fly to the rightfielder, Doc Gessler. The swarm of fans seated along the perimeter of the outfield was supposed to dutifully scatter under these circumstances, but one boy was not nimble enough. Gessler tripped over the tyke, and the ball fell for a double, the A's only hit of the game.

But no sense crying over spilt milk. Taft and Johnson put on such a show of arms that even should diamond scholars "go back to the very inception of the national game — there will be found no day so altogether glorious, no paean of victory chanted by rooters and fanatics half so sweet as that witnessed yesterday." Perhaps proudest of all were the two managers, the storied Cornelius McGillicuddy (a.k.a. Connie Mack) of the Athletics (a.k.a. Mackmen) and James McAleer of the Nationals. They went to Taft's box to meet him, and while he greeted both courteously, the president disclosed his allegiance for the home nine by saving "a subtle wink and a double-action smile" for McAleer.

Despite his girth, Taft was no slouch when it came time to deliver the mail. Let the *Post* correspondent recapture that moment for us: "A mighty cheer swept across the crowd as President Taft showed such faultless delivery. . . . He did it with his good, trusty right arm, and the virgin sphere scudded across the diamond, true as a die to the pitcher's box, where Walter Johnson gathered it in. . . ."

In a sense, the presidential tradition started that day by Taft has outlasted the Senators, because the consecutive-president streak goes on. Jimmy Carter served up the opening pitch twice in Atlanta (1972 and '73), and Gerald Ford is one of only three politicians in the last decade to have first-balled two clubs, working Cincinnati as vice-president in '74 and Texas as president in '76. (Senator Henry Jackson pitched the first ball for both Seattle franchises, Pilots and Mariners, and Ronald Reagan did the honors for the A's and the Angels.)

But then, politicians are not as fashionable as they used to be, especially in the National League, which is ahead of the American even in this department. The most somber openers occur in Milwaukee, which always has the county executive throw out the first ball, and in Detroit, where gaiety is manifest when the fire department trots out its traditional floral horseshoe with its clever message "Good Luck Tigers!" and presents it to the manager.

On the other hand, San Diego once had a fellow dressed up like a chicken throw out the virgin sphere, and Philadelphia, which always confuses good humor with tackiness, employs the likes of Kite Man, Cannon Man, Sky Cycle Man, and Parachute Man to deliver the ball into the park. A number of clubs have taken to using old ballplayers instead of politicians. Poster children are also somewhat in vogue, and two clubs have called upon local centenarians. The Dodgers used an umpire once, Jocko Conlan, and the Angels went with Mickey Mouse.

Predictably, Charlie Finley marches to a different Opening Day drummer. The likes of Governor Reagan aside, Finley has often preferred to have singers throw out the first ball, because then he can entreat them to warble the anthem on the cuff. Just imagine how Finley would have gotten the presidents to work freebies if he had owned the Senators: notarize contracts, naturalize players, pardon the ones with paternity suits, lead the pledge of allegiance.

Down in front! Pass the Cracker Jack!

Perhaps the best thing about Cracker Jack is that it never goes away, but you think it does, so it is a pleasant surprise when it reappears. This is not just me talking off the top of my head. Ask, say, an unmarried man, age 26 or so, would he like some Cracker Jack, and he will stare at you as if you had just inquired if he would like to watch *The Donna Reed Show* on a Muntz TV. People are bonkers about Cracker Jack as kids, and then they forget about it until they have kids of their own.

It also works this way: After a lousy week, during which no visions of Cracker Jack danced through your aching head, you finally get to a circus or a game, and Cracker Jack pops right into your mind. It would probably do it at the ball park even if a fellow named Jack Norworth had not, in 1908, been fishing around for some confection that rhymes with "back," hence: *Buy me some peanuts and Cracker Jack, / I don't care if I never get back.* Next question.

Who invented Cracker Jack?

The Rueckheim Brothers, F. W. and Louis, German immigrants. When F. W. came to the Windy City from down on the farm in 1872 with $200 in capital, he and a partner set up a sidewalk popper.

Popcorn was not invented in a movie theater by Thomas Edison. It is the oldest corn going. One ear was found in the Bat Caves of New Mexico. It was 5,600 years old. But nobody had ever done a whole lot with popcorn. Then at the World's Columbian Exposition in 1893, F. W. and his brother (who had bought out F. W.'s former partner) wowed the innocents with a popcorn-peanuts-molasses snack.

Unfortunately, Cracker Jack is a sticky business. It was blob-sized until Louis figured out how to break up the gooey mess — by banging it against baffles in a rotating barrel. Then F. W. gave the new, improved bite-sized confection to a salesman. "Whaddya think of that?" F. W. asked.

The salesman replied, "That's a crackerjack of an idea."

That's a true story. Now do you want to go on with the history or get right into the prizes, the same way everybody does when they buy Cracker Jack?

Yeah, the prizes.

There is a very pretty woman at Cracker Jack, a former art teacher named Susan Reedquist. She is known around the plant as the "prize girl" or the "prize lady," depending on how up-to-date you are. She is in charge of selecting the 1,000 or so prizes that go into 420 million boxes of Cracker Jack each year. No fewer than 400 different prizes are packaged every day, and these are deposited manually — fourteen prize sorters dropping 128 prizes a minute. It is the only unautomated part of the process, but there are also three mechanized checks to ensure that a prize gets into each package.

Of course, just like you and me and batting averages, the prizes are not what they used to be. The prize lady has a vault that contains virtually every Cracker Jack prize ever produced, back to 1912, when prizes were introduced. Their heyday seems to have been in the 1930s, when the prizes included intricate metal and wooden toys. Once, during these halcyon days, there was an episode of *Amos 'n' Andy* in which de Kingfish went to a ball game and dropped a diamond ring he had bought for Sapphire. It fell into the Cracker Jack box out of which a fellow in the next row was munching. Of course the stranger thought the diamond ring was his prize. Ohhhh me, Andy! Imagine anybody today thinking that even a zircon ring could be included in a Cracker Jack box. Down in front!

But for goodness' sake, let's understand what the prize lady has to put up with. The Food and Drug Administration, for example. Nitpickers, all of them. You can't use sharp metal; you can't have any rough edges; you can't have toys that break into pieces. If it's not one thing, it's another. You could never in your wildest dreams imagine what is sitting prominently on the prize lady's desk. A simulated child's esophagus, that's what. If a toy can fit into the simulated esophagus, the prize lady has got to scratch it.

Worse, the prize lady has to accommodate today's TV generation. "The toys have to provide instant gratification," she says. "That's the effect of television."

The prize lady selects the prizes that will be tried out on whole children, as well as on their esophagi, and only the items that score high on the "smile scale" qualify for Cracker Jack. "You've got to remember that these kids have grown up in a paper and plastic world," the prize lady says. What the little shavers don't know won't hurt them.

Cracker Jack is one of the four or five most recognized brand names in the country. Ninety-nine percent of Americans are aware of it. And yet Cracker Jack is hardly in the mainstream in the way Coke and Ford, two other of the most familiar brand names, are. Undoubtedly, Cracker Jack owes much of its fame to its felicitous inclusion in the one sports anthem in the country.

But as you careful readers of the *Wall Street Journal* have learned, there is no such thing as a free lunch. Cracker Jack has been terrific for baseball, too. Why, Cracker Jack is still made with all natural ingredients: popcorn, peanuts, molasses, corn syrup, salt, and sugar. There are still the same number of peanuts — nine to fourteen — in every box. And they use the exact same formula they've always used; connoisseurs can tell that the goo covering the peanuts is different from the goo covering the popcorn. You still get "A Surprise in Every Package." Take a hike, Mom's apple pie.

Think about this: Suppose Norworth had not used Cracker Jack in his song. Has baseball ever thought about that? Suppose Norworth had used Moxie: "Give me some peanuts and cold Moxie!" Or Sen-Sen. Or JuJuBes. Wouldn't that be a fine how-do-you-do? Every time baseball played its theme song, it would be connecting itself with things that hardly exist anymore. That's all Bowie Kuhn needs, to be defunct-linked. And football. What a time it would have rubbing it in. Ha, ha, ha, baseball and Sen-Sen! Ha, ha, ha! Football would not let baseball hear the end of it.

So it has been a fair trade-off between Cracker Jack and baseball. And if Cracker Jack was struck by dumb luck in getting featured billing in "Take Me Out to the Ball Game," it has looked out for number one very well indeed. The name itself is a dandy, the prize idea a gem. It has two famous slogans: "A Surprise in Every Package" and "The More You Eat The More You Want." And everybody instantly recognizes the symbol of the little boy and his dog that has graced billions of Cracker Jack packs since 1919.

Actually, Sailor Jack and Bingo (for those are their names) are touched up every now and then, restyled to look more like a modern sailor boy and a fashionably precious mutt. For a number of years Bingo appeared forlorn; his head drooped. Now his puppy countenance has brightened. Jack has put on a white hat in recent years and is saluting much more proficiently than he did in the early going. That's the good news.

The bad news is that Jack is dead.

The sailor boy was modeled after F. W. Rueckheim's young grandson Robert, but alas, shortly after posing, the lad succumbed to pneumonia. He was buried in St. Henry's Cemetery in Chicago. On the child's tombstone is the friendly commercial image of Sailor Jack and Bingo.

What were your favorite wirephotos? There were two types I most admired. One was from Election Day and showed the president/governor/mayor emerging from the voting booth in his precinct grade school or church basement. This was democracy's pictorial equivalent of they-put-their-pants-on-one-leg-at-a-time-too. It made all the afternoon editions.

The other wirephoto jewel showed bat-kissing. If a fellow got a clutch bingle, he was shown bussing his lumber. If he hit three round-trippers he was photographed kissing one of a like number of bats, held rather like a bouquet. The most bats I ever remember a hero holding and kissing was four. When the operative number was five to nineteen, only one symbolic kissing-bat was employed for the wirephoto. (I always imagined these strict canons were spelled out in the UP, AP, and the INP manuals.) From twenty on up, the number celebrated was formed by baseballs, the digits created by dots on the order of a Seurat painting.

Once in a blue moon a player was shown kissing a baseball, but he *never* was pictured kissing his glove. In wirephoto protocol, glove-kissing was considered kinky. But bats were there to be kissed. And the bats were always Louisville Sluggers. You could see the little oval trademark. So ingrained in the consciousness of American youth was the dictum "Keep the label up" that players made sure to do it even when kissing bats for wirephotos.

In Slugger Park there is a bat museum — tours daily — and amid the display of famous bats is an endorsement for Louisville Slugger from Babe Ruth. He raises a hymn to the cudgel, praising its "driving power and punch that brings home runs." As a child, I never saw such a testimonial, which is just as well, because it would have utterly confounded me. Why would any major-leaguer, Babe Ruth or anybody, bother to endorse a Louisville Slugger? Why, this would be as unnecessary as endorsing food or shelter. "Hello, I'm Julia Child, and I'd like to urge you to eat food!"

Oh sure, I knew there was such a thing as an Adirondack, and whenever anybody's dim-witted visiting maiden aunt bought a bat as a gift for a nephew, she got stiffed with a little brown number named Hanna Bat-Rite. But these were aberrations. A baseball bat was a Louisville Slugger . . . and if you threw it after hitting a ball you were out.

The Slugger is almost a century old. The baseballs are made in Haiti, and it is estimated that 85 percent of the gloves are manufactured in the Orient, but Louisville Sluggers are constant, immutable. Henry Aaron hit with a slimmed-down version of the model that Babe Ruth used. The official name of the company is still Hillerich & Bradsby, it is still 100 percent privately held, and a member of the Hillerich family's third generation of bat executives — John A. Hillerich III — presides as president.

The Hillerichs, like the Cracker Jack Rueckheims, were immigrants from Germany, where J. Frederick Hillerich was born in 1834. By 1859 he was sufficiently established in Louisville to open his own woodcraft shop. It had a reputation for quality manufacture of items like balusters and butter churns. His son Bud, a fan of baseball and an instrument of destiny, soon joined the enterprise.

One day in '84 (so our story goes), Bud was at the ball field, watching the local pro team, the Louisville Eclipse of the (then major league) American Association. The star of the Eclipse, Pete Browning, broke his bat, and young Bud offered to make him a new one. Browning looked askance at Bud (the tale continues), but he accompanied him to the shop. Any port in a storm. Bud turned out an ash bat to Browning's specifications, and as you fable fans might imagine, Browning went 3 for 3 the next day. Soon Browning's teammates, and then visiting opponents, were beating a path to the quaint little woodshop on First Street. The elder Hillerich (the story guffaws) fumed; one can almost hear him bellowing at Bud in a Katzenjammer dialect, "Vat iss diss mit das crvazy baseball schtick?" Fade out. . . .

Fade in the Slugger factory. Portentous bass voice-over: "Today that quaint little woodshop on First Street makes three and one-half million bats a year!"

The Pete Browning tale is promulgated in all hallowed Slugger chronicles. And why not? Browning was a period superstar, lovingly known as the Old Gladiator. But there is a skeleton in the closet. On the wall of the company president's office is a clipping from a 1912 *Louisville Herald.* It relates a story told by Bud Hillerich that does not mention the Old Gladiator. Instead, Hillerich explained how he had made his own bat when he was playing on a semipro club. A teammate, Augie Weyhing, had asked to use it, and Bud had made one more for another teammate, Monk Cline. Monk Cline? Augie Weyhing? Down in front!

Anyway, the rest is history. The bat was known as the Falls City Slugger until 1894. In 1905 Honus Wagner signed a contract with Hillerich, permitting his signature to be branded on bats. He thus became the first baseball player ever to ink an endorsement pact. In 1911, Frank Bradsby, a sales expert, came on board, and the corporate name was altered in 1916. The factory was moved across the Ohio River to Indiana in 1974. Otherwise, business as usual.

More than 90 percent of all pros sign up with Slugger. Most join on as minor-leaguers earning a small fee and the promise that Louisville will make them personalized bats for as long as they play for pay. On semiautomatic lathes, consumer bats can be knocked out in eight seconds flat, but the pros' personal models are still turned by hand. Bats are never made or cut or formed. They are turned.

In the old days players used to make special trips to Louisville to talk to the craftsmen, to pick out their own timber. Not surprisingly, Ted Williams was the most persnickety. Players tended their bats, "cooling" them in alcohol, "tightening" the grain by rubbing them with a bone or a pop bottle. Today Louisville hears only from agents trying to renegotiate the old service contracts.

Styles change, too. Generally, handles have gotten thinner. Still, the most popular bat with the public is the Jackie Robinson model that has a relatively stout grip. The other retail autograph models are named after Aaron, Clemente, Mantle, Frank Robinson, and fourteen current hitters including Pete Rose, who is trying to get out of his Slugger contract so he can Charlie Hustle aluminum bats.

An original model is catalogued in a very simple way — by the initial of the player's surname and a number that indicates how many players with the same initial have had distinct models turned for them. Thus, the first bat made with a concave end is designated as C271 because it was turned for Jose Cardenal, who is the 271st player with the initial C to have had a Slugger model created for him.

A small room at Slugger Park holds file cards on every major-leaguer who ever had a Slugger turned for him. There is an eerie feeling there, a sense of time having stopped. A man can go into that file cabinet and determine what bat it was that Home Run

Baker used on April 14, 1910. And in a few minutes a craftsman can turn that exact bat. There are thirteen check points on every bat. It is always made from a white ash that has grown for forty-five to fifty years in New York or Pennsylvania. The tree has to have grown on a ridge top or have been exposed to the north and east for the right amount of sun. Then it is cut and dried. Finally it is turned by an artisan who does it precisely as one of his predecessors did it decades ago, about the time the seed went into the ground and Home Run Baker took his cuts.

Unfortunately, it is hard to find young men who want to be woodturners. It requires a long time to learn this honest craft, and young people do not want to invest that time. Besides, there are aluminum bats. They already take up 35 percent to 40 percent of the total bat market, and their share increases every year. A Slugger will cost you nine bucks tops, but it will break and sting your hands, and you must remember to keep the label up. Aluminum bats sell for as much as $50, but they last and last, whichever way you hold the label. It is also alleged that a baseball jumps off them faster. The sound is different, too. It is more modern, like an automobile crash.

Aluminum bats are now allowed in every game but Organized Baseball. There, as always, the law reads that a bat must be turned out of one solid piece of God's own wood. Someday soon a phenom is going to step to the plate in the majors, fresh out of college, and he is going to be swinging with a wooden bat for the first time. *Que será, será.*

None of this upsets Hillerich & Bradsby as much as you might imagine. Remember, these are the same fellows who got out of butter churns when the time was ripe. Now their brand is pressed on aluminum bats, too. And the Slugger people are especially proud of their top-quality magnesium bats. Magnesium bats made by Louisville Slugger! Why, you might as well tell me there is magnesium Cracker Jack.

Bill Williams, Hillerich & Bradsby's vice-president of advertising, says, "The crack of the bat doesn't seem to mean that much to kids anymore." He spoke that not in anger but merely in resignation, with a hint of pity. Imagine never getting good wood on a ball. Imagine not knowing what a loud foul off Home Run Baker's bat sounded like.

*   *   *

Comedy is not the most dependable traveler through time. Many people now find the mots of the wits of the Algonquin Round Table forced and leaden. And Abbott and Costello, those purveyors of the broad and foolish? They appear downright puerile. Consider their horse routine, when Abbott, the tall one (he was 5' 11"), brings Costello to blubbery tears by telling him deadpan about the mudder who had no fodder. Our first reaction is wonderment: Did a nation laugh at this?

You bet it did. Except for Laurel and Hardy, there has never been a pair of comics who were so enjoyed for so long. They were Top Ten box-office draws for more than a decade; in 1942 they were Number 1, just ahead of Clark Gable. They struck some simple child-like chord in us and strummed it again and again.

The pair broke up in 1957, and Costello died two years later when he was 50. Abbott, ever the happy wastrel, had to scuffle with the IRS over back taxes for most of his sunset years, but he lasted till age 78, dying four years ago this month. But they remain as much in evidence as ever. Their movies — and they churned out three or four a year for Universal — are everywhere on TV, usually during the children's hours, harmlessly washing our minds without leaving a trace upon our consciousness. But hush, my children, here is the one heirloom of Abbott and Costello that endures:

COSTELLO: I would like to know some of the guys' names on the team. . . .

ABBOTT: Oh sure. But you know baseball players have funny names . . . nowadays.

COSTELLO: Like what?

ABBOTT: Well, like Dizzy Dean and Daffy Dean.

COSTELLO: Oh yeah, a lot of funny names. I know all those guys.

ABBOTT: Well, let's see now. We have on our team: Who's on first, What's on second, I Don't Know's on third.

COSTELLO: That's what I want to find out, the guys' names.

ABBOTT: I'm telling you: Who's on first, What's on second, I Don't Know's on third.

COSTELLO: You're going to be the manager of a baseball team?

ABBOTT: Yes.

COSTELLO: You know the guys' names?

ABBOTT: Well, I should.

COSTELLO: Will you tell me the guys' names on the baseball team?

ABBOTT: I say: Who's on first, What's on second, I Don't Know's on third.

COSTELLO: You know the guys' names on the baseball team?

ABBOTT: Yeah.

COSTELLO: Well, go ahead — who's on first?

ABBOTT: Yeah!

COSTELLO: I mean the guy's name.

ABBOTT: Who.

COSTELLO: The guy playing first.

ABBOTT: Who!

COSTELLO: The guy at first base?

ABBOTT: Who's on first. . . .

That, of course, is just the beginning of the Who part. Not until considerably later do they introduce What. It goes on and on. To-morrow is pitching. Today is catching. Why is in left, Because is in center, and finally, I Don't Care is at short. For some reason, there is no rightfielder.* The routine could be played at any length. Maybe at one point there was a rightfielder, but it didn't work. No one knows for sure. Strangely, even though *Who's on First?* is far and away the best-known comic bit in American history and even though Abbott and Costello played it more than 15,000 times — including a dozen times for President Roosevelt, who never tired of it — and even though they did it in vaudeville, in burlesque, on radio, on television, and in the movies, there seems to be no ac-count of what inspired it, who wrote it, or even what Abbott and Costello thought of it.

Studio publicity had it that the comics introduced the routine in 1936 at the Oriental Theater in Chicago, but almost surely its ori-gins date to 1931 or 1932. The two men had become a team shortly before. William A. Abbott, a theater box-office employee, filled in one night when Louis Cristillo's straight man didn't show. Both men were from New Jersey, although Abbott grew up on Co-

---

*There is a similar incongruity in another famous piece of baseball literature, *Casey at the Bat.* In the poem's third stanza, the two batters preceding Casey are identified as "Flynn" and "Jimmy Blake." In the next stanza, after Flynn has singled and Blake doubled, Ernest L. Thayer writes: "There was Johnny safe at second and Flynn a-hugging third." Why did Jimmy become Johnny? Why didn't anyone ever catch this? How could the poet have made such a mistake? What does it all mean?

ney Island until, at age 15, he was shanghaied. Slipped a Mickey Finn, he woke up a seaman in the middle of the ocean. He later returned to show biz, the family profession.

Costello had a more uneventful childhood in Paterson, where, despite his short stature, he played baseball and other sports. Later he had fourteen professional prizefights and became a Hollywood stuntman. He was always interested in sports. In 1955 his two-year-old colt, Bold Bazooka, equaled the world record for five and a half furlongs, and two years before that he had spent $5,000 of his own money on a vain campaign to have the Dodgers moved to Los Angeles. (Now you know that number 8 is a trick question; all the answers are correct. The other answers are: questions 1 to 7, c; 9 to 16, d.)

Given Costello's interest in sports, it is more likely that *Who's on First?* originated with him. Certainly no one claims that anyone but the two comics themselves wrote it. Betty Abbott, Bud's widow, believes that her husband and Costello first performed the routine — a version about one-third as long as the final one — at the Eltinge Theatre in New York late in 1932.

Almost from the first it seems to have been the centerpiece of their act, but it did not receive national attention until 1938, when Abbott and Costello got their big break, appearing on the Kate Smith radio show. Two years later they used *Who's on First?* in their first movie, *One Night in the Tropics,* in which Robert Cummings and Allan Jones starred. Because the comedians and the routine were a big hit in this film, Universal signed them, and they later used *Who's on First?* in movies of their own.

"They kept embellishing it," their manager, Eddie Sherman, recalls. "Initially they didn't do the entire routine the way it's been recorded or the way they did it in pictures. They added on a thing they called 'Naturally.' They were always adding things to it over the years."

The official version, if there is such a thing, was enshrined in the Hall of Fame at Cooperstown in 1956. The gold record and script usually are displayed on the second floor, next to the National League centennial exhibit. Recently, Universal bought the rights to *Who's on First?* so it can use the bit in a movie and a TV show. This is business, of course, but it is also altogether silly. You can no more sell the rights to *Who's on First?* without Abbott and Costello than you can sell the rights to Sally Rand's fan dance without Sally Rand, or Babe Ruth's home-run trot without Babe Ruth. Oh well, never mind. Down in front!

It is hard to pin down why *Who's on First?* became so popular and enduring — especially at a time when sports material usually bombed on the stage. For obvious reasons, the bit must have appealed to baseball fans, and probably it also appealed to those who laugh at baseball fans for being so devoted to the sport's minutiae, its names and statistics. It goes without saying that the routine never could have worked for another sport. Who's at Halfback? No way. Baseball is the only popular American sport in which every position is permanently set at a specific location. The one thing you can count on in life is that there is a first baseman and a shortstop and a catcher, and they are right where they were last month. The second baseman is not going to vanish — poof — and materialize down the leftfield line as something known as a nose guard or a power forward. Baseball positions are anchors in a shifting world, and to have given the most indefinite names to the personnel at these most dependable positions is to have made brilliant use of comic irony. That is the genius of *Who's on First?*

Obviously, two burlesque comedians did not sit around and ponder all this, but their routine has a sort of uncultured existentialism. Costello is like a Sartre character in *No Exit,* stymied at every turn despite being on the most familiar, comfortable territory. Abbott is a seminal bureaucratic figure, ever helpful, never helping. Maddening.

The routine was written in the depths of the Depression, a time when the nation was still as confounded by this unforeseen calamity as it was hungry. Without warning, unseen forces were frustrating, then destroying common folk in ways they could not comprehend. Who? What? I don't know. Tomorrow! Why? Because. Economic disaster aside, the modern, impersonal, urban, red-tape society had just begun to crank up. You see, Abbott and Costello were saying, you can't depend on a damn thing anymore, not even baseball.

This is why, I think, they never came up with a rightfielder.

You might say that this is all a lot of gobbledygook. These were two downtown comics who worked bawdy routines out front while the strippers were getting ready backstage. Maybe, but genius pops up in funny places, and those who have it are often unaware of it.

On the afternoon of March 3, 1959, right after the Dodgers went off to spring training, Bud Abbott turned on the television in L.A. to watch an old Abbott and Costello movie. *Who's on First?* was in the film. Near the end of the routine the phone rang, and Abbott answered it. He was told that Lou Costello had died. "Tell me," Abbott would often say after that, "why did I happen to be watching that picture at that time? Will you tell me why?"

Probably because all along, surely, the rightfielder in the routine was God.

When All the World Is Young, Lad

1977

THE high school in Walton, Kentucky — of red brick, fringed by a garden of daffodil buses — lies in the lee of the Interstate that winds out of the Bluegrass, roaring north toward the Ohio and the city of Cincinnati, twenty miles away. The school is the largest building in Walton, for it must be big enough to hold all the children of the town, and all those of the neighboring hamlet of Verona, and all the high school myths and memories of anybody who visits.

High schools are our commonest common denominator. Good Lord, they all even smell the same, that stale institutional odor that can be disturbed only by another ringing bell. End of the period. The children fall out into the corridors, moving with a special rhythm, at a pace they will never again employ in life. Nothing else in the human experience resembles the break between classes.

In a room just beyond the clamor, the assistant principal, Mr. Tyler, muses: "Let's see now, Steve would be a junior if he were still here, wouldn't he?"

"A senior, I think."

"Oh, yeah, that's right. He used to go around with Gordon and Stephenson, that crowd." There was nothing special about the boy: a nice little fellow, good family; an industrious enough student, but capable of the usual adolescent high jinks. He liked to trampoline, and some people knew he rode horses at 4-H.

There is peace in the halls again, between-classes concluded, and soon only an outsider's heels click upon the linoleum. Almost as one, the students of Walton Verona High School stare curiously out their open classroom doors. Who dares violate these halls before the bell? And only now, looking back at these children — in this everyday setting, observing their normal, everyday routine — only at this moment does the full incongruity and enormity of what Steve Cauthen has done loom clearly.

It is not enough to marvel that at the age of 17 he has accomplished more in a year than any jockey in history. It is not enough that already there exists the mad school of thought that this little boy is the finest rider of all time. These are incredible things to ponder about someone so young, but somehow, as young as he is — and younger-looking still — the immensity of his achievement in 1977 cannot be properly understood until you stand in his high school and see the open country faces of the other children of Walton and realize that Steve Cauthen should be there among them still. He should be a senior in high school this day, hearing the bells and whiffing the smell.

And he would be . . . but for the coincidence of his size and his family background, but for the depth of his desire and some amazing gift of God that no one can comprehend.

Instead, almost at this very moment, several hundred miles away, when a bell rings, Steve Cauthen will burst from the starting gate at Aqueduct, bound to his horse in consummate harmony, seamless, one with the creature — a prodigy like none we have ever seen before, the leading money rider of any year, a fearless athlete, a resolute little doll-person, so very tiny, so very young, so very extraordinary and ageless in his grace at this one thing he does that he always calls "race riding."

His home is crosstown from the school, a horse farm of forty acres, hard by a train track and the county line. His room has been left untouched, so that there is the sensation of boarding one of those ships in the Bermuda Triangle, where everything is in perfect order, but there are no people. Steve's textbooks — *Modern Biology* being the most imposing volume — and the ribbons he won at horse shows stand out as artifacts from that distant era.

In New York, he boards with old family friends, but Cauthen's real habitat is the jocks' room at Aqueduct (or Belmont or Santa Anita in season), where he has the honor of an end locker, catty-cornered from Jorge Velasquez, who, coincidentally, held the old

New York riding record of 299 wins in a year. Cauthen will top that by almost 150, which, if you will, is comparable to a rookie hitting 90 home runs in the big leagues. His mounts have won more than $6 million, exceeding Angel Cordero's record by a full 27 percent. Three times this year the kid rode six winners on a nine-race program; four times he rode five; one week he rode twenty-three. His best mounts, the two-year-old Affirmed and the grass-running Johnny D., won Eclipse Awards — top U.S. honors — in their categories, because Cauthen gave them perfect rides in a couple of their major races. Withal, he missed a whole month of work after a gruesome spill in which his mount broke a leg, and he broke a wrist and two fingers, cracked some ribs, took twenty-five stitches and a concussion. He came back, galloped horses two days, and won his first race out on a colt named (no doubt by angels in heaven) Little Miracle.

In the process, Cauthen also became a phenomenon, which is really neither here nor there, but which does help us understand better the person and the exalted place he suddenly assumed in his sport's orbit. So much of Cauthen's saga is tied to the peculiar institution that is pari-mutuel horse racing, which has always been a hybrid entertainment and which recently has become a distressed industry as well. For a time the kid blew a breath of joy and humanity into a callous and cynical wheel. That moment is gone — the business of thoroughbred racing is business — but in the nuclear glare in which young Cauthen was scrutinized, we could discern the man's elegance behind the boy's downy countenance.

But make no mistake: While all of racing is a bet, each race is a sport. What Cauthen does is as athletic as what Lydell Mitchell and Pete Maravich and Guy Lafleur do with their bodies. In a way it is even more so, for their bodies are their own, not, perforce, attached to some 1,000-pound beast, charging thirty-five miles an hour, with brains as fragile as its sesamoids. "The horse is such a beautiful animal," Cauthen says. "When you're on him, in control of him, moving with him as one, it is a beautiful feeling." And then, in some reverie: "The best is when you're almost getting him to know what you want to do."

Almost. The very best is only almost. And sometimes you are all out, in close, side by side with jockeys who are as dim-witted or panicky as their mounts. Or, you are dead clear, unbothered — like in the fourth at Belmont on May 23, on Bay Streak. "What happened?" a microphone-person demanded a few days later, as the child in the wheelchair came out of the hospital with his mother. "Horse snapped a leg," said Steve Cauthen into the metallic thing thrust into his bruised little face.

And Velasquez's mount, onrushing, had stumbled over him. Horse snapped a leg. Horse will snap a leg in some other race, too. "I haven't got any fears," the kid says now, summing up this old inconvenience.

Racing has few heroes. The Secretariats are shuffled off to the equine massage parlors as soon as they attract some fond attention to the sport. Jockeys are too small to identify with, and the general public perceives them as crooked little Munchkins at that. Besides, most of the good ones these days are foreigners — "the Spanish boys," as they are dismissed cavalierly at the track.

Unlike other well-known athletes, jockeys appear from thin air. This makes them even more suspect. Who *are* these elves? Had Steve Cauthen been comparably talented in any other sport, he would have been a community celebrity at 13, a high school demigod, his value certified by the presence of scores of college and professional scouts. Everybody in Boone County knew about Lenny Spicer, who graduated from Walton Verona High in 1975 and signed with the Pittsburgh Pirates.

But few in Boone County were aware that Steve Cauthen was even contemplating a career. And you can't ride a race until you ride a race. There is no spring training. "I was ready to die after I rode my first race," he says. "There's no way to get fit galloping. People have no idea."

People had no idea that, for years, the little boy had sat up nights with his father, a racetrack blacksmith, studying patrol films from River Downs. No one knew that he had worked summers at the track, mucking stalls, walking hots, staying around the starting gate; listening, learning, ingesting every nuance of race riding. Who had any idea? His friend Todd Stephenson stayed over at the Cauthens one night, and so he found out that Steve would get up at 4 A.M. and, in the pitch dark, dress and go out to the barn and sit on a bale of hay, and for two hours, in the still predawn silence that might be disturbed only by a train whistle, he would practice whipping. Alone, in the red barn, he learned to switch the stick from one hand to the other, to tag the horse precisely upon his tailbone.

His father gave him the anvil, but it was Steve Cauthen, the child, who heated the metal and banged himself into the shape that stunned experts when they first saw him ride. "A lot of jockeys start training a few months before they start riding," Cauthen says. "I grew up to be a horseman, not just a jockey."

Because he was such a mysterious new presence and such an appealing figure (and because he was native-born), he captured the imagination of the country. Johnny Carson told Steve Cauthen jokes, gen-u-wine media celebs like Barbara Howar chased him cross-country for an interview; and such was the everyday journalistic crunch that once, by the scales, two TV crews fought a pitched battle over camera locations. "I'd come into the jocks' room in the morning, and there'd be five guys waiting," the kid recalls. "And they'd be screaming: 'I was first,' 'I'm next,' begging me to talk to them. It was ridiculous."

But if Cauthen was a comet in the insatiable Famous People Industry — in the 1977 parade, videotape highlights will show him marching somewhere between Anita Bryant and R2-D2 — he threw a monkey wrench into the machinery of racing wherever he rode. Until June 28 he kept a five-pound apprentice allowance — hey, gang, let's give Rod Carew four strikes! — that utterly destroyed the equipoise of the ancient system. Worse, there was no price to be had on his races.

Strangely, Cauthen's success proved how far horse racing is out of the mainstream of American life. He didn't sell. To be sure, for a substantial fee, he rode Steve Cauthen Days at various outback ovals — Penn National, Latonia, Hazel Park, etc. — and invariably he pulled warm, record-type crowds, but this was largely an intramural matter of churning up a devoted existing constituency. Horse racing has no rub-off. While Cauthen is the Bruce Jenner of 1977, the Simpson or Seaver of his sport, while he grossed six hundred or seven hundred grand, he made little beyond the fringe; not a single endorsement.

Thus, in a perverse way, while Cauthen is the biggest star in the most crass sport of all, he has quietly returned to his roots, as pure a major athletic commodity as there is to be found. Often nowadays he rises at dawn and goes to the track just to drink coffee and hang around. "Saturday was always my favorite day when I was growing up, because then I could be around racetrack people," he says. "Nobody makes me come out mornings now. I just like the atmosphere. I like the people at a racetrack — that's my people."

His is a scrawny little voice, rather what you might expect, given his size. But it is of honest timbre, almost devoid of backwoods inflection, and those grown-ups who have spoken to Cauthen intelligently about things within his ken have found him articulate, even garrulous.

"I'm not a headline freak," he says. "I never wanted the publicity. All I wanted was to be appreciated by the people around me, race-track people. But I understand the publicity stuff. In New York, everything's got to do with business. Somebody comes to you because they need you. They don't necessarily have bad intentions. They just need you at that time. I don't mind. Now last spring, I was a tired kid. But it's OK now. I always wanted just the one thing, to be a race rider, and this is the place to be one."

Professionally, Cauthen is bred as well as any foal ever dropped in the Bluegrass. On the home side is the father, the blacksmith, Ronald (Tex) Cauthen. On the shop side is his agent, Lenny Goodman. One was raised in Sweetwater, Texas; the other come outta your Brooklyn. Between the two, between Sweetwater and Brooklyn, there is no virtue or value in race riding that has not been imparted to the child.

Tex Cauthen is the salt of the earth. He grew late, to 5'9", and so no matter what the doctors say, he is not altogether convinced that his oldest son won't shoot up a few more inches from his present 5'1". If so, if so. Even now, the father's primary emotion about his son is being happy for him. The rest he takes in stride. "I just feel that Steve's doing what he's supposed to be doing," he says.

His wife, Myra, has trained horses, as have a brother and a brother-in-law. And her father owned horses. It's in the family. She met Tex at the track. They are nice-looking people, but they don't look a thing alike. He is dark and rounded, and she is light and angular. And Steve doesn't look at all like either of them. Apparently, he got the least of their height and the best of the rest of them.

The Cauthens bought the farm in Walton in 1965, when Steve was five, and they keep broodmares there. At tracks like Latonia, a few miles up the road, or at River Downs, Tex Cauthen earns $27 for shoeing a horse. It is one of the most honest professions. There are no shortcuts. All about the Cauthen living room are pictures of horses winning races for members of the family — trainer or rider — but the one large painting over the fireplace is of a smith shoeing a bay. This helps to keep things in perspective. The Cauthens remain very much in perspective. The neighbors, ever-vigilant watchdogs in strike-it-rich cases such as this, detect no new airs. The *Walton Advertiser* wrote a nice story on the local boy when he passed Cordero's earnings record, but, in keeping with priorities, the lead story that edition featured John Williams of Bracht Piner Road, who was cited for raising a 17¾-pound muskmelon.

The Cauthens did splurge and buy a phone recording machine, but this marked change in life-style mainly assists strangers who mispronounce the family name. Most say the first syllable as in *coffin* or *cough,* while correctly it is as in *cotton,* with an h: Cothin.

The family is from England, possibly Cornwall, and moved west to Sweetwater via the Carolinas. Myra Cauthen is a Bischoff, from the Bluegrass. She grew up on a horse farm not four miles from where she is raising her family. Besides Steve, there are Doug, 14, and Kerry, 8. The house is comfortable, and the home is filled with ample amounts of affection and respect.

"I got everything from my mother and father," Steve says. "They're loving parents. And the main thing is, they gave me the love I needed when I needed it. And that's why I'm where I'm at."

Nonetheless, to maintain this felicitous location, it helps to have Lenny Goodman sharing the address. A jockey's agent is crucial to the rider's success, as his fee of up to 25 percent attests. Agents are allowed only one customer, so a kind of symbiotic relationship develops. This is revealed best by the agents' sloppy use of pronouns. They say things like "I ride the six-horse," when, to every other naked eye, it appears that the 75 percent is in the irons.

As Tex Cauthen discovered when he went comparison shopping among agents, Goodman is regarded as the best in the land — a view that probably is shared by Goodman himself. Quite often he prefaces remarks with: "Tell me if I'm wrong" — which a person never dares say unless he is secure in the knowledge that no one will and he isn't.

In tandem, Goodman and Cauthen resemble characters out of Dickens. A single glance suggests that this backstreet sharpie must have obtained this innocent child from a foundling home in order to perpetrate some nefarious caper. But stay around, and see that it is no overlay. The kid, in his way, is every bit as dapper as his emissary. Cauthen finds it hard to pass a mirror by without slyly inspecting his profile and searching for wayward hairs to put back into place. In civilian attire he favors a soft camel-hair cap of a sort fashionable half a century ago, and his dark, melancholy eyes give the eerie sensation that this 95-pound child is Babe Ruth, shrunken by jungle specialists.

Goodman, on the other hand, comes prepackaged: Guccis, pinkie ring, hefty cigar, color coordinates. His silver hair, brushed back, glimmering, suggests that he has watched too many Victor Mature movies. And tell me if I'm wrong: Lenny Goodman can touch his tie. This is a lost art, going the way of shooting cuffs. Just a touch at the knot at the right time. Very few gentlemen can still do it just so. And, for that matter, with all the Sunbelt turning away from four-in-hands to wearing chains and necklaces, you are not going to see much more tie touching.

There is a wonderfully sly communion between this disparate pair: Goodman, with his crinkly eyes, jesting with his pink-cheeked meal ticket. The kid does a great deadpan. "I'm riding this in th' ninth Sat'day, yahear," Lenny announces, making subtitles in the air with his big cigar. The farm boy cocks his head, just enough to indicate which one it is who is still drawing the 75 percent. Lenny smiles. Neither one of them is going anywhere. "Lenny's making more money than the United Fund," another agent explains.

"Natural talent, sure," Lenny says of his boy. "But tell me if I'm wrong. There is no one around with a head like this child. Instinct, talent, intelligence. Put it all together, it spells Mother . . . or somethin'."

Cauthen goes back to his locker to prepare for another ride. He is truly scrawny, a fact accentuated by his ghostly complexion. But then, all jocks must be transformed. Their room is like a wizard's laboratory — such a surprisingly drab place of browns and blacks, tack and trunks, peopled by tiny specimens in white knickers and, even, terrycloth robes. Only at the last do they change and leave, suddenly adorned in gaudy colors, flicking whips in the air with bravado.

Cauthen inspects his whips before the day's races, testing them. Then, carefully, one selected, he trims it with scissors. A whip is a crucial implement, but ultimately it is merely an extension of the hands. It is his hands that measure a jockey. "A horse gets the knowledge through your hands," Cauthen says. "He gets confidence in the way you use your hands." In the final strides of a close race, the accomplished jockey puts the whip away and rides the horse a cappella, tight to the body, flowing with him, lending him energy and the human competitive element in ways that a whipping cannot transmit. The whole body is intimately involved in the exercise. The thighs, the feet, the shoulders, all pumping. But always it has been known as a *hand* ride, for it is the hands that tell the tale in race riding.

Cauthen's hands are outsized, the only large aspect of his body. But they are not farm-boy ham hocks. Even with the mean scar from the Belmont spill cutting across the top of his right hand, Cauthen's hands appear to be the fine, long instruments of the esthete. And down to the wire, they ride a horse. Already, on the back side, there are whispers that some of the very best riders are spooked now when they hook the kid in the last furlong.

There is no way to explain this magic that Cauthen has with horses. He is a natural athlete, of course. He has the necessary instincts. He senses pace: the clock in his head. Reflexively, he stays out of trouble. Joe Hirsch, columnist for the *Daily Racing Form,* who has seen the boy ride a thousand or more races, swears he has never once seen him make a mistake. Never.

But nothing else matters if the jock lacks the ability to inspire the animal. That is the mystic gift, which none of them — Shoemaker, Cordero, or the child — can explain. Cauthen says that the horses he rides again exhibit no recognition of him on sight, but they often do seem to remember him when he settles upon their backs. Somehow this is revealing. Perhaps the horses sense that he cares.

"You always want to win, sure," the kid says, "but the important thing is to get the most out of your horse. If he runs the best he can, wherever he finishes, I feel good — for him and for me. And when you cross that finish line first on a horse who is not the best — and you know it — that's the greatest feeling of all."

There is a moment, somewhere, when the most beautiful and accomplished part of sport turns to art. But athletes are probably wrongly identified as artists. Rather, they are the art, not the author of it. Julius Erving is not a poet of the basketball court; he is a poem. As Reggie Jackson is not a drummer, but a tympani flourish; Muhammad Ali not an actor, but a prime-time series. What more shall we say: that Walter Payton is a brushstroke, Jimmy Connors a rousing chorus, Pelé a hymn? And Cauthen, what is he? It is hard yet to be certain. There are times, at the wire, when he reposes upon an easel, but other times when he seems too lusty for that, and we think of him as a ballad:

> *When all the world is young, lad,*
> *And all the trees are green;*
> *And every goose a swan, lad,*
> *And every lass a queen;*
> *Then hey for boot and horse, lad,*
> *And round the world away. . . .*

Hey, hey, for boot and horse, lad!

Yes — but in the end, Steve Cauthen remains a fairy tale, for it is not only that he has come so far so quickly, so improbably, it is that he has come from one existence to another, overnight, like frogs and princes. He may be the last of the line. Cincinnati will swallow up Walton, Kentucky, soon enough. Horses and blacksmiths will be confined to racetracks, as hoop skirts and carriages are to Williamsburg. No boy will grow up as a horseman, riding horses from childhood, feeding and tending them, practicing to master them upon bales of hay before dawn.

Riders will be made in Taiwan.

Walton will be made into suburbs. Already, says Ab Ryan, down at his implement store, his business in Walton is going toward lawn mowers, away from farm equipment. The kids drive up the Interstate to Florence, where the big shopping mall is, and kick tires over at McDonald's; the town got government money for city-style sewers (instead of septic systems) and now ranch houses are flying up.

Oh, it is not all gone yet. There is still a town water tank, inscribed with high school class numerals and the names of first loves. The main street, named Main Street, still features an inordinate number of houses of worship, beauty parlors, and auto body shops, and a billboard at the edge of town urges that citizens rethink this business about our getting mixed up with the United Nations. Posters advise that a turkey shoot is coming up: "So come out and enjoy a shoot and win a little something."

And there are still the trains in Walton. Two tracks run through town: the L&N, which stands for Louisville and Nashville, and the Southern, which goes by the Cauthen farmhouse. The engineer pulls his whistle right there, as the freight chugs into Walton, and it sounds loud and clear in the house, shrill enough to disrupt conversation, and shrill enough, for sure, to nourish the dreams of any child who ever heard it there, just as train whistles have sung to ambitious farm boys down through all the years.

Steve Cauthen knew exactly where he was going. He would tell his friends he was leaving very soon to become the best race rider in the world. He would tell them that flat out, says his classmate Mark Gordon, who will himself be leaving Walton after graduation this May, to join the Marines. And the other kids would hoot and mock Steve, call him "Superjock," and flick towels at him. But it was in fun, and Steve would keep saying it, matter-of-factly. It was no big deal, it was just that he thought he could go out and be the best race rider in the world.

And he was absolutely right. "What Steve has done, you can compare it with soap opera," says Mark Gordon.

Steve Cauthen, his old friend, class of '78, says: "It's a pretty good achievement. It never happened to any other kid in the business."

Tell him if he is wrong.

*   *   *

In his second year as a rider, 1978, Cauthen continued his historic spree, riding Affirmed to the Triple Crown. But then, the next summer he fractured his knee when a mount at Saratoga fell, and when he came back that winter he suffered through a horrendous (almost impossible) string of 110 races without a win. Shortly thereafter, Cauthen accepted an offer to ride in England, and the change rejuvenated him.

Today, he is perhaps as famous as any American expatriate, both the leading and most popular jockey riding in England. He speaks with a "mid-Atlantic accent," and is something of a country squire, often known to his new, adoring public as "Gentleman Steve."

All-American,
All the Way

1972

HE was in New York to attend a board meeting of the YMCA, and he was standing there, of all perfect places, under the Biltmore clock. There have been so many rowdy, bumptious years of change since he was an All-American, boy and halfback, but he was instantly recognizable. He does not look older; and, of course, the way things are in his line of work, his hair is not that much longer these days.

There is real comfort to be had waking up one fine, polluted, polarized morning and discovering that there still is a Biltmore clock and a YMCA and a Pete Dawkins. These things actually have survived. Perhaps each morning one last hero should be assigned to stand under the Biltmore clock so we can hear the ticks from the good old times, when peace and prosperity were both lit up at this end of the tunnel and the only shaggy-haired perverts were the four who were making noise in a Liverpool cellar.

Used to triggering such reveries, Dawkins suddenly dropped his smile and spoke almost plaintively. "Do me one thing," he said. "Just one thing. Don't treat me like just another piece of nostalgia. You know, I don't live in the fifties anymore, either."

The trouble with Pete Dawkins, All-American, is that despite his protests he is locked into time. In a professional era when great athletes are ongoing household names from puberty to pension, Dawkins's career seems to have lasted only somewhat longer than a halftime show and hardly as long as a twi-night doubleheader. So much of him was jammed into that glorious Eisenhower autumn of '58 that, like Conway Twitty, much of him must always remain there.

The other youthful stars of that year — Aaron, Unitas, Palmer, Shoemaker, Robertson, and West — still ride shotgun across the sports pages. And those athletic eminences of '58 who have left the scene — Russell and Mantle, for instance — did not retire before spending the prescribed number of seasons as "aging veterans." Of course, they all took home a lot of money. Dawkins's trophy was his calendar year.

He was the very essence of that time, a period that prized humility, respect, and clean-cut-ness from a silent generation. By now we have forgotten that those well-rounded, level-headed scholar-jocks who succeeded Dawkins — men such as Jerry Lucas, Terry Baker, and Bill Bradley — were pale imitations of the original Joe Renaissance. There was nothing Dawkins was not, that dreamy senior year of his.

He was appointed first captain of the Corps and elected class president. He was a Star Man, tenth in a class of 499, and accepted as a Rhodes scholar. He was captain of the football team, everyone's All-American, the nation's leading scorer, and winner of the Heisman and Maxwell trophies.

It was written, first facetiously but gradually at face value, that it was unfortunate that Cadet Dawkins and General MacArthur could not have matriculated at the same time at the Academy since MacArthur would have made such a serviceable adjutant for Dawkins. There were so many New Testament metaphors applied to the young man that, it was reported, he grew sensitive at the sacrilege. After all, he was a former acolyte, a member of the cadet choir, and he collected the offering.

Dawkins could play six musical instruments, he was the highest-scoring collegiate hockey defenseman in the East, he had constructed his own hi-fi (as he had previously built his own soap box derby vehicles), and he went about industriously lifting rocks when he had no quick access to his body-building weights. He was modest, had a sense of humor, and made out all right with the honeys, too. Moreover, breathless journalists informed America that Dawkins was actually given to such State U. vernacular as "no sweat."

All accounts of Dawkins began by reporting how he had "con-

quered polio." He had, in fact, suffered a spot of the disease as a
child, which had left him with a slight curvature of the spine, but
the implication usually was that he had burst forth from a sideline
iron lung midway through the Navy game.

In the Academy yearbook, his classmates wrote a truly incredible
encomium, a reverent tribute that began simply: "We have stood in
awe of this man." And ended: "We were not completely sagacious,
but we knew a great leader, a great friend, a great man." It was left
for Colonel Red Blaik, the coach, to say aloud what everyone else
was whispering, that Cadet Dawkins was destined to be chief of
staff of the United States Army.

And, oh yes, perhaps more than all these things, this too: at that
time, 1958, professional soldiers were not popularly dismissed as
blackguards. Soldiers were even generally considered to be quite
respectable people.

Major Pete Dawkins, at home in faded blue jeans and boots, listening to the music of his friend Kris Kristofferson: "When I was
studying at Princeton [at the Woodrow Wilson School, 1968–70],
that was the most heated time of the war. People were very suspicious of me, of anyone military, though after a while some people
would condescend to say: 'You know, you're really not like those
soldiers.' That was supposed to be a big compliment. I'd reply: 'But
don't you see, I am a soldier? I am what I am.' Nobody wanted to
hear that. Nobody wanted to believe that it was their stereotype
that was wrong. I didn't fit the popular stereotype, therefore I was
out of place.

"Then one day during that same period at Princeton, somebody
came up to me and said: 'You know, looking back, I think of you as
the Bob Dylan of the fifties.' That's the greatest compliment I ever
received."

Last January Dawkins's orders to return to Vietnam were pulled,
and he was assigned to SAMVA, the office of the Special Assistant
for the Modern Volunteer Army. SAMVA appears to be both a think
tank and a lobby. On the one hand, it must make the new Army
attractive for volunteers. On the other, it must convince the old
Army (which is still the only Army) that modernization is not necessarily a sign of frailty, that the Republic will be safe even if doors
are put on soldiers' toilet stalls.

Dawkins, if the truth be known, is not overly optimistic, but he tries. As soon as he settled himself at SAMVA, he wrote a couple of memos. The subject was hair, that is to say, the length of hair. "I simply maintained that we could not win over the hair issue," Dawkins says. As a reward for his interest he was taken along to a high-level briefing on the subject that General Westmoreland was conducting. Before Dawkins knew it, Westy had him up before the gathering posing as the military hair model. As Colonel Blaik predicted, the kid was really going places.

In the upper echelons of the Pentagon, some of the old soldiers still wax rhapsodic about the halcyon war years when any man in Army issue with a dandy regulation whiffle cut would be set upon by all available women, beside themselves at the very sight. It came as some surprise to a number of officers that a) this was no longer the case, and b) it had nothing to do with Communism.

Symbolically, nothing speaks more directly of declining military prestige than hair. At the time when Pete Dawkins entered the Army, the whole nation aped the military haircut, just as the whole nation — and not just the American Legion and defense contractors — cared deeply about the outcome of the Army-Navy football game. Now a military haircut is a source of shame. The PXs do a thriving wig business, and many of the most dedicated career men try to assuage their social embarrassment by letting their hair sprout some on top. Unfortunately, that only makes the wearer appear as if he had submitted to one of those two-bit Depression bowl cuts. Many of the most outstanding officers in the Pentagon look like members of *Our Gang*.

"You know," Dawkins began tentatively at another of the hair hearings, "it's not just the new recruits who want long hair like everyone else. It's my wife, for instance, and a lot of the wives of my friends, of good officers, who want to know why we can't have longer hair."

A bull general rose, horrified at this clear endorsement of henpeckery. "By God," he thundered, "do you mean, Major, that now the Army should be run by what a bunch of women want?"

Dawkins bowed his head, believing he had been defeated, but happily another general took a stand in his defense. "You know," he said, "the Army's in a lot of trouble these days, but it's nothing like the mess we could be in if all the women turn against us."

So the battle for longer hair turned; but how much longer? The debate raged. This long and that long, how long for hygiene, and how long for discipline; so long for white people, and so long for black people, and what about sideburns vis-à-vis ears, which is all the more complicated because hardly anyone is familiar with precise ear terminology except for lobes. (At West Point it is decreed that for Duty, Honor, Country, sideburns must terminate at the top of the tragus, which sounds like something you should not be talking about in polite company.)

At the Pentagon the hair dilemma remained unresolved until Major Dawkins devised a strategy. His maneuver may not go down in tactics textbooks along with Jackson's Valley Campaign, but it was a bold stroke just the same. Major Dawkins suggested, "Let's not say how long the hair has to be. Let's just take pictures showing how long." Stunningly, the Dawkins Arrangement was accepted, giving him the honor of fathering the only visual — rather than verbal — regulation in the history of the U.S. Army.

"We must make changes in the Army, if only because everything is changing," Dawkins says. "Too many people in the Army still think that if we can just hold the line, be the last bastion of traditional America, that the country will come to its senses, get its hair cut and form up again around the Army." He shook his head at this hypothesis.

"You know, to much of the military, Vince Lombardi remains the greatest contemporary civilian hero. I believe that he was so genuine that his teams experienced a contagion for winning that overrode the exceptional demands that he placed on players. But I also believe that his methods — arbitrary and imposed — have become anachronistic. But Army people don't want to believe that. It is like, if you were a theologian, trying to apply things to the present that Reinhold Niebuhr said years ago. Possibly, Niebuhr and Lombardi would have had new approaches for this time. It is wrong to assume that their attitudes were ever intended to be pertinent today. Understand, I am not critical of the way Lombardi operated: I am critical of those who continue to hold this model reverently. I know Lombardi's methods will not succeed in the Army today, and I suspect they would have even less of a chance of succeeding in football.

"Kids demand room for expression in sports as much as in anything else. It may sound frivolous, but I don't believe that enough significance has been attached to the popularity of Frisbee. Think of it: It's the ultimate of its kind, a complete free form. There aren't any rules unless you make them up. The fact that so many people everywhere are devoted to such an unstructured sporting expression says something, I think."

In a poll of the 1971 Army football team to determine the players' sporting idol, Dick Butkus was the overwhelming choice.

Captain Dawkins, in 1966, while he was in Vietnam: "This is the big stadium. This is the varsity."

Pete and Judi Dawkins, and their children, Sean, 7, and Noel, 4, live a half-hour's commute from the Pentagon in one of those developments that has streets named for chic colleges. Their house is on Vassar. The Heisman Trophy is in the living room. Until this past year his parents kept it, but now Dawkins feels enough time has elapsed for the sculpture to become a period piece, so he has taken it on. Sean Dawkins has only one observation about it. "Nice carving," he says. Maybe somewhere a developer is naming streets after Heisman Trophy winners.

Most career servicemen move so regularly that they invariably rent housing. The Dawkinses have bought their home, however, because Judi Dawkins comes from the Washington area, and she and the children will stay there when the major is shipped back to the Far East for a year. "It is not just that Pete has to go, like any other husband off on a long business trip," Mrs. Dawkins says. "It is that he might always be away from us." She means that he might be killed.

Dawkins was first posted to Vietnam in 1965. "We found out in 'sixty-three that Pete would have to go two years later," Mrs. Dawkins says, "but that didn't bother me at all, because of course I was perfectly sure that the war would be over by then, by nineteen sixty-five." She shrugs, smiling at the innocence of the time, not the irony.

Though the children are too young to know much, or care, about their father's profession, the Dawkinses have experienced something of the alienation the war has brought to many American families. Dawkins has an older brother, Dale, who is an automobile executive; he also has a younger sister, Sue, who is a full ten years his junior, and an even younger brother, Mike, now 18.

Mike was only 5 when Pete was America's hero, and he would toddle about in a sweater with a big, proud Army "A." But as Mike and his sister grew and the war wore on, they more often came to look upon their older brothers not as model successes but as the personification of the military-industrial complex, infiltrating their very family.

"One effect of the tragedy of Vietnam," Dawkins says, "was that the Army was profoundly baffled by the attitudes developing toward it. We didn't understand why we were blamed. The vast majority of soldiers, of lifers, viewed the war with no joy. Just a sense of responsibility.

"Guys picked up and left their families simply because events had occurred and their duty was advanced. Somehow, because of the nation's frustration, the attitudes of these men, our soldiers, were perverted to mean that most of them were opportunistic and self-seeking. Good God, would you want a military that shrank from combat when combat presented itself?"

The twenty men of SAMVA are assigned to the C-Ring of the Pentagon, an area where everyone uses the word *synthesis* profusely. The offices of SAMVA are well lighted; that much can be said for them. Three posters serve as the only decoration. One is an *Easy Rider* photo with Dennis Hopper providing a naughty hand signal. Another, over Dawkins's desk, is by Ben Shahn and carries the message: "YOU HAVE NOT CONVERTED A MAN BECAUSE YOU HAVE SILENCED HIM." The third poster features a model posing as a t.t.u. soldier — a t.t.u. soldier is a tough, thoughtful, unarmed soldier — which is about the only breed of that cat the public will accept nowadays. Around SAMVA, only "synthesis" is heard more often than "tough, thoughtful, unarmed."

Dawkins, having spent much of his career studying at Oxford and Princeton, teaching at West Point, and on policy assignments in Saigon and Washington, is, obviously, very much a living, breathing t.t.u. soldier. He did win an array of impressive medals for his courage in Vietnam, but he does not wear them as a rule, limiting himself to the most austere ornamentation and, of course, his West Point ring. Other officers know Academy graduates as "ring knockers."

The higher up Dawkins moves (and his promotion to lieutenant colonel has been approved), the more scrutiny he will receive. Already, old-line lifers, in from another bivouac, grumble about Dawkins's pantywaist desk tours, and an Iowa congressman once rose on the floor of the House to protest that the government was paying for Dawkins's fancy book learning.

Nevertheless, Dawkins is escorted by two totems as he ascends the hierarchy, and one is his football reputation — or, anyway, his overall cadet fame that was founded on the playing fields. In a business that treasures tradition, Dawkins is tradition on the hoof. Moreover, his celebrity gives him a potential outside the military that translates to leverage within. Says Major Josiah Bunting, a close friend who is a novelist and a history professor at West Point: "If ever a time comes when Pete is faced with compromising his principles, he can always say, 'OK, I'll go be a senator instead.' Now how can they handle that?"

In fact, most people wonder why he bothers to keep tilling the feudal Army soil. Says Kris Kristofferson, the songwriter, who was also a Rhodes scholar and a combat helicopter pilot: "It used to bewilder me why someone with Pete's intelligence and charisma would stay in the Army. I have such tremendous respect for him. But he sold me. Look at it this way: It's great just to have someone like Pete Dawkins in the military."

Dawkins's biggest edge, however, comes from his contemporaries who have stayed in the service and continue to hold him in awe. Fort Leavenworth, Kansas, sits in the middle of the country, and, in the insular manner of most Army posts, in the middle of nowhere as well; the denizens refer to "the outside world." Leavenworth is a large post, and it can be an important one, too, a crucial station for rank-conscious young officers.

A lanky career major, Ranger and Airborne and bowl-cut, drew on his cigarette. "Sure, you find it here at Leavenworth, you find it anywhere in the Army," he said. "There is always a certain amount of resentment about Dawkins — you know, the glory boy. It comes especially from guys like myself who didn't go to the Point. Everybody knows he did only one tour of Vietnam, but that he got special attention from the press. He's on the five percent [early promotion] list, but he hasn't had to get all his tickets punched, like everybody else. But you see, every time this comes up, there's always somebody around who was with Dawkins at the Point or somewhere, and they say, 'Hey listen, he's special, he really is, and the Army would be crazy to make him go through the same garbage as everybody else.'"

The major put out his cigarette on his boot and intently field-stripped it. "You know," he said after a while, "that's a helluva thing when you think about it, when you realize that kind of talk comes from his rivals, so to speak."

Jonathan Swift, in *Gulliver's Travels*: "A soldier is a Yahoo hired to kill in cold blood as many of his own species, who have never offended him, as possibly he can."

Dawkins, stuck in rush-hour traffic near the Pentagon: "The military is never so evil as some would have it, nor so gallant as others. If you do believe that we live in a world where we can abdicate forces, then yes, obviously, the Army is a caricature. But if you read the tea leaves of history, one is obliged to believe that we cannot possibly get by without a competent military force, that we cannot achieve decisions other than in consonance with a military reality."

Defense Attorney Barney Greenwald in Herman Wouk's *The Caine Mutiny*: "See, while I was studying law 'n' old Keefer here was writing his play for the Theatre Guild, and Willie here was on the playing fields of Princeton, all that time these birds we call regulars — these stuffy, stupid Prussians in the Navy and the Army — were manning guns. . . . Of course, we figured in those days, only fools go into armed service. Bad pay, no millionaire future, and you can't call your mind or body your own. Not for sensitive intellectuals . . . [but] a lot of them are sharper boys than any of us, don't kid yourself, best men I've ever seen, you can't be good in the Army or Navy unless you're goddamn good."

Dawkins at 33 is a trim 6′2″ with large sloping shoulders. He moves with purpose at all times at what may be described as an organized lope. Tennis is his sport now, although he began playing it just two years ago. He took up skiing a while back and was winning slalom races before the snows were gone. If anything, he took longer to master football than any other game. Baseball was his best high school sport. He scored nineteen runs in his first cricket game, he made the West Point hockey varsity shortly after he picked up a stick, and he earned his Oxford blue in rugby only eight weeks after he first saw a scrum.

In football, though, Dawkins was nothing special in prep school, a weak-passing, left-handed plebe quarterback and a fifth-string sophomore halfback. He was a starter as a junior but merely the other halfback; Bob Anderson was the All-America. It was as if they were saving 1958 for Dawkins. He started off with four touch-downs in the opener. Army never lost, and all along Dawkins drew an inordinate amount of publicity because of the Lonely End formation. Colonel Blaik, nobody's fool when it came to destiny, just upped and quit after twenty-five years of coaching following that season.

West Point makes it especially easy for Dawkins to haunt Saturday afternoons. There is still a ring dance in the fall at the Academy, a formal, no less, with corsages. The lettermen wear dated little malt-shop zipper jackets with those big fuzzy A's on them — no sweat. Pep rallies are fervent large productions, and football players are treated with deference by their classmates. The Academy chaplain, the Reverend James Ford, thinks it's helpful to hire former football stars as preaching assistants.

"It's important to have a winning attitude," says Colonel William Schuder, the director of athletics who was first captain of the Corps in 1947, a classmate of Davis and Blanchard. "It's one of the things that encourages a young man to try the Army as a career. You can't have an Army with a losing image."

In support of this widespread notion, bad news has no place at West Point, and, like PDA (public display of affection), simply is not tolerated on the premises. When the superintendent was removed last year to face trial for having concealed war atrocities, the cadets were ordered to go mill under his window as a spontaneous warm tribute. When the football team went 1–9–1 in 1970, the Academy yearbook declared: "It can truthfully be said that bad breaks prevented us from enjoying another successful season." It can also truthfully be said that this is the same rationale which gave us fanciful body counts all these years, too.

The first of Dawkins's classmates to die in Vietnam fell in January 1963, when the present plebes were in the fourth grade. It has been that long that the funeral barrages have been cracking above the Hudson, and almost that long that the Army has wrestled with its soul and the Academy has fought to preserve the middle word — Honor — in the motto it venerates. "It's particularly hard to be an artist as a soldier," Dawkins says, "and if you do have pride, life is trying to be an artist in your job. But being a soldier must always be a derivative value. There is no absolute value in performing the soldier's manifest task: that is, killing. A soldier's life can only draw value from the society that gives it meaning, by preserving those qualities that society believes are worth preserving. The Army must always gain a sense in itself that derives from the public."

When Dawkins first set out to be a soldier in the summer of '55, that sense was easy to behold. A military man, the absolute t.t.u. soldier, sat in the White House, presiding over the nation's massive deterrent. The star-spangled heroisms of Iwo Jima and the Bulge were only a decade past, and the soupy words from the general that the civilian had fired had hardly left the top of the Hit Parade: "Old Soldiers Never Die." It was so easy to want to be a young soldier then.

"You must remember those times," Dawkins says. "I was so ripe for it all. I was obnoxiously headstrong. I'd show them. I was just seventeen. I had guys in my plebe class who were twenty-one. I never would have taken that crap they threw at us if I had been twenty-one. But everything up at the Point was right for me the summer when I was seventeen."

No one at the Academy likes to believe that the supply of quality plebes may have diminished in these times less congenial to military evangelism. "We still get those typical red-blooded American kids who have wanted to come here since they were eight or ten years old," says Brigadier General John Jannarone, the academic dean. Obviously, the general does not mean it exactly this way, but implicit in that assertion, one often voiced, is the fact that the U.S. Military Academy is largely inhabited by young men who have not been moved by the events of the 1960s. Certainly, to see Dawkins return to a football game is not so much to watch him come back to West Point but to watch him come back to 1958.

In the huge mess hall the air is feverish with glory be. Nothing seems forced; it is for real. The occasion: Army plays Rutgers tomorrow. That Rutgers has not been a gridiron juggernaut since it won the lidlifter in stocking caps a century ago is of small moment. Army is meeting *somebody* in football.

The band plays rugged martial music, interspersed with lively modern pop. As the meal nears an end, some cadets, as if suddenly infested with demons, climb on their chairs, take off their jackets and wave them like banners, around and around over their heads. This is a tradition.

Other cadets sit backward on their chairs and bounce them

about, yelling like banshees, as if they were astride cavalry stock. In one wing of the hall, masters of the art start hurling cakes thirty feet into the air. It is announced that Army has this day defeated Rutgers in 150-pound football, and the hall explodes with cheers that, surely, could not have been rendered any louder or with more pride on the day the word came in that both Gettysburg and Vicksburg were won.

Dawkins, his chest ablaze with ribbons, marches out of the hall, looking self-conscious, as the cadets give him the once-over. "He's still top priority around here," says Bob Antwerp, first captain of the Corps. There are not many celebrities, never mind heroes, left in the U.S. Army of 1971.

Outside, in the chill winter air, cheerleaders are setting up a rally on a balcony of Washington Hall. The cadets begin to gather below in the courtyard. A cheerleader offers a rocket cheer as something of a benediction, then cries: "We got a super guest star here tonight."

The cheerleaders proceed next with a skit, which ends in a jousting match between the Scarlet Knight of Rutgers ("Hey, youse guys, I'm from Rutgers, New Joisey") and a Black Knight of the Hudson — who is, however, carefully identified as a janitor, not a cadet. This dramatic device is employed so that the Scarlet Knight can win the joust and gain rights to the beautiful Rapunzel without shaming the corps. But, alas, the Scarlet Knight is incapable of climbing up to the buxom lady's lair, which sets the stage for the guest star.

General George C. Marshall: "I have a secret and dangerous mission. Send me a West Point football player."

Cheerleader: "So who could be more worthy of this fair damsel than SAINT PETER DAWKINS!?!?!?!"

On cue, from the back of the courtyard, there is a tragus-shattering roar, and the beam from an unmuffled mighty motorcycle begins to lurch about. On the cycle, dressed in a silver lamé helmet, large yellow sunglasses, fatigues, and boots, is a cadet obviously playing (broadly, to the crowd) the role of the largely mythical St. Peter Dawkins. The chopper caroms about the crowd, at last finds a path to the stage, and zooms toward it.

It screeches to a halt at a ladder, and the Dawkins character leaps toward the balcony stage, with, suddenly, the strains of "Jesus Christ Superstar" swelling to crescendo. On the balcony he removes his helmet and glasses and fatigue jacket, revealing a red-white-and-blue, stars-and-stripes Captain America shirt under-neath. He also reveals one more thing: that the actor playing the part of St. Peter Dawkins is none other than Major Peter Dawkins.

To the throaty cries of "Give me some skin," Dawkins smiles bra-zenly and pulls off his shirt, to stand there, bare-chested in the freezing night. This is another tradition, and Dawkins decides to take it one step further. "OK, we'll find out the ones who really have spirit," he howls into the microphone. "Everybody, take off your shirts."

In the bitter cold, only a few at first comply. Even for cadets with winning attitudes, there are, after all, some discernible differences between playing Rutgers and Notre Dame, especially as they relate to creature comforts. But Dawkins keeps after them with the old-time religion. "The thing that this corps has got to do for the foot-ball team is take off their shirts together." In the face of this logic, more in the crowd strip, clutching their biceps and jumping about to stir up circulation.

At last, when only a few misfits remain clothed, Dawkins rears back with a zealot's patter. "One way, one corps, together, always!" he cries with a frightening fervor, ravishing the crowd with frenzy. If, on that balcony, it had not been just Pete Dawkins carrying on but Patton himself firing off his handguns, Sergeant York turkey-gobbling, U. S. Grant taking a Breathalyzer test, and Nathan Hale being executed half a dozen times, the audience could not have responded more wildly.

In bedlam, the cadets pile onto each other's frozen shoulders, waving their undershirts and shouting, "Go Rabble!" There is so much shirt waving that, in the spotlight beam, lint particles fall like a heavy snowstorm. The cadets settle down to listen, chattering and slapping at their goose pimples, as Dawkins assures them how special they are and how vital their cheers will be in determining the outcome of the game.

A few days later a visitor made the idle comment to an Army lineman named Jay Kimmitt that the rally had been "quite a scene." Kimmitt, otherwise a most cordial young man, suddenly became testy and on edge. "I wouldn't call it a scene, sir," he snapped. And, well, this much we do know: Army beat hell out of Rutgers.

MacArthur was talking of games and wars when he expressed this homily, adapted from Wellington. It is displayed in a prominent place in the gym, as if to prove that sports have a solid vocational tie-in with battles and are thus deserving of the taxpayers' largesse: "Upon the fields of friendly strife are sown the seeds that, upon other fields, on other days, will bear the fruits of victory."

Dawkins may have been a better soldier in Vietnam for having played football. Bill Carpenter may have had the courage to call napalm down near himself because he had learned, as the Lonely End, how to stand out there naked and vulnerable and still make the right moves and judgments. Maybe these things do count. Don Holleder, another West Point All-America of that period, was killed in Vietnam, and someone once said that Holleder and a couple of journalists were the only *names* ever to be killed in that war.

Imagine that: *names.* This is not a MacArthur time anymore, certainly not so much as it is a McLuhan time. Dawkins's roommate used to tell him: "You're the figment of a sportswriter's imagination," and Dawkins, laughing, reveals that the press "homogenized me." No matter, really: He is close enough to being what he has been portrayed as. Besides, it is not significant in his case whether or not he learned to react or think fast when midway between the sideline stripes. What is important is that Dawkins was ordained a celebrity for his part in the friendly strife.

One military expert blithely writes that Dawkins is "the most highly regarded young officer in the Army, the surest bet there is for chief of staff in the 1980s," and surely Dawkins would have reached this estate had he never played a down of football. But he profits that he did, and when he did — and not just like some other Whizzer White or Jack Kemp or Vinegar Bend Mizell. Sporting successes certainly helped those men demonstrably because they gained exposure in the stadiums: but exposure is just the stuff of TV spots these days.

Dawkins is defined in quite different terms. As the Army has fallen to its low ebb, it has come to mean a great deal to many people that Pete Dawkins ran wild as the leaves changed above Michie Stadium that autumn of 1958 — and that he is still there on the team. At the age of 33, damned if he isn't a symbol.

A colonel's wife, sitting across the crowded living room from Dawkins, was on the defense about the Army for no good reason, except perhaps that she has become accustomed to that stance. "Only the bad, that's all you ever hear," she exclaimed. "Is that fair?" She suddenly thrust out her hand and pointed toward Dawkins.

"Why do people think he stays in after all that has happened? He could do anything on the outside. Anything. Doesn't that mean something that Pete Dawkins stays in the Army? They all remember him.

"Good God, at least they still remember Pete Dawkins, don't they?"

*   *   *

For another dozen years after I wrote this piece, Pete Dawkins stayed on track to become chief of staff. He was the first to rise to lieutenant colonel, the first to colonel, the first to brigadier, the first to major general. Then, abruptly, in 1983, he announced his retirement from the Army, refusing to give any reasons, just saying that if he wanted to do anything else with the rest of his life, he would have to move on at this point.

After considering many spectacular civilian offers, he accepted one on Wall Street. He and Judi reside in a cooperative just off Park Avenue, and Pete is regularly mentioned as a possible Republican candidate for high New York State office.

The Tacky Tour

1975

THE rented car with the Monkey Jungle bumper sticker banked off the expressway onto Route 1, south-southeast out of Miami, heading on a course charted directly for the Serpentarium. The car was never seen again. The last contact placed it somewhere near the Orchid Jungle checkpoint. And then, nothing. "It is just like it was swallowed up by exhaust fumes, vanished into fat air," said one tourist official. Yet another victim of (ta-daaa) the Tacky Triangle!!!

Well, as Wink Martindale used to say as he closed his inspirational record *Deck of Cards,* "I know, because that soldier was me." I know, because that rented car was mine. In the days that followed, from one tip of the Tacky Triangle to the others, my family and I visited:

The Serpentarium, Monkey Jungle, Parrot Jungle, the Coral Castle, Tiger's Air Boat Rides, Miccosukee Indian Village, the Waltzing Waters Aquarama, the Thomas Edison Winter Home, the Shell Factory, the National Police Hall of Fame, the good ship *Bounty,* Potter's Wax Museum, various glassblowers, Spook Hill, Cypress Gardens, the River Ranch rodeo, the Tower of Peace, the Citrus Tower, the Singing Tower, the Tupperware Museum of Dishes, the Museum of Sunken Treasure, the Fountain of Youth, Ripley's Believe It Or Not Museum, the Castillo de San Marcos, the Old Jail, the Oldest School House, the Museum of Toys, and the Tragedy in U.S. History Museum.

I know, I know. You're saying, Why would anyone ever do a thing like that? And my answer to you, from the heart, is: Taste. Discernment.

The decisions were not made lightly, understand. When we took the trip last winter, we could have seen: the Orchid Jungle, Jungle Larry's African Safari, Lion Country Safari, Sarasota Jungle Gardens, the Gardens of Light, St. Petersburg Zoological Gardens, Busch Gardens, Masterpiece Gardens, Sunken Gardens, Everglades Wonder Gardens, and Weeki Wachee Springs. Also: Ringling Museum, Circus World Showcase, Circus Hall of Fame, Marco Polo Park, Cars of Yesterday, Six Gun Territory, Tombstone Territory, Parrots Paradise, Flipper's Playground, Alligator Farm, Florida Reptile Land, Marineland, Treasureland, Fairyland, Sea World, Ocean World, Pirate's World, and Jacksonville of the World Football League.

This is the first honest travel story ever written. It is about the real places that real people really go to. Most travel stories are not at all about where people travel to, but only about where travel writers can cadge the best trips to. Hence, the emphasis on the Taj Mahal, Rome, Italy, the Serengeti, and whatnot, while genuine places like the Tacky Triangle go begging for exposure. I hope this is just the beginning, one small step for touristkind. In fact, what this country needs, travelwise, is its own version of the Michelin Guide.

The Michelin Guide is, of course, put out in France, where food is the thing. Chefs over there drown themselves in A-1 Sauce if they drop in the Michelin ratings. Well, we are not a strong food country, unless you want to count the Colonel and his sort, but we have our own hang-up. We devour tourist attractions. Wherever we are going, we say, "What have they got there?" If St. Augustine's City of God was located, say, in the middle of Iowa, people would not go there unless there were mechanized angels at God's Gardens or God's Paradise or Godland or what-have-you. Unless something is a specific, authentic, by-admission-only Attraction, it does not exist for us.

Although this is the way of life for American tourism, we have no unbiased, comprehensive Michelin Guide–like authority to instruct us. We must depend on unsightly self-interest brochures to advise us which are the best tacky things to see and revel in.

Now understand, when I say tacky, that is not necessarily disparaging. There is tacky and there is *tacky*. If you go to an American tourist spot, you expect it to be tacky. What is the point of being a tourist attraction if you can't be tacky? You might as well get the environmentalists all involved and settle on just being a scenic overlook, right? The Pennsylvania Dutch country was once merely quaint. But recently it has been tackyized to the point of plastic, and I'm sure you'll find it an infinitely finer place to visit than before.

So you see, I'm not putting down Florida. On the contrary. Florida is not alone in tacky endeavors, merely exemplary. A great deal can be said for many parts of California. The strip between Dallas and Fort Worth is a real comer, too. And New Jersey cannot be sneezed at. The finest tacky symbol in America (this is your traditional tacky now, not your *nouveau* tacky) is the sea horse, and these positively abound at establishments along the Jersey shore. In this respect, New Jersey far surpasses Florida, which relies on alligators and dolphins. But town in and town out, no other place can boast the Attractions that the Sunshine State does.

While we are on the subject of alligators and dolphins, if tourist Attractions were like the stock market, my advice to Florida would be to get out of alligators and dolphins. Sell. There is a glut. Dolphins perform in Maine malls now, as well as in movies and on television. And if they're so darn smart, why do they always perform the exact same act? Midway through the last dolphin show we saw, my daughter Alexandra said, "Oh, here comes the hoop bit." I realized then it was time to knock off dolphins.

Alligators, even alligators wrestling Seminole Indians, are another old-hat theatrical property. We're jaded. Besides, the scare value of alligators has diminished with the animal goings-on on television. There must be about fifty-three wildlife animal shows on TV each week. Kids may see 50,000 people murdered on television by the time they are old enough to read, but surely they see even more beasts being done in. The law of the jungle prevails every night at 7:30 in our house. What is an alligator wrestling a Seminole Indian, when in the preceding days kids have seen leopards ripping the guts out of wildebeests, polar bears gobbling up fish, snakes and birds eating one another, tarantulas doing their mischief?

I have always been keen on monkeys, but these little primates are also in for hard times. We started our Tacky Tour in Miami, so one of the first attractions we visited was the Monkey Jungle, whose yellow bumper stickers adorn most rented automobiles in Florida. (If *you* put a bumper sticker on your car, you are tacky. If you park at an Attraction and come back and find that someone else has put a bumper sticker on your car without your permission, that's not tacky; that's common.)

Everything considered, the Monkey Jungle is a pretty nice Attraction. It has a grand collection of tacky souvenirs and postcards. Alas, it does not offer for sale the tackiest thing in the world — a shiny black throw pillow inscribed with a Day-Glo map. Despite the classic tackyism of pillow-maps, they are, increasingly, an endangered species; on the Tacky Tour, I found them only in the gift shoppe of the *Bounty*. The Michelin Guide uses stars to rank establishments. When I bring out my tacky guide, I am going to award little pillow-maps for quality. Four pillow-maps is supreme. I give the Monkey Jungle two pillow-maps.

But, as I was saying, monkeys are up against it now. My kids are 6 and 3, my wife and I somewhat older. We liked the monkeys much more than the kids did. They didn't even work up much enthusiasm for Peanut, who wore a Dolphin helmet and rode a bicycle. A monkey on a bicycle? What kind of big deal is this? On television the children have seen monkeys torn limb from limb by lions; they've seen monkeys cross the entire African veldt in a half-hour, minus the dog-food commercials; they've seen monkeys jump across raging rivers, outwit warthogs and eagles; they've seen monkeys copulate at a quarter to eight in the privacy of the family room. So why get excited about a monkey riding a bicycle? The man said, "Please applaud for Peanut, folks, it's the only reward he receives," which made me feel sad, because that is almost exactly what MCs used to say about old, drooping strippers.

You can see an animal Attraction every day wherever you are in the Tacky Triangle, but after the Monkey Jungle we laid off the animals. There is no sense going to Florida and seeing pale facsimiles of TV shows.

Almost as big as animals in the Tacky Triangle are wax museums and glassblowing. You are familiar with wax museums, which go back at least as far as the heyday of Vincent Price. We visited the one in St. Pete, where, as in all wax museums, the wax people looked almost like real people and also almost like wax. If I ever open a wax museum, I am going to advertise: "Wax-like!"

Glassblowing seems to hypnotize people in Florida, which leads me to think that instead of putting on just another animal show, a TV network should schedule glassblowing at 7:30. There is a great demand for it.

Also in ascendancy in the Tacky Triangle are towers and museums (other than wax). The Tower of Peace in Lake Placid and the Citrus Tower in Clermont are tall and thin as towers should be, and sure enough, as advertised, you can see a far piece from these structures. That's about it with towers. The Tower of Peace gives away orange juice, and at the Citrus Tower you can watch glassblowing for free. Neither has a revolving restaurant on top, which is the prime selling point of towers these days. Worse, the Singing Tower in Lake Wales is just a carillon, and you can't even climb to the top, never mind eat a meal there. My son Chris was flabbergasted. "You mean you just look at it?" he asked, stupefied.

A minister we drank bourbon with in Jacksonville informed us, with disgust, that the clergy in St. Augustine had decided that a good way to advance the Word would be to construct a majestic Tower of Love. It is in the planning stages. The view of this particular cleric was that when it becomes necessary to build towers to promulgate love and Christianity, both institutions are in trouble. Towers without revolving restaurants are lackluster Attractions, and I would be hard pressed to give any of them more than a single pillow-map.

I can, however, proudly award three pillow-maps to Coral Castle, located twenty-five miles south of Miami. The children will have no interest whatsoever in Coral Castle, as mine didn't, and my wife and I found it boring and unappetizing and rather ugly. But you should not miss anything so tacky as Coral Castle.

It was built by a nutty fellow with a long last name — the guides refer to him as Ed, as if he had just gone over to Burger Chef and would be right back. Ed has been dead lo these many years, which is not surprising, since he constructed the whole dreadful place himself, toting huge rocks around. Possibly, Ed believed he was a forklift. He built a coral sundial and a large table shaped like Florida, a nine-ton swinging gate, a Feast of Love Table and, as the brochures say, "other thrilling wonders."

The icky part of the saga is that Ed built this monstrosity in honor of a lady back in Latvia who had jilted him. It is easy to see why she did: Ed was nutty as a fruitcake. Would you want your sister to marry a forklift?

The best part of the story is that as heartbroken as Ed was, as distressed, as pained, as upset, as distraught, he was clever enough to construct his secret love palace right there on Highway 1. Ed was crazy like a fox. Just think how much better Gettysburg would be doing now if Lee and Meade had been smart enough to have fought right off Exit 9 of the New Jersey Turnpike.

Another recommendation for Coral Castle is its brochures, which are done in one color, a sort of dirty pink, and drenched in hyperbole: "The Coral Castle of Florida encompasses all the beauty, mystery and romance associated with the ancient wonders of the world. . . . Considered to be the greatest creative achievement by one individual in the history of America." Wow! That is brochure writing of the first water. Most brochures in the Tacky Triangle are slick, sterile items, and all of them hedge their bet by trading off and mentioning a bunch of other Attractions. Very dreary and very corporate.

(There isn't a four-pillow-map brochure in the whole Tacky Triangle. For that you have to go to South Carolina, where there is a motel named South of the Border — so called because it is just below the North Carolina line. South of the Border, which calls itself, fondly, SOB, has forgotten more about tacky than most establishments will ever know. The SOB brochure is a classic in its field. It is written entirely in Mexican dialect, to wit, or rather, to witless: "Ees onlee wan South of The Border, amigos, where Pedro has put eet all together to make ze mos' exciting vacation stop between Maine and Florida! Ees leetle Mexico on 100 acres weeth 300 beautiful rooms, shops, 3 sweemeeng pools . . ." Stop eet queeck, stop eet!)

Museums have more room to move around in than do towers and monuments. Now that animals are passé, you are going to see more and more tacky museums, halls of fame, and walls of fame. Surely, that is how come we have the National Police Hall of Fame in North Port Charlotte: 1½ pillow-maps. Admission entitles visitors to a flag decal, membership in the Dick Tracy Crimestoppers Club, and the opportunity to inspect a haphazard collection of law enforcement paraphernalia. There is a guillotine, an electric chair ("used in many states for the execution of condemned prisoners"), and the very first handcuffs used in the territory of Alaska. Also prominently displayed is a license plate from the 1935 Shriners parade in Washington. No explanation is offered for its enshrinement, and I did not inquire for fear of being slapped in those Alaskan handcuffs and called "an alleged perpetrator." Finally, for no apparent reason except titillation, a significant part of the museum focuses on President Kennedy's assassination.

In this respect, the National Police Hall of Fame imitates most wax museums and my favorite-named exposition — the Tragedy in U.S. History Museum. Tragedy is located in St. Augustine and features, besides the obligatory J.F.K. assassination material, the Wreck of the Old 97, plus some World War II newspapers.

Being the oldest city in America, St. Augustine comes down heavily on the oldest this-and-that and on museums in general. It lacks only the Oldest Museum. Its most ballyhooed is Ripley's Believe It Or Not Museum, about which Chris said, "There's not much there I didn't believe." Half a pillow-map.

Northern Florida, like the southern part, is also thick with menageries, while in the middle, on both coasts, pirates are big. Tampa is top-heavy with pirates. I don't want to be unkind, but I was not impressed with the level of pirates in the Tacky Triangle. They seemed entirely too cutesy-poo, much like dolphins. From Tampa to the Museum of Sunken Treasure on Cape Canaveral, which is easy to locate as it is across the street from the City of Jerusalem Museum, the only pirates that unnerved my children were the mechanical ones at Disney World. That's a fine how-do-you-do.

You have noticed, no doubt, that I have not mentioned Disney World until now. Naturally, not wanting to be sacrilegious, we went to Disney World. But Disney World, for us, was like a busman's holiday. I wanted the family to see the Duck Follies at Masterpiece Gardens in Lake Wales, a town that also has a mosaic of da Vinci's *Last Supper,* boasting 300,000 pieces of 10,000 colors. Regrettably, the children were not primed this particular day for Duck Follies. So I said, "Listen, if you aren't good at the Duck Follies, I won't take you to Disney World." You find out very quickly that once kids have to go to Attractions they weary of them quickly. Another day, another dollar.

If I were going to open a tacky Attraction in Florida, it would be a simulated motel. Kids like tacky motels near the tacky Attractions more than the Attractions themselves. Go to any motel near Disney World and after a full day of Fantasyland, Frontierland, Magic Castle, the works, you will find kids riding up and down on elevators, pushing buttons, messing around with the ice machines, jumping on beds, locking one another out, throwing things in the pool, and so forth. Having a whale of a time. This is because at Disney World everybody says you are here to have a good time, but at the motel everybody says you are here to behave. So there is the challenge. Instead of another museum or tower, gardens or hall of fame, I am going to build a simulated motel. Around it I will build real motels — Holiday Inn, Ramada, Howard Johnson's, Best Western, and so forth. And the whole complex will be called Motelworld.

Another thing the Tacky Triangle is lacking these days is gift shoppes. At a number of places in the state, such-and-such is touted as the largest gift shoppe in the world (likewise, many places advertised the largest alligator farm in the world), but the selections on display are not up to the tackiness of years past. The postcard situation is outrageous. The only postcard in the whole state that I can, in good conscience, award even two pillow-maps to is from the Fountain of Youth; it is of 1955 vintage and shows a lady toasting you with a tiny paper cup. I give the Fountain of Youth itself a high rating — 2½ pillow-maps. The Fountain, which has a dubious affiliation with Señor Ponce de Leon, is not a fountain but a well. Visitors sip from those tiny paper cups reminiscent of Amtrak. There is also an Indian burial ground, although we were advised that it has lacked buried Indians ever since one particularly testy hurricane.

Finally, there is the Historical Space Globe, which lights up, showing the voyages of exploration. I went out of my mind over this. Here comes Columbus on the heavy line, Vasco da Gama on the broken line, Sir Francis Drake dots and dashes. All lit up on the huge globe. One thing I never understood about learning American history is why half of everything you're taught before Pearl Harbor concerns the idiotic explorers, bumping around, stumbling into things, especially when we know that they were only looking for the Northwest Passage. It would make more sense to have school kids in America come down and see the Historical Space Globe for a few minutes, get the explorers out of their system, and then spend their time studying people who actually did things, who didn't just chance upon things.

But back to the gift shoppes. This may be damning with faint praise since the species is in an awful slump (can we ever top Stuckey's old advertisement of pecans and free water; free *water*?), but the top gift shoppe in the Tacky Triangle must be the Shell Factory. It is located on U.S. 41, alias the Tamiami Trail.

The Tamiami Trail is a bonanza. It offers linear archeology. Archeologists traditionally dig down, discerning the age of something by the level at which it lies. On the Tamiami Trail and similar classic Florida boulevards, a traveler can pinpoint age by other methods. A shopping center featuring a pancake café is obviously quite new. In my family, we speak of "pancake modern."

Going back a bit, we come to mobile estates or planned communities, or signs that boast "Appearing Nitely in the Lounge." These edifices date from the early to mid-1960s. And then the Thunderbirds, another distinct archeological layer. Throughout the Tacky Triangle, one finds hundreds of establishments named Thunderbird, most of which, it is my understanding, were built and named in the same week of March 1957. I would never dare enter an establishment named Thunderbird because I fear that Connie Francis surrounded by five boys in boat-neck shirts would not be there.

The Shell Factory is of earlier vintage, done in Early Airplane Hangar from the pre–*I Love Lucy* era of American tackyism. But let us not tarry. I am, as you can see, saving the best for last: three pillow-maps — no, make that 3½ — for the Waltzing Waters of Cape Coral.

Here you get not only a dolphin show, but also Aqua Follies, which is waterskiing in sort of a big tub, and at last, the pièce de résistance, that "fairyland of sights and sounds," the Waltzing Waters themselves. They are fountains of colored water that go up and down in time to show tunes and love songs. The night we were there one of the songs that the waters waltzed to was "More," which made it perfect. "More," as you know, is the national anthem of Muzak and piano bars. To witness water dancing to "More" strikes me as the epitome of tourism.

As good as the Waltzing Waters are, for total effect nothing matches Cypress Gardens. People rave at what Disney wrought, and properly so, but the mistake is to suggest that his two places are American. Not so, not at all. They are mechanical and nonsectarian, belonging to the world at large. The uncomfortable feeling I get at Disneyland or Disney World is that people are not acting like themselves. They are acting like the stylized puppet people in Small World.

Cypress Gardens, though, is American to the core. If you could show a foreigner only one of each thing in America — one natural splendor, one historical site, one downtown, one national park — Cypress Gardens is what I would choose as the one American amusement, over a baseball game or a football game, over a state fair, over Disney World.

Cypress Gardens is incredibly original, yet basic and unchanging, like the Harlem Globetrotters or Lawrence Welk. That is why it works. One feels a certain purity at Cypress Gardens. At places like the Disneys or Williamsburg, as much as you may enjoy them, there is a natural tendency to marvel at *how it was done.* That is a distracting kind of curiosity, like kissing with your eyes open, which takes away from the pleasure. There is no such problem at Cypress Gardens. It is just gardens and waterskiing. Disney World requires something new — a haunted house, Space Mountain — at each turn of the season. Something new at Cypress Gardens would constitute tampering.

You come to it down narrow country roads, wandering past orange groves, and all of a sudden it looms, pristine and pastoral, the fairyland America. On the hotel marquee at the entrance, the message reads "Music of the Forties." Of course. It hits me. People are always saying that the big bands will be back. Maybe yes, maybe no, but it never occurred to me that the big bands had not disappeared, that all this time they have been waiting to come back from somewhere. Of course. All this time the big bands have been *at* Cypress Gardens.

Parking is efficient and, on admission, your hand is stamped, just like at the racetrack. The shopping promenade is classic: a Florida fruit shop, caricatures, pastel portraits, signs to be made, monograms to go on anything, postcards. Glassblowing. There is a throne where you can pose for pictures so you can look like a king and a queen.

For the show, the stands with cantilevered roofs fill quickly, and people often sit on the ground, on borrowed cushions. Just before the show begins, music is played, tunes like "No Business Like Show Business," "More," and "Everything's Coming Up Roses." Soon the Aquamaids will be here.

But first. The announcer achieves new heights of tackiness by reading the dismal reports of freezing weather in cities up north. The places with the most inclement weather get the best responses. I only wish I had been at Cypress Gardens on the day there had been a cattle-killing blizzard somewhere; I'm sure that would have brought the house down.

But Cypress has a warm spot in its heart for its frozen northern neighbors. Every day, the PA salutes a different state. This particular day Michigan was honored. For those in the crowd who might not be too sure, Michigan was identified as "the home of the NBA Pistons, the baseball Tigers, and the automobile industry." In that order. You're only as good as your last assembly line, baby. The people cheered for frozen Michigan.

When the time came for the Aquamaids to climb on the boy skiers' shoulders, to make the famous pyramid and zip around, carrying flags, the announcer said that this was still the favorite at Cypress. More postcards are sold of the pyramid than of any other scene.

People say to me, "Have you seen the Taj Mahal, have you seen the Eiffel Tower, Westminster Abbey?" I say to them, "Have you seen the Aquamaids' pyramid at Cypress Gardens?" I have, and I give it four pillow-maps.

On the way back to the motel we saw Spook Hill and the Singing Tower.

Aloha

1977

EXCUSE me, could you tell me whether you pronounce the fiftieth state Ha-wah-ee or Ha-vah-ee?

Certainly. Ha-vah-ee.

Thank you.

You're velcome.

I have always thought of Hawaii that way — in flashes, a one-liner. Say Hawaii to anyone and sudden brief images wash over him: undulating grass skirts, Waikiki, Haleloke doing the hula on *Arthur Godfrey,* Arthur Godfrey strumming the ukulele, Duke Kawhats-hisname swimming, *From Here to Eternity,* surfing, leis, and Sugar-loaf — which is actually in Rio de Janeiro, but which I have always confused with Diamond Head, which looms over Honolulu. Never mind; you get the picture. Aloha.

It is not surprising that Hawaii is so popular. At a time when theme parks are all the rage, Hawaii is the biggest theme park in the world. Theme parks are amusement parks with an identifying gimmick. To wit, Disney World, or Opryland in Nashville, which celebrates country music. Nashville itself used to perform this function, but now Opryland has been built to pull it off, with an entrance fee. Ultimately, there will be the ultimate theme park, Worldland: the African veldt will be over here, and hard by it, sepa-rated by a replica of the Berlin Wall, will be the Best of Westminster Abbey. Worldland will be ideal for Americans because no one will have to worry about going anywhere to see the world, or about un-English tongues, un-American currency, and "the water."

In the meantime, Hawaii is the best we have in theme parks. Aloha.

Hawaii, you see, is perfect. *Officially* it is every bit as American as Evansville, Indiana, or Greater San Jose — those little beige people can vote and get into Diners Club, just like you and me. But it doesn't *seem* American. Hey, present company excepted, not *really*. The people are different sizes and colors and they wear funny clothes. There's a toy language and live volcanoes and special music being played all the time. I took my first trip to Hawaii well before Christmas, but I always felt it was Christmas because Hawaiian music is played constantly, like Christmas carols in season. Aloha.

It is all indoctrination, which we undergo at the age of channelization, which is when we learn to recognize 1 through 13. By the time anyone actually arrives at Hawaii, the place is already constructed in the mind. It is propaganda. "Hey, we been working at this for fifty years," says the Hawaiian Visitors Bureau man, with a devilish smile. That which has lain in the mind for years is brought to a fever pitch by the airlines even before you arrive. Departure lounges, thousands of miles away, are done up in Hawaiian decor. The stewardesses wear Hawaiian muumuus, the stewards aloha shirts. There are Hawaiian place mats, Hawaiian pineapples, something dreadful named Aloha Punch. There is, of course, Hawaiian music. There are macadamia nuts. On United, you are given seven, in the same sort of triangular packet that usually contains a "nondairy creamer," whatever, pray God, that may be. I love macadamia nuts, but just for the record, do not travel to Hawaii under the impression you can load up on them there cheaply. If anything, macadamia nuts cost even more in Hawaii. Aloha.

Even on the plane they start saying aloha. The only thing in Hawaii that comes cheap is aloha. If you have any sensitivity, you will come to shudder at those three little syllables. But it is a magic word, the key to the kingdom, the ticket to all the rides in the theme park, to Waikiki and luaus and Don Ho, to Mai Tais, the hula, and Sugarloaf. In the old days aloha had help. It had the leis, which everybody got right after the boat docked, and you threw coins in the water for the "natives" to pretend to retrieve. But now, the boats are gone, the jumbo jets disgorge tourists at a dizzying rate, and the only ones who rate leis are members of tourist groups who are prepaid. Aloha.

* * *

My first impression of Hawaii — and the purpose of my visit was to record first impressions — is that it surely must be as glorious a resort as there is in the world. According to the Visitors Bureau, which will very shortly possess such sophisticated data that it can tabulate tourists by zip code and by "what side of the street they live on," 89.9 percent of the tourist sample queried in 1975 said that Hawaii provided an above-average or superior vacation. In terms of climate, ambiance, activity, beauty, and so forth, Hawaii is simply very hard to beat. It is in the middle of nowhere, of course, but that is probably a saving grace, inasmuch as it keeps down the teenagers with their transistor radios, who overrun mainland vacation spots.

But it is the aloha connection that makes the islands so alluring for most Americans. Nothing else would account for the incredible popularity of certain awful institutions. The luau, for example. Many hotels feature weekly luaus, most of which are conducted as engagingly as a lube job down at the Sunoco. Before the roast pig is brought by (some hotels use the same show porker over and over, returning it to its residence in the freezer after displaying it), before the tedious historical hula show starts, the tourists are shepherded into line to have their pictures taken. The male visitors are photographed standing next to a picture-book hula beauty in artificial grass skirt, real bra, and lei. The women are placed next to a bare-chested Hawaiian male. The camera snaps, the next tourist moves into place. The pictures are up on the bulletin board the following day. Buy yours and take it back to the mainland as proof that you actually consorted with genuine hula natives. Aloha.

Surely, American tourists want desperately to believe that the islands are the racial paradise they are made out to be, that Hawaii, our last hope, has achieved the racial serenity the mainland never has. It has always seemed to me that even the worst American bigots would prefer not to be what they are. Thus, it is easy for the island flacks to perpetuate the myth that Hawaii is still destined to produce "the golden man," to be the place where everyone has the same perfect hue and heart. In fact, the melting pot simmers. Racial resentments have not affected tourists the way they have, say, in the Caribbean, but out of sight of visitors, relations are uneasy and often raw. The Japanese (known slightingly as Buddha-heads), who were first brought in as contract laborers in 1868 and have long since become the largest ethnic group, compete with mainland Caucasian Americans for control. The whites are called *haoles* (howlees), once a passive word meaning newcomer, but now a pejorative on the order of honky. The Filipinos (frips) are down at the bottom with the few remaining full-blooded Hawaiians (pineapples) and with the Portuguese, who figure in the local version of Polish jokes. But the theme park runs smoothly; the single most favorable response the Visitors Bureau gets is that the locals are "warm and friendly," and I would certainly subscribe to that.

I cannot help but wonder, though, if it is a put-on, if the Hawaiian-Americans who service the tourist-Americans don't view us as enviously and suspiciously as Jamaicans and Mexicans and Virgin Islanders do. That feeling is heightened away from the glitter of Waikiki, and especially in the other islands, where the country does not appear at all like the United States. It is poor and it seems very Caribbean: corrugated tin roofs on old houses that often sit on stilts; skinny dogs pawing around; dirt roads and dirty children; faded Coca-Cola signs. There are many banana trees, too. Banana trees always seem to signal poverty. They are squat and off-green, and while they are cousins, more or less, of palm trees, the one makes us think of style and opulence, the leisure of the tropics, while the other recalls the hot squalor and ignorance of those latitudes. There is no Banana Beach, no Banana Springs for the beautiful people. Get away from Waikiki and all the magnificent resorts on all the islands, and there are a lot of banana trees in Hawaii. Aloha.

And then, as in any resort, where separating wayfarers from their cash is the perennial pursuit, there is an inordinate concern about money in the islands. Because it costs a great deal to ship anything to Hawaii, prices are high, and the inhabitants, isolated on their Pacific Eden, resent this presumed inequity. Now the tourist boom has escalated the price of things already there, the very earth. Can the Hawaiians afford Hawaii? On a guided bus tour I took all around Oahu (or Alohaland, as it actually said in the bus destination window), the driver kept telling us the prices of houses, the rents of apartments we passed. He was obsessed by real estate. "Eighty thousand, and only three bedrooms," he said, shaking his head. "Five hundred and seventy-five dollars, including utilities," he revealed over the microphone. He pointed out shopping centers as if they were unique indigenous attractions. Coming back into Honolulu, he said, "On my right is where the *Utah* went down with fifty-four men, and on my left, the new Sears warehouse." Periodically, he would cry out, "Aloha," and everybody would obediently chant "Aloha" back at him.

Japanese vacationers take their own tours, and while American and Japanese tourists never seem to have to deal with each other except when their buses pull up to the same scenic overlook, the Orientals definitely add foreign luster to the place. They are also very business-like, even about their holidays. Although it takes several hours longer to fly to Honolulu from Tokyo than from California, the average Japanese stays only five days, while the average American stays ten (and Canadian fifteen). Of the five days, the Japanese often turn one over to a pilgrimage to the site of the sinking of the *Arizona,* where they listen uncomfortably to the toll of the dead and injured, and shift from foot to foot behind their Nikons. American tourists tend to check about for concession stands, so they can ship pineapples home.

But the Americans seem very aware of the Japanese. Hawaii is the last outpost of the United States, the extension of the West and the Sunbelt alike. All these years it has been a dream, a Shangri-la, and now we have met somebody else coming round the other way. A lot of U.S. tourists don't quite know what to make of this.

An elderly gentleman from suburban Buffalo struck up a conversation with me on the bus tour because he wanted to buy the right aloha postcards, and he couldn't remember which island we were on. This seemed to be a constant problem on my bus. I told him it was still "Aloha from Oahu," and then I asked him what he thought of his first visit to Hawaii. "Well," he said, "it's a lot like Florida, weatherwise. It's a lot like Tucson, too. Tucson in Arizona. We went there last year. Hawaii's a lot like Arizona, only it's got all your special elements, your luaus, your hula. And, of course, it's also got all these Japs around."

In keeping with this spirit, I pointed out how your Arizona likewise had Indians and Mexicans, and your Florida had Cubans. He shook his head at my ignorance. "No, no, no," he said. "I mean the Japs are around, in hotels and on buses, just like us Americans."

While Hawaii works so well because it promulgates its theme park "elements" so well, its diverse beauty is surpassing. "The loveliest fleet of islands that lies anchored in any ocean," wrote Mark Twain (who is referred to in Hawaii as "our first copywriter"); Hawaii is so lovely that it is beautiful even when it is not. Sugarloaf, for example, is really quite brown and scruffy up close, barely a large knoll, and a romantic is terribly hurt at this revelation, like when you at last personally encounter a movie star and discover she is merely photogenic, only the sum of her best angles. Sugarloaf is like that: perfectly positioned and nothing else. How much did NBC pay to create its stylish new N? How much is that ship worth to Cutty Sark? Other theme parks have to hire all sorts of specialists to get a symbol, but Hawaii was given the perfect one — looming, backgrounding.

One can almost see God after He was finished making the Hawaiian Islands. They are volcanic, and an eon or two newer than typical American mainland. God was more practiced at making land by the time He put together Hawaii. And He was admiring His handiwork with some angels, and He asked for opinions, and the head marketing angel said, "I like it. It plays. But islands are islands. It needs a logo." So God gave Hawaii Sugarloaf.

The logo aside, everything else is so vivid. The colors come in great separate chunks: green land, blue water, white surf, black rocks. There is not much blending; it is not a peaceful beauty but a striking one. And it is disconcerting to think how much of it came from somewhere else: the pineapples from Jamaica, the macadamias from Australia, the hula from Polynesia, the leis from India, the ukuleles from Portugal, the people from all sorts of distant islands — even the sand on Waikiki is alleged to have been imported a half century ago from Manhattan Beach, California.

The Hawaiians never had a written language. The missionaries put letters to the sounds they heard and found out they needed only twelve letters, which is why Hawaiian sounds like baby talk. The whalers brought prosperity, but it took the Spanish-American War to illustrate conclusively how strategic the islands were. By the latter part of the nineteenth century, the native rulers were an anachronism. The last king, Kalakaua, is said to have once beaten three aces in a poker game by uncovering three kings and pointing to himself as the fourth. A man named Dole thought pineapple might work out. Others built a couple of Victorian hotels on the strip of beach in Honolulu that the island royalty had always preferred.

It used to take great investments in time and money to holiday in Hawaii. The rich came for the whole summer; as recently as 1933, barely 10,000 tourists visited the islands during an entire year. But so well had Hawaii marketed its exotic themes that people lusted after the place, and with each succeeding mode of more advanced transportation, the tourist numbers fairly leaped: first with the Pan Am Clippers, then the four-engines, the jets, the wide-bodies. Visitors topped the 100,000 mark in 1955 and went past a million in 1967; now the figure has reached three million a year, which translates into well over $1 billion. So anxious are people to see Hawaii — just to be there — that they will spend way beyond their budgets in plane fare and the $50-a-day hotel tariff, and then eat all their meals at McDonald's.

Almost all first-time visitors deplane at Waikiki, stay for a few days, and then move on to one or more of the outer islands — or the "neighbor" islands, as they are known now, so their feelings won't be hurt. Waikiki is only seven-tenths of a square mile and is saturated with 23,000 hotel rooms, up eightfold in barely twenty years. Drains and sewage, never mind muggings and parking, are becoming problems, so it is to everyone's benefit to shuffle tourists on to Maui, Kauai, and the title island, Hawaii, which is always referred to as the Big Island. Of these, Maui is now the hot one — "where Honolulu was twenty-five years ago" — and it will not suffer itself to be lumped with the rest of the neighbors as "the other Hawaii" in advertising.

I chose the Big Island; and, surely, nowhere else, in such a relatively small space, could so much that is representative of this earth be jammed. On mountains, still growing, that now crest at close to 14,000 feet, there is skiing much of the winter; below, there are beaches of black sand. There is Kilauea with its great moonscape crater that smokes and simmers and spatters, where Pele, the fire goddess, resides, and Mauna Loa, the volcano, always grumbling, ever ready to show us a sneak preview of hell (eruption information may be dialed twenty-four hours a day). The road from this charred furnaceland winds into displaced pastoral highlands that lack all tropical touches, where cattle and horses graze on large ranches, where the citizens wear cowboy clothes and tote firearms. There is no blue Hawaii here. And yet, just minutes from this rolling piedmont, there is stark desert, and, minutes away from that, the harsh rocky coast where fancy hotels must patiently wait more millennia for the lava flows to provide them with beaches.

Such wondrous diversity seems impossible. By the lewd standards of our "adult" society — isn't it revealing that adult is now a synonym for dirty? — Waikiki is a very sensuous place. Who could ever forget that X-rated film classic *Hawaiian Thigh*? For anyone who loves this earth we live on, who marvels at its voluptuous body, a visit to the Big Island is like a torrid, lustful weekend affair. Waikiki is merely a party, maybe a party girl. The Big Island is a heavy physical relationship.

I stayed on the Kona coast a cove or two away from where Captain Cook met his grisly fate. A small statue, at a point inaccessible by land, commemorates his death. He was the first of his race to reach Hawaii, stumbling upon it on January 18, 1778, when Washington lay huddled at Valley Forge. The Hawaiians had never before seen large boats (the word *moku* still means ship and island alike), and they took the captain for a god, an impression he did little to dispel. It was more in disappointment than anger that the natives turned on him when at last it seemed rather certain that he was something less. Aloha.

Ah, how quaint those illiterate primitives! One day, at my hotel on Waikiki, *Hawaii Five-O,* the TV show, filmed a segment around the pool. The tourists didn't act any less deferentially in the presence of the show's star, Jack Lord, than the natives could have responded to Captain Cook. One woman, her bikini in nearly as much disarray as her mind, fairly ran into the ice-cream shop, screaming, "And Dane Clark is guesting! Dane Clark is guesting!"

Hawaii is a place where most people are active. One of the reasons why Waikiki Beach never seems to be as crowded as you would expect is that the average tourist in Hawaii only spends an hour a day baking in the sun. Waikiki is an open beach, too. There is still access from the street; there are no uniformed guards to scream at you if you don't have the right hotel key. But the hotels employ people to take care of the beach. It is clean and white. Generally speaking, you can tell all you need to about a society from how it treats animals and beaches.

Almost from sunup, Waikiki is active, exuding a good feel. Soon after dawn, the surfers take up their places far out, where the waves break (it almost seems the surfers have been assigned the display role for the day, not unlike Sugarloaf, which surely must be put away at night, like the flags). Joggers splash along on the hard, wet sand, moving among fishermen, who still patiently ply the surf. There are only two strictures posted: "No Frisbee Playing Allowed" and, under a huge banyan tree just off the beach, "Warning/Beware

Bird Droppings." Otherwise you are on your own. The beachboys come out with rakes and begin to scrape the sand clean. Two aging gigolos take up a shady bench and scan the sports pages. One has his college ring on — a college ring on! — and wears tinted glasses and Adidas track shoes. The other, from the texture of his skin, appears to have once been trapped in a tannery. And as his pelt has been bronzed by the sun, so has it blonded his hair (his eyebrows are dark). He wears sandals and short-shorts. He is too old for short-shorts. There is no hair on his legs. The saddest of male creatures is the old beach type, hanging on past his time. This guy was probably a lifeguard or a surfer once; every Boat Day was a score. It was too easy, he never got over it, and now he is coming hard on 60, still wearing short-shorts but reduced to having to get up at dawn to check out the outfield talent that the young beach stars wouldn't look twice at.

A group of Japanese come out of a hotel onto the beach. The men are proper in coats and ties, the women prim in long skirts and stout high heels. Yes, of course they have cameras, and a couple of ladies even make a concession to the sand and remove their shoes. They all take pictures of each other on the beach, posed so Sugarloaf backgrounds. The two old gigolos and other Americans glance up idly. The Americans all wear loose-fitting, casual kimono-type clothes. The Japanese appear to have just stepped off Fifth Avenue.

The Japanese go back to the hotel for morning tea — or coffee, regular, and a Danish, I suppose. A catamaran lands. Pigeons with cherry-red eyes pick at the sand. The place is filling up. The gigolos put down the sports sections and contemplate a chubby middle-aged arrival, deftly evaluating her with the caustic code language of their trade. She has a T-shirt over her bikini; it says "Here Today, Gone to Maui." She takes it off, sits on her towel, and begins to put on her special Hawaiian tanning lotion. Hawaii has got everybody who comes to the theme park so buffaloed that visitors are cheerfully deluded into believing that somehow the sun that shines on the islands is different from the one that beams down elsewhere.

The sun is hot by now. On the principal Waikiki thoroughfare, Kalakaua Avenue, the puka-bead shops are already in full sway. Aloha postcards, aloha hats, scarves, decals, panties are beginning to move. If this were Dallas, there would be the same junk with "Cowboys" stamped on it. They probably sell a ton of Jayhawk panties in Lawrence, Kansas. The tourists are eating Eggs McMuffin or meeting the day's tour guides. Many are reflecting solemnly about how commercial Waikiki is. The most unfavorable comment that the Visitors Bureau receives is that Waikiki is too commercial.

This, of course, is our great modern affectation: that something is too commercial. It is supposed to prove how sensitive we are. I was at a party not long ago where a guy said he and his family were swearing off national parks (that's what he said: "swearing off") because they had become too commercial. Everybody nodded sorrowfully at this disgraceful condition and commended him on his noble sacrifice. Every pseudo-doomsayer provides the same woeful expertise. Sports have become too commercial. Christmas is too commercial. The elections are too commercial. Toys are too commercial. Doctors are too commercial. The Bicentennial was too commercial. What was the first thing Jimmy Carter said after he was elected? The inauguration was too commercial. So Waikiki is too commercial.

Well, yes, hey, life is commercial. Surprise. This is no longer the Fertile Crescent with everybody sitting around eating nature's own pomegranates. If something is good in 1977, it is going to be commercialized. In the old uncommercial days, you had to be discerning about many things now taken for granted. You had to make sure the food wasn't spoiled. You had to stock firewood and make educated guesses about birth control. The least we can demand of people nowadays is that they don't just rail at everything being commercial, which it is, but that they apply some old-fashioned discernment to the matter. Just because there is a whole lot of commercialism running around doesn't mean you have to indulge in all of it. It is my experience that precisely the people who put on the phony hair shirt and moan about things being too commercial are the ones who would expire from lack of pollutants, who would go berserk if they had to endure two days on vacation without scuba lessons at the pool and left-hand-turn lanes.

Of course Waikiki is too commercial. Of course most all resorts are. If they weren't, people wouldn't go to them. But the point is, Waikiki is not too commercial unless you let it be. I found it — the beach, the bustle, the tumult — to be very real, as genuine in its way as smoldering volcanoes and sultry rain forests. What is so patently false about Hawaii is all the pretentious rubbish pawned off as culture and tradition. If I was told once, I was told 100 times that there are now twenty-five McDonaldses on the islands. This was always said with a sense of doom, and so I never knew how to react properly to the news, because McDonald's neither frightens me nor heralds the end of civilization. The people I saw eating at McDonald's appeared infinitely more contented than those who` had forced themselves to attend a luau.

My advice is, if you are looking for the most real glimpse of Hawaii, go see Don Ho perform. The hula and the luau — all that stuff was culture once upon a time, but it is a straight-out fraud now. Don Ho is culture now. He is also commercial; also, I could not abide his act. It was boorish and overdone, and often puerile. But it is utterly fascinating, because when you get up to go, you recognize, as I did, that you have experienced what Hawaii truly is.

Don Ho (it is impossible to call him Ho) somehow bestrides the confluence of what Hawaii has become and what the tourists expect. He is the personification of the islands (something the mainland *haole* Jack Lord could never be), Chinese in name, but "chop suey" when all his strains are totaled up. It is not true, but a revealing rumor nonetheless, that he is paid $1 million a year by the Visitors Bureau not to defect to Vegas.

Many cities used to be instantly connected with an entertainment star, but most cities (or states) now are associated with sports people: Johnny Bench of Cincinnati, Bear Bryant of Alabama, and so on. Al Hirt in New Orleans might be one exception to this rule; Don Ho is certainly the other. And he has the place completely to himself. World Football and World Team Tennis are the only "big league" operations ever to try to make a go on the islands. Don Ho is the only superstar on the Aloha team.

He operates out of a supper club located in the heart of Waikiki next to Don Ho Lane. It is known as the Polynesian Palace, and for the twoshowsnitely the tourists are jammed in like cordwood. The people on tours, with prepaid tickets, get the best seats, the ones with tables. The minimum is two regular drinks or one "exotic" drink — a Mai Tai or a Chi Chi or a Tahitian Itch or a Surf Sunset, any of those sugary treats that come with pineapple slices and little parasols sticking out of them. Don Ho bellows "Suck 'em up" periodically throughout the show, and the *haoles* respond dutifully. If you order the exotic drink, you get to keep the special Don Ho glass.

Don Ho suddenly emerged as Mr. Hawaii several years ago, notably on account of his theme song, "Tiny Bubbles." He succeeds, I am sure, because while everyone else in Alohaland puts on a stylized little happy face, he scowls. After days of hearing alohas rained on you like call letters of a rock-'n'-roll station, there is something dear about a mean little man who refuses to smile, who, in fact, glowers and shouts "Suck 'em up, gran'ma." Don Ho also professes to despise "The Hawaiian Wedding Song," and between numbers he enriches the audience with crude jokes about honeymoons, bathrooms, and ethnics. The night I saw him, by far his own greatest amusement and that of the adoring crowd came from his considerable repertoire of gags about passing wind. That brought the house down. (Of course, to give the devil his due, Don Ho did restrain himself for 45 minutes — 44½ over the aloha average — before delivering a double entendre based on the word *lei.*)

Don Ho's constituency is older women, a singular honor that he shares with one other crooner, the rosy-cheeked Las Vegas staple, Wayne Newton. But whereas Newton is all confectionery, the consistency of cotton candy, Don Ho is lecherous and lewd, an exotic tough guy. Newton is the safe good son; Don Ho is the daring bad son.

When he growls, "Where are all my favorites, the gran'mas?" they hop up, the old gals, drop their canes and the scales from their eyes, and scurry up to the stage where they gladly wait in line as Don Ho plants a wet, open-mouthed kiss on each. For the most favored, he also pinches rear ends and speculates on the sexual activity of the aged. At one point he takes his shirt off and carries on that way for a time, and whenever he deigns to sing, the room turns instantly reverent. Don Ho does not miss a trick. Near the end, juxtaposed with his final dissertation on stomach gas, came a reverie about the glory of being an American. The final number, I want to tell you, was not "Tiny Bubbles" but "God Bless America."

It was a mighty happy bunch that poured out of the Polynesian Palace, clutching their special Don Ho glasses. Certainly, all the gran'mas had them and almost all of the couples in matching muumuus and aloha shirts. I suppose Wayne Newton makes women feel safe in such a hard, evil place as Vegas, and I suppose Don Ho provides the reverse function in Hawaii, supplying a little candor and edge to all the sugar goo. A little eruption now and again is not all bad. Eruptions made the place, after all. Suck 'em up. *Au revoir.*

Little Irvy,
the Only Twenty-Ton
Traveling Whale

1969

Charlotte goes first, driving the camper. She handles such an outsized vehicle well, but in the cities she usually forgets after a turn and leaves the blinker light on. Jerry, her husband, follows her in Old Blue, which is a whitewall, wide-nosed Kenworth with $6,000 worth of highly polished chrome, a 335 Cummins diesel engine, a four-by-four gearbox, a Jacobs brake, and forty-six dashboard dials and buttons.

Jerry has a special contoured driving seat for himself and snappy tuck-and-roll upholstery in the air-conditioned cab, although, of course, he never has to curl up in the sleeper behind the cab since he and Charlotte have a queen-sized bed in the camper and all the other comforts of a stationary home. Still, Little Irvy, lying on his I-beam cradle inside the Thermo King trailer in the back, appears even more comfortable.

The people wave in the passing cars, and Jerry pulls his horn in acknowledgment, although he is never quite sure whether they are greeting Little Irvy or Old Blue, since both are one of a kind. Little Irvy is the only, and the ugliest, traveling whale in the world. Old Blue is the most beautiful truck in the world: all shades of blue — powder and azure and deep royal — the prize of the interstates, a glorious galleon tossing along the swells of the highways. Just the thought of it all makes Jerry break into song sometimes, as he does now, shifting through some of his sixteen gears down toward the crest of a hill:

"Little Irvy, Little Irvy, colossal 'n' frozen, what a show,
Little Irvy, in Old Blue, they're always on the go."

Little Irvy weighs twenty tons, most of it blubber, the rest meat and oil, and he reclines at something more than thirty-eight feet long. He has been dead — or more euphemistically, refrigerated — for more than two years now, and more than half a million people have seen him, including at least 50,000 underprivileged children that Jerry has let in on the cuff. All the others are separated from 35 cents for the privilege.

Everybody the world over, it seems, has a fascination for whales, and people have been paying to see them exhibited at least since 1861, when P. T. Barnum himself brought two small dying white whales to his New York museum. It was left, however, to Jerry Malone, onetime used-car salesman of Visalia, California, to first manage to freeze a whole whale and put it on the road. By now, Little Irvy, who debuted at Fisherman's Wharf in 1967, has traveled about 25,000 miles of the United States and Canada, which is probably more than he ever managed without Old Blue in the Pacific Ocean. This thought pleases Jerry, for he has grown somewhat attached to Little Irvy, invariably referring to him as "my whale" and to the whole enterprise as "the whale business," as if it were a thriving national industry on the order of electronics or life insurance.

Certainly, he prefers not to dismiss Little Irvy as just another large meal ticket. "I've thought about my whale so much," Jerry says, "that most times it seems like he is part of me. I look at it this way: If Little Irvy wasn't here in my truck, going all over the country and becoming famous, he'd just be oil and dog meat by now. So I can't feel bad about him frozen. I just pat him and say, 'Hey, you ugly, smelly son of a gun, I love you.'"

Little Irvy is entitled to such a wealth of affection. To bring him in and refrigerate him cost $12,000. Old Blue is an $80,000 truck. The camper, incidentals, and the interest on the loan have made "framing" Little Irvy, as they say in the amusement world, a $125,000 proposition, but the American love of whales (and trucks) should pay that off in less than the four years Jerry originally figured. Then, as humorists tell him about 593 times a day, he will really have a whale of a deal.

The scheme is marred only by a few disgruntled patrons. "Many people," Barnum wrote, "have such a horror of being taken in, or such an elevated opinion of their own acuteness, that they believe everything to be a sham, and in this way are continually humbugging themselves." The modern examples of this thesis are upset when they discover that Little Irvy is not frozen alive. Presumably, these people are under no parallel delusion that the Bird's Eye Brussels sprouts they purchase at the supermarket may be thawed and replanted, but they pay their 35 cents on the premise that Little Irvy, though somewhat larger than a garden vegetable, will himself be brought back to a more active existence. "What, you mean that whale is dead?" they declare after careful examination. "I paid 35 cents to see a *dead* whale?"

Others are even more disturbed, since they altogether overlook billboard references to Little Irvy's glacial status and actually expect to find him, all twenty tons and thirty-eight feet, splashing about in the forty-foot trailer.

A few weeks ago in Portland, Oregon, a woman in pink plastic hair curlers asked if Little Irvy did any tricks. "Yeah, he does one trick and he does it real well," Jerry said. "He plays dead." Hardly had she left before a sedate, well-dressed older gentleman inquired: "Do they take him out and let him exercise in an aquarium every now and then?" Such sorts have periodically sicced societies for the prevention of cruelty to animals on Malone. Others have asked Charlotte in the ticket booth if peanuts could be obtained so that they might feed Little Irvy. Still others, extreme self-humbugs, have simply cursed her graphically for exhibiting a dead whale.

Charlotte is a pretty, 25-year-old redhead who met Jerry when she was working in a Visalia bank. This was a good place to meet, since Jerry's roller-coaster business career has made him at home in loan departments. Bright and friendly, she has learned to shrug off the vitriol. "It used to bother me," Charlotte says, "but then I've seen people get mad at *free* shows, so at last I just decided it wasn't us — it was them — and I forgot about it."

Jerry says: "People want to know, why don't you put 'Dead Whale' in big letters on the side of your truck, and I tell them I don't put 'Dead Whale' in big letters on the side of my truck for the same reason that banks don't put '12½% Interest' in big letters on their front windows."

Anyway, Jerry views Little Irvy as more of an adjunct to institutional education, and the 4½-minute recorded lecture that a visitor hears while inspecting Little Irvy details various habits, dimensions, and peccadilloes of whales. Such as, "He is not dangerous, but capable of swallowing a man over two hundred pounds." Jerry is disappointed to hear that the Smithsonian has no real whale on display, and he toys with the idea of offering them Little Irvy when his traveling days are through.

Already Malone is looking ahead to an especially sophisticated whale show that would ply a more cosmopolitan circuit than Little Irvy's tour of shopping centers and fairs. "Now, when I get my *second* whale," Jerry says, his blue eyes dancing, "I'm going to get me a professor to travel with it and make it real educational. We'll play schools and colleges. I was thinking maybe I'll get a much bigger whale than Little Irvy and cut it in two and carry it in a set of doubles — that's a cab pulling two trailers linked together. I'll have to work it all out but then I'd have it so you could look right inside the whale, and when you got out of there, hey, you'd *know* whales."

To help patrons become more familiar with whales now, Malone not only has the recording going, but little signs describing various points of interest are pasted all over Little Irvy, making him look rather as though he has been stamped for mailing by a haphazard post office employee. "HERE IS WHERE LITTLE IRVY EXHALED HOT AIR WHICH CONDENSED AND TURNED TO STEAM," says one. And: "IF YOU WERE TO WET LITTLE IRVY'S SKIN, IT WOULD BECOME SOFT LIKE VELVET." The latter is important, because in the dry cold of the trailer Little Irvy's skin has begun to peel with a freezer burn, making him rather unsightly. "Believe me, madam," Jerry told a suspicious matron, "if I was gonna make me a fake whale, you don't think I'd make him as ugly as this, do you?"

However, despite all the signs and other visual aids — including color pictures of Little Irvy being harpooned and the actual murder weapon itself — many whale watchers leave unimproved. In the South they depart still calling him "Little Ivory," and now, in Portland, following the most careful recorded explanation about how whales are mammals, a large woman in tight-fitting pastel slacks points and tells her barefooted son: "There, you see, that's the biggest fish in the world."

A helpful bystander, moving the six feet down from Little Irvy's forty-two teeth to his glass eye, politely corrects the mother. "No, ma'am, he's not a fish, he's a mammal." The woman, turning away from an inspection of Little Irvy's fatal harpoon wound, only glares back, at last addressing herself again only to the boy. "Fish are in the sea," she tells him, and the youngster, a bit shaken by the giant squid perched on Little Irvy's back, nods gratefully at this assurance of the verities of life.

Outside now, Jerry beckons to Charlotte to abandon the ticket booth. "Come on," he says, "we got to pull a Hank Snow." Hank Snow sang a big hit once called "I'm Moving On." It takes an hour or so to strike the set, to pull the sides over Little Irvy's glass window, and to be on the way to the next stop, this time Winnipeg. Jerry is already in the cab, warming up Old Blue for the long trip. Charlotte starts to move out. "Well," he says, looking back fondly, "there's eight thousand more people walking around without thirty-five cents in their pockets."

The desire to see whales never seems to lag. In the nineteenth century the fact that they were the prime source of oil and that Melville had glamorized them with Moby Dick — who, like Little Irvy, was a sperm whale — may have accounted for the fascination. But then, and always, it is just that they are so big. For every year since 1908 the most popular exhibit at the Museum of Natural History in New York has been the replica of a blue whale, the largest creature on land or sea that God ever put the breath of life into. The newest model is ninety-four feet long, made of polyurethane foam and fiberglass, and it cost nearly $300,000.

Whales petite enough to remain alive in confinement are always the hit of marine shows, and Namu, the five-ton killer whale who was captured and held in a Seattle aquarium four years ago, became a nationwide celebrity before he passed on. Mrs. Haroy, a seventy-ton finback who had been hollowed out and reinforced with steel and concrete, made a small fortune for her Danish owner with European appearances in the 1950s. Despite being soaked with 8,000 quarts of formaldehyde, Mrs. Haroy became somewhat odiferous on her maiden visit to the United States and was at last dispatched to a grave on Staten Island. Presumably, there are enough other exotic beasts in the heart of Africa to diminish whale curiosity, but only two years ago a dead whale named Jonas, sixty-six feet in length, tumbled off a flat truck taking him to display at the annual Zambia trade fair and blocked traffic on the main road from Rhodesia for some time.

It was not uncommon in the United States well into this century for entrepreneurs to haul dead whales about on railroad flatcars. The fly-by-night promoters would run a spur line right down into the ocean, hoist a harpooned whale on the car, and tote the monster around until the stench overcame even the most determined curiosity. Too often, when a whale reached this state of decay, the quick-buck operator would simply have him pried off the flatcar, leaving a dandy problem for the surprised local firemen and constabulary to argue about. There were a sufficient number of whale carcasses dropped throughout the country so that ordinances were hastily drafted in several states prohibiting the immigration of deceased whales.

Occasionally, a modern trooper conversant with such an obscure law has detained Little Irvy as he crossed a state line, but so far Little Irvy has eventually been accepted in all the states and nations that he has desired to enter. Malone, the signal authority on the subject, says that Little Irvy only smells "twenty percent as bad" as he originally did and, besides, however gamy he might be, he is prevented from assaulting the noses of customers and law enforcement officials by two thicknesses of glass. A regular Thermo King truck refrigeration unit that costs only 25 cents an hour to operate keeps Little Irvy's quarters at approximately 5 degrees below zero Fahrenheit, and the carcass itself measures down to better than 300 degrees below. It took forty tons of liquid nitrogen, pumped in and around Little Irvy, to freeze him. "I could keep Little Irvy frozen and run my show if it were a hundred and twenty degrees in the middle of the Sahara Desert," Jerry says.

"I knew if I was going to make it, I had to be self-sufficient. That, and the whole thing had to be framed beautifully. I knew I had a good thing — nobody would ever call Little Irvy a 'California show,' which is what they call them if they're all flash outside and nothing inside — but even if you really got something inside, you've still got to be beautiful outside. And you can't beat Old Blue for that. The only thing I changed was at first Charlotte and me were in all these special blue-and-white outfits. Why, I had forty-three-dollar Bostonian shoes, thirty-seven-dollar slacks, the works. But people figured we had to be making too much money to be dressed like that, so we just started dressing regular."

Now, he shifted gears down again, because they were heading up past Mullan, Idaho, into the mountains on the way to Missoula, Montana, which looked like a good place to spend the night. They never really stay anywhere; they just pull off the road and sleep wherever it is convenient and there is room for the rolling stock.

This night, it was on a lot full of John Deere tractors and Case-Beloit industrial machinery right on the main drag in Missoula next to the 4Bs Café. "We never slept in a tractor lot before," Jerry observed to Charlotte.

There was an old man with his pickup truck there to greet them in the morning. He was walking around Old Blue, communing with it, wanting to touch it but not daring to. Jerry came out of the camper and told him all about Little Irvy inside, twenty-ton, thirty-eight-foot, etc., but the old man didn't care. "You can keep the whale," he said, "just let me have this here truck. This truck is too pretty for any man to drive on the road." Jerry gave him a picture postcard of the truck. At most cafés and diesel stations where he stops, the people want to have a picture of Old Blue and, in fact, Jerry estimates that fully one-third of Little Irvy's paying audience is really more interested in getting a closer look at the truck. Little Irvy himself has been named an honorary Teamster.

Jerry Malone began life as an Okie, born in 1930. Destitute, his family came west from Apache, Oklahoma, in 1936 — with thirteen in the car — and the whole way Jerry took turns with his cousin Odell sitting on the cookie jar that held a good bit of the family's sustenance for the trip. The Malones settled in California's San Joaquin Valley, in Corcoran, and the first morning there Jerry's father started walking, knocking on every door, asking for work. Three miles down the road he got a job cleaning out chicken coops. From the age of 7, Jerry spent his summers getting up before dawn and, with the other members of his family, picking prunes for 2 cents a fifty-pound box until twilight and exhaustion. Eleven years after they had arrived in Corcoran, Mr. Malone — who had progressed to digging cesspools, carpentry, and contracting — was able to buy the same prune patch his family had worked for so long.

Jerry started slowly; he quit school to work when still in the tenth grade; he was married at 19, a child was soon on the way, and then he went into the Navy. Before he was discharged, though, he talked a loan company into setting him up in a trailer rental business in San Diego. It failed when a larger rental firm moved across the street, just as there were to follow a succession of car enterprises that were all signal in their auspicious debuts and dismal conclusions.

"Some guys called me a loser," Jerry says, "but the same guys who did always wanted me to come to work selling for them whenever I went under. Sure, I went broke a lot but I knew how to go broke just right. I never went bankrupt, and I could have, it's the easy way. And I learned things from going broke. You learn or you quit, you die. I think a lot of people have become the biggest successes because they did go broke once.

"The trouble was, I could never get an edge. I was always operating on borrowed money, so I could never get far enough ahead before something would happen. But I'll tell you one thing: I don't ever think it's a crying shame to go broke in America. It's a crying shame only if you stay broke in America."

The trouble with Jerry Malone was that he was never satisfied working for someone else, even though he was an outstanding salesman and made a good living at it. But financial independence always meant more than financial security; he was a capitalist, pure and simple. And he could sell a bank or a loan company on a scheme almost as easily as he could sell used cars.

Jerry came to the whale business relatively late in life and, indeed, he is still known in his new trade as a "JCL," a Johnny-come-lately. Bald and 39 now, with three teenage daughters from that first marriage that ended in divorce, he has had experience as, among other things, a farmer, a school-bus driver, a bartender, an automobile racing driver, a maître d', but mostly as Jerry Malone, used-car dealer. There was Jerry's Auto Sales, M&M Auto Sales ("Our cars melt in your heart, not in your hands"), the Wild Irishman, Auto Liquidators. Jerry Malone sold a purple Edsel once.

It all fits in: Malone grew up as part of the first generation to have clearly exhibited greater admiration for the speed, show, and breeding of mechanized vehicles than for animals. And nowadays, too often, Jerry is less celebrated as the man who owns Little Irvy and created the whole scheme than as the man who *drives* that gorgeous Kenworth. A frozen whale inside? It might just as well be a payload of lettuce or strawberries.

Indeed, though he has been involved with motor vehicles all his life, Malone admits that even he was awed by the growing mystique of truck and trucker. "When I was getting started with the whole idea," he says, "getting money, getting my whale — all that was only a challenge. There was only one thing that worried me and that was whether I could handle the truck."

He laid on the Jake brake down a steep incline. "Now, here's what I'm going to do next," he said. He was really excited, and the red was coming to his face. "I am having the first drag truck built, the first one. Just the cab, and it will be something. I'm calling it the Boss Truck of America, and it will be all red, white, and blue. The whole frame will be chrome, and nobody's ever done this in the history of the world — four thousand dollars in paint and upholstery, six thousand in chrome and, remember, this is just the cab. More than six hundred horses, a V-twelve Jimmy diesel engine with Allison automatic transmission instead of gearboxes. It'll weigh nine tons, and when I drag — get this — it'll need special chutes coming out the back to stop me. There's about fifteen hundred fairs in the U.S. and Canada, and I can play auto shows and trade shows, and when I come roaring out of there, red, white, and blue, I can hear it now, that announcer saying, 'Hang on with Malone, ladies and gentlemen, because here he comes in the Boss Truck of America!'"

There was a knock on the camper door, and Jerry got up to answer it. The man standing there was perhaps a few years younger than Malone, a well-built, healthy-looking fellow with his wife and daughter. Jerry recognized him; the man, who said his name was Carl Perleberg, had stopped him earlier to talk about the truck. "It's a good show inside," he said. "We liked it."

"Thank you," Jerry said.

Perleberg is an apple grower in Quincy, Washington. He had come out there from Fort Lee, New Jersey, because outdoors was the life he wanted. His wife worked and he moonlighted when they first arrived in the Northwest, and they saved enough to buy some land and plant 9,000 apple trees five years ago. Perleberg kept putting his profits into more orchards, and this year he cultivated 170,000 apple trees.

"Yes, it was a good show," Perleberg said, "but you know what really impresses me?"

"No," Jerry said.

"What I like most is the idea," Perleberg said. "It means something to me that if a man wants to catch a whale and cart it around this country, he can get the money and do it. Take off, live a free life, show the whale, and in the end I guess you end up giving more to Uncle Sam than I do. Now, that's all good. There's something very good about that. If this were some Communist country, I guess you would need an act of Congress to do a crazy thing like this."

"If they have a Congress," Jerry said.

"Right. Well, I know you're busy but I just wanted to say thanks, because I enjoyed this and I like the truck, and most of all because I kept thinking that what you are, carrying a whale around — you are a perfect example of the free enterprise system of this country."

Jerry nodded bashfully at the grandeur in that, and the men shook hands and, when Perleberg left, Jerry mused on how growing apples and trucking a dead whale around weren't all that different. It was both a case of wanting and trying, improving and expanding. Americans of Malone's age have been shaped by the sharpest of contradictory economic experiences — first, growing up in the harsh, sore days of Depression and then suddenly being tossed on the labor market at the instant of boom when all of the rules of a childhood are out the window.

The generation is hybrid, related neither to those who came before with Calvinistic devotion to long hours and frugality, nor to those who followed, who have known only affluence and the leisure and idealism it affords. Instead the Malones believe, on the one hand, in the honor of good, old-fashioned employment and, on the other, in risking the fruits of all that on speculative home runs. Hard work, easy money. You really must work for yourself if you are to manage as an apostle of these twin faiths.

Malone has always been an overextender. The Little Irvy scheme did not just happen. It sort of took shape in the marvelous sequence of Jerry's life and, as soon as the whale business began to look successful, Malone was promptly off spreading himself thin again.

Rambling in some disorder, he explains: "See, here's what happened. First I had bought these two cute little Casey Jones trains, kiddie rides, and then I bought a trailer and put a monkey circus in it," says Jerry, getting started. "I brought in an artist from Albuquerque, and many people said he painted the most beautiful trailer front they'd ever seen. I bought ten monkeys, bars, rings — everything for the kids — and then I got Eric Rasmussen, who has the most successful Arabian Giantess in the business, and, also, everyone thinks he does the best bally. And he was great. He gave it all this stuff on a recording about how this one monkey shaves and that other one does something else like that, but even with this and the trailer front it just never caught on. Because, like Charlotte had told me, what do I know about monkey circuses?

"Not only that, though, but then in Phoenix I saw a friend, Mr. Kelly, and the world's largest alligator, but his alligator just died, so he gave me a good price on his trailer, and I fixed it up and put two seals in there. So you see, by then I had two Casey Jones trains and two trailers.

"But what I found was that a show can't work just with a beautiful paint job. People want beautiful equipment, like the truck. I had to do something. I sold the two Casey Jones trains. Then I was down in L.A. and I ran across this guy doing shopping centers named Bebe the Clown. We made a deal and I took my monkey circus trailer and fixed it up different inside with a little theater and pillows all over the floor for the children. Then I got Bebe to change his name to Macaroni and we bought a St. Bernard dog and called him Noodles — so now you got Macaroni and his friend Noodles, and maybe we can find a spaghetti company somewhere to work something out with. Macaroni shows movies and jokes with the kids. It's going very well. There's a lot of shopping centers in L.A.

"I've still got the seal trailer setting back in Visalia. We had a fire and one of the seals was killed, and the other I put in a friend's pool in Bakersfield, and it was stolen out of there. Now I'll be damned if I can figure out who would want to steal a seal in Bakersfield, California, but they did. Now the trailer in Visalia, the trouble was, it was never meant to be a seal trailer. That was my mistake, but it'll sell because a lot of guys know I got it and, if you do have the world's largest alligator, it's perfect for that."

Charlotte was with Jerry that day in 1964 when they visited an aquarium and he first got the idea of freezing a whale. Increasingly intrigued, Malone performed his own market research at truck cafés. He would sit down at a counter, order coffee, and say, to no one in particular: "I saw the damnedest thing today." Then he would drink the coffee, until at last someone could stand it no longer and ask him what, in fact, he had seen.

"I saw a whale, a twenty-ton whale, frozen in a truck. Would you pay to see a thing like that?" Better than a third of those interviewed in this unique random survey allowed as how they would. Jerry figured that was potentially 75 million Americans times 35 cents.

Malone's car lot(s) had folded by then, and he was married and making $1,575 a month in commissions selling cars on the lot of a close friend, George Zarounian. Finally, he gave Zarounian notice and told him he was going after his whale full-time. "It's crazy," Zarounian said.

"Crazy things work these days, George," Jerry replied.

By now, Jerry had already named his future whale after an uncle, Irv Mulanax, the other half of M&M Auto Sales and various other defunct ventures. Jerry bought business cards with gold-leaf lettering and headed out in search of investors. Potential dead-whale angels, however, remained more prone to place their savings in convertible bonds, the American Stock Exchange, and other such investments, and Zarounian pleaded with Malone to come back.

Finally, he made a proposal. If Malone could march cold into three shopping centers (selected by Zarounian) and sell them all on the idea of booking a frozen whale, he, George Zarounian, would co-sign the loan. When the third straight shopping center went for Jerry's pitch, Zarounian — who, it is said in Visalia, resembles Gilbert Roland — leaned back in his chair, sighed in exasperation, lit up a Bering cigar, and said: "Well, I guess I'm in the whale business." Stunned but game, the United California Bank approved the loan application.

The risk on Zarounian's part was considerable. There was no guarantee, first of all, that Malone could even get a whale to put into his $80,000 truck, which he was already committed for. There is only one U.S. whaling station, at Point Richmond, California. Malone had to get permission from the Department of the Interior before dealing with the whalers, who had little margin for error themselves. There is a $10,000 fine for harpooning a sperm whale under a thirty-five-foot minimum, and Malone could not fit one in his truck if it was more than forty feet or twenty-one tons. Besides, even at that point, some cryogenics experts that Malone consulted said they didn't think he could freeze a twenty-ton whale anyway.

On June 30, 1967, Malone was already out $100,000, with no whale and no assurance he could keep it from deteriorating even if he had it. On July 1, after almost two months of searching the Pacific, the whaler *Alan Cody* harpooned Little Irvy; on July 2 he was at Point Richmond, and on Saturday, July 8 he was frozen solid. Nobody really was bothered with the detail that Little Irvy had turned out to be a girl whale.

Little Irvy was still caked in ice when they finished cleaning up the truck that night about seven o'clock. Malone had somehow obtained the rare permission to bring his traveling exhibit to Fisherman's Wharf, and Uncle Irv Mulanax allowed as how they could open up bright and early Monday morning with his namesake. "Are you kidding?" Jerry asked. "Two years I've been working on this and I'm going to wait two more days?"

He and Charlotte were parked and setting up for customers by nine o'clock. At this point they inventoried, and between them their resources totaled one nickel and four pennies — 9 cents. Charlotte worked the entrance and Jerry went inside and started explaining about Little Irvy to the patrons, because, of course, they had no recording set up yet.

After an hour or so Jerry's voice was wearing thin from the lecturing, so he walked down the steps to Charlotte. They had already welcomed their first 100 paying customers, so Jerry kissed her and took a couple bucks from her and walked over to a bar. The bartender came around and Jerry said: "Give me a tall VO and water." The bartender started to mix the drink, and Jerry put both dollars on the counter and said: "Make that a double, because you can call me Mr. Success."

*   *   *

I have gone through various phases of interest in my career, and Little Irvy was at the height of my Americana period. I subscribed to an entertainment industry periodical named Amusement Business *at that time, and there was an item in a dot-and-dash column about Jerry Malone and Little Irvy. It just jumped out at me. A frozen whale.*

I went to an editor named Ray Cave, who subsequently became the boss at Time *magazine. It was a crazy idea, and hardly sports in any normal sense, but, like a good editor, Ray could recognize my crazy passion for this. "All right," he said. "Go out and try this. But don't tell anybody." Little Irvy was more than I could have ever dreamed, of course, and it turned out to be a very different and important story for me. After you've written about a dead whale and made that work, editors are more prone to listen to you.*

Eighteen years later and Little Irvy is still on the road, frozen.

Jerry Malone changed his name to Tyrone Malone, and, just as he'd dreamed, went heavier into trucks. At one point he set the speed record for trucks on the Bonneville Flats, and I did another story on him. But it wasn't anywhere near up to Little Irvy.

In March of 1957, a school friend and I were driving back to our homes in Baltimore, after spring vacation in Florida. We were high school seniors. Suddenly, driving through North Carolina we couldn't get any rock and roll music on the radio because the team from North Carolina had just come back from the NCAA finals in Kansas City, and all the stations were at the airport, reporting on that.

Later, Tommy Kearns, one of the Carolina stars, became a good friend, and he would often tell me tales of that wonderful season. Finally I decided I had to write about it.

A Team That Was Blessed

1981

THE United States of America was much more regional a quarter of a century ago. This was before designer jeans. People could be distinguished by what they wore and how they talked and what they ate and on a variety of other indigenous counts. For example, when Frank McGuire left St. John's, in New York City, to become the coach at the University of North Carolina in 1952, he had trouble persuading players to go south with him. This was because most of the best city players then were Roman Catholic, and the other coaches, friends, and hangers-around, even a few priests, would tell a player and his parents that if the boy went with Mc-Guire down to the Protestant Bible Belt, he would surely "lose his soul."

McGuire points out now, "This was my biggest hurdle — souls."

Sometimes parochial schools would even refuse to mail a prospect's transcript to heathen Carolina, but McGuire learned, to some extent, how to fight fire with fire. He would tell parents to look at it this way: Their boy wouldn't just be a basketball player, he'd also be serving as a missionary. And at some of the kitchen tables where McGuire raised this point, it went over very well.

Recruiting at that time largely took place right there, at the kitchen table.

The move south wasn't an easy transition for McGuire himself, either. He had come from the big time. The first game he coached at Chapel Hill, about 1,200 fans showed up in a gym that held only 5,632. His office was a shabby, reconstituted section of an old men's room, unable to accommodate two grown men standing shoulder to shoulder. The Carolina team traveled to away games in crowded private cars, and when the players arrived at the distant campus, they slept on cots set up in the host's gym. This was called "local entertainment."

For this bush stuff McGuire never would have left St. John's except for his son, Frankie.

McGuire was a New Yorker through and through, and one of the biggest names in college basketball, having taken the Redmen to the NCAA finals in 1952. Frank McGuire knew everybody in town, and everybody returned the honor. He had the gift of gab, a fine Irish way about him. He had a handsome, open face, and he parted his golden hair high and made you think of Dan Duryea — that is, if just once Dan Duryea had played the good guy. Certainly, McGuire would never have left New York, but in 1951 he and his wife, Pat, had a boy who was named Frankie. Frankie was retarded and had cerebral palsy, and it was very difficult caring for him in a small apartment in the big city. So it was that McGuire took little North Carolina up on its offer and then started to try to spirit the flower of high school basketball out of the archdiocese of New York.

It helped McGuire that a lot of the big city colleges recently had been caught fixing games; it also helped that Uncle Harry continued to work the territory for him.

Consequently, in their crew cuts and car coats, four defenders of the faith gathered as freshmen in Chapel Hill in the autumn of '54: Pete Brennan and Joe Quigg from Brooklyn, from St. Augustine and St. Francis, respectively; Bob Cunningham from All Hallows, residing just over the color line, in West Harlem; and Tommy Kearns, who had grown up in the Bronx and moved across the river to Jersey, but commuted an hour and a half each way into Manhattan to play for Looie Carnesecca at St. Ann's, where he had a basketball scholarship. In those more freewheeling times, the Catholic schools serious about basketball held tryouts, citywide, and practice began the week after school opened. It was pretty much the only dream in town. "We played some softball, too," Kearns says, "but it couldn't take you anyplace."

At the time Kearns made this observation, a few weeks ago, he was lying on the beach in Uruguay, a well-tanned role model.

Already ensconced in Chapel Hill, a year ahead of the other New Yorkers, was Lennie Rosenbluth, from the Bronx, a somewhat mysterious, wraith-like figure, 6'5" and maybe 170, a Jew who didn't arrive at college until he was almost 20, after a high school career that consisted of seven games, total. Rosenbluth had played at playgrounds, Ys, parks, church halls, "the mountains" (i.e., the Catskills, a.k.a. the Jewish Alps), and, finally, a military prep school in Virginia. McGuire had never even seen Rosenbluth play; he'd taken him blind on the recommendation of Uncle Harry, who was Harry Gotkin, his main talent scout back in the city.

McGuire had implicit faith in Uncle Harry's basketball judgment, doubting it perhaps only once, in Rosenbluth's sophomore year, when Uncle Harry called up and told McGuire he had a hot prospect named Lotz. "Dammit, Harry, all you get me is Jews and Catholics; can't you ever get me a Protestant?" McGuire snapped. He was thinking of lox and bagels. In fact, as Uncle Harry then tried to explain, Danny Lotz's father was a Baptist minister. They had really struck it rich, Protestant-wise. Later on, even, Danny Lotz married Billy Graham's daughter.

But getting back to Rosenbluth. In his junior year at Carolina he was joined on the varsity by the four Catholic boys, and the team began to shake out. The Tar Heels went 18–5 in 1955–56, and the next season they were a set piece from the first victory, in Asheboro, over a semipro club known as the McCrary Eagles. About then, the jokes began about "the four Catholics chasing the Jew upcourt" and other hilarious variations on this theme.

And a true story. Waning seconds, close game, Rosenbluth at the line. McGuire: "Say a Hail Mary, Lennie, and make the shot."

Lennie: "But I don't know how to say Hail Mary."

Brennan: "We'll say a Hail Mary. You make the shot."

And so forth and so on.

Hopes were high that the Tar Heels would win the Atlantic Coast Conference, because that would have redounded not only to the glory of the university but also to the repute of what all the principals still pronounce as "Noo Yawk" basketball. While the college game was almost exclusively sectional then, the four major teams in North Carolina constituted an exception. For years N.C. State, perennially the team to beat, was stocked with Hoosier sharpshooters that Coach Everett Case, the Old Gray Fox, imported from Indiana. Duke featured Philadelphia players — good ball handling was their trademark — just as Carolina now had its Noo Yawkers and Wake Forest had its Southern Baptists and a Methodist ringer or two.

To win the ACC was the Tar Heels' great goal that year. That would make a grand double victory, for school and style alike. The latter was known as give-and-go.

The Foe

There was indeed an NCAA tournament then, had been for years, but Carolina dared harbor no serious aspirations of winning the national title, because everyone everywhere simply assumed that Kansas would win the crown in 1957. And in '58 and '59, for that matter. This was because a young giant from Philadelphia, Wilt Chamberlain, had decided to play for the Jayhawks, and now he was entering his sophomore year, his first of varsity eligibility.

He was then perceived as superhuman. "People today cannot imagine the impact that man had on us all at that time," Joe Quigg says. "Wilt was just a colossus." He stood somewhat over seven feet, he was powerful and quick, and he was black! His reputation preceded him to Lawrence, Kansas, because he was surely the first high school athlete whose recruiting was coast-to-coast news. "I don't mean these things to sound wrong, but I was above all the other guys then," Chamberlain says. "I guess I was just ahead of my time."

The only question seriously debated was whether or not Wilt would destroy college basketball.

It didn't take long for teams that were playing Chamberlain to figure out that their only chance was to collapse the defense around him and hold the ball on offense. Kansas would even lose twice — both times by a basket in a low-scoring game on the road. "What they did to Wilt would have provoked you or me to distraction — two or three bodies always packed up against him," says Dick Harp, who was his coach. "He never got any breaks from the officials, but he never lost his composure."

"Looking back, I don't ever remember feeling any pressure that season," Chamberlain says. "All I can remember is getting bored so often." The championship would be restorative. Kansas drew San Francisco, the defending champ, in the semifinals. A 6'9" guy named Art Day jumped against Wilt. "So you're Mr. Chamberlain," he said, and Wilt only snarled at him and made it a point to "crush" Day's first shot. At that, Day looked up awestruck. "So, you *are* Mr. Chamberlain," he said, and Wilt broke out laughing, right on the court. Chamberlain scored 32, at will, and Kansas won 80–56.

It was so devastating that most people forgot which team was coming into the final game undefeated.

The Season

Midway through their schedule, with their record 16–0, North Carolina traveled to Maryland on a train and played the Terps before the largest basketball crowd in the history of the South, 12,200. When Maryland got possession of the ball, leading by four with forty seconds left, McGuire called time out for the purpose of reviewing how the Tar Heels were to act — like gentlemen — in defeat. They won in overtime. "After that, after I called time out *to tell them how to lose,* and still they couldn't, well, from then on I knew they were really something special," McGuire says.

But it was McGuire who set the tone. "The best thing he did was he left us alone, five guys who played Noo Yawk style," Brennan says. Much of the strategy, the matchups, McGuire turned over to his assistant, the late Buck Freeman, who had, years before, been the head coach of the St. John's Wonder Five. Freeman was tall and white-maned, leonine, but he was also a fussy old bachelor who liked his whiskey. Above all, he was an utter technical genius, perfectly complementing the younger McGuire, who was a master of tempo, of game and group psychology. It's said that no coach has ever better understood when to call time-outs than Frank McGuire.

The Tar Heels aligned themselves in such a way as to defy conventional defenses. "There was a chemistry, patterns, not plays," Rosenbluth says, "and when you have that, scouting reports don't mean a thing." In fact, broken down, the Carolina offense more closely resembled that used by the Harlem Globetrotters than any other. Rosenbluth was in the middle, back to the basket, the "showman," as the Globies call their "lead" (Meadowlark, Goose, Geese, whoever). Kearns was the "floorman" (Marques or Curly) out front with the ball. The two more traditional sturdy-center types, Quigg and Brennan, weren't under the basket, where they might get in the showman's way, but were put out in the corners.

Cunningham, at 6′3″, tall for a 1950s guard — and to gild the lily, McGuire listed him at 6′4″ — was the other starter. Just where were you, Bobby? "Sneakin'. Always sneakin' around," he says. "Lookin' after my children." He means the four more visible starters. Cunningham was the classic fifth man.

As a high school junior he scored more than twenty points a game and got thirty college offers. But, in November of his senior year, he took 100 stitches in his shooting hand when it went through a window. The doctors wanted to amputate his thumb right away, and would have but for the pleas of his father, an immigrant laborer from Ireland. So the thumb was salvaged, but only McGuire kept his promise of a scholarship, a display of loyalty that also had much to do with cementing Kearns's decision in favor of Chapel Hill.

His touch gone, Cunningham accepted the grubby tasks. "After where I came from and what I'd been through, I was just glad to be a part," he says. Even Rosenbluth, the big name, the big scorer, says that Cunningham, the least renowned, was "the key." But they all had to give up something. Rosenbluth would take himself out of the flow and let his teammates score more if he was double-teamed.

But none of the others ever resented sending the ball in to Lennie, because they'd never seen a man who could shoot as he could — spinning layups, hooks, turnaround jumpers. Three of the other four starters — Kearns, Cunningham, and Brennan — all proudly, distinctly recall being *the* one who threw the pass to Rosenbluth when he scored his most extraordinary basket, a fourteen-foot hook shot, in traffic, against Wake in the ACC tournament, in the final minute, down a point. Kearns, although the cockiest of the lot, probably had the most difficult time adjusting, both to the team and to "the foreign country down there." As popular and smooth as he was, Kearns was more of a loner than his classmates on the team, and would have left Carolina as a freshman except that his father, a cop and a Coast Guardsman, wouldn't brook that kind of move. "I had real culture shock," Kearns says. "I mean, trees! And I'd be walking around the campus, and all of a sudden everybody is saying hello to me: *Hi, how you?* I kept thinking, What do they want out of me? What's the con?"

But Kearns found new friends, joined a fraternity in which he was the only member from north of the Mason-Dixon, fell in love with a bank president's daughter named Betsy over at Duke (McGuire feared Kearns would give away team secrets between kisses), and at last acclimated himself to that strange existence beyond the subways.

It may seem odd, perhaps, that it was the playmaker and the leading scorer, the two who started and ended most of the action, who were the two most distant individuals on the team. But interpersonal dynamics are often overrated. They were Noo Yawk when it mattered. As Rosenbluth, the captain, the old man, remembers, "We got so close on the court that we got to know exactly what everybody else was doing — and we were free-lance, too. For example, I knew that if Pete put the ball on the floor, it was going up."

But certainly, everybody rooting for the Tar Heels had fallen in love with them. Even the most devout Catholics could see some advantages in that. McGuire received this advice from a bishop: "I know you're making a lot of converts down South, but tell the boys not to bless themselves on the free-throw line unless they're sure they can make the shot." Coincidence or not, the roughest games tended to be against Wake, where anti-Semitic remarks had been directed from the stands against Rosenbluth. Carolina played Wake *four* times that season and beat the Deacons each time. But each game was tight, and when Rosenbluth won the last one with his miraculous hook, McGuire was moved to observe, "The Catholics and the Baptists were having a helluva battle, until the Jew took over and broke it up."

And the Tar Heels were good public relations for the state. To have Carolina associated with urbane, ethnic New York was hardly all bad, especially since New York was the limited partner in this endeavor. In a way, you could say that with McGuire's team, the Sunbelt, as we know it, began its transmutation — visibly, anyway — from the Bible Belt. Lennie Rosenbluth was this century's Virginia Dare.

Even if you never thought about it in quite those terms before, Carolina moved on to the Final Four at 30–0, 31–0 counting the lidlifter over the McCrary Eagles, which some people still did. Unfortunately, if the Tar Heels got past Michigan State in the semis, their opponent in the championship game would surely be Kansas and Chamberlain, and they would have to face them in the Jayhawks' home territory, in Kansas City. As the Tar Heels' play-by-play announcer, Ray Reeve, was to say over the radio from K.C.: "Nobody's given them a Chinaman's chance."

The Final Four

Point of fact: Carolina had no business beating Michigan State. The Spartans' coach cried in the locker room afterward because he knew his team should have won. It took three overtimes. Rosenbluth went for twenty-nine, but he forced his shots, often firing attempts that Jumpin' Johnny Green slapped away. Kearns played his worst game of the season, and Quigg got only one shot before he fouled out.

So Cunningham, realizing he had to shoot, scored twenty-one, his career high, and he and Brennan saved the streak. Still, it almost ended in regulation when, at 58 all, the Spartans' Jack Quiggle threw in a desperation try from past half court at the buzzer. But the referee said time had run out before the shot. "All the luck we had that year," Rosenbluth says. "I guess we used it up for all the Carolina teams that followed."

Chamberlain was to have the best word for it.

Then, at the end of the first overtime, it was truly finished. As they said in North Carolina at the time: "That's all she wrote." Reeves said that on the air. State was up 64–62, six seconds left, Jumpin' Johnny at the line, one-and-one. Kearns remembers how desperate the situation was. The little guy he was guarding just walked over to him and, with a big grin, said three dirty words, "Thirty and one."

But Green missed the front end, and on the left side, Brennan came down with the rebound. He didn't call time out. He didn't look to pass out. He turned and dribbled. *If Pete put the ball on the floor, it was going up.* Only this one time Pete was eighty feet away. He started upcourt by himself, and suddenly he found himself near the other end, twenty feet from the hoop, two defenders in front of him, all his teammates behind. So he pulled up and fired. The buzzer sounded just after the ball went through the twine.

The Tar Heels won, anticlimactically, two overtimes later.

Then they watched for a while as Chamberlain annihilated San Francisco. Far from being intimidated, though, they came away calm in the knowledge of how they had to play him. "San Francisco let him get away with too much," Brennan says. "I don't care how awesome he was. We had to be physical with him." The next day, in the lobby of their hotel, the Continental, Kearns hung out, loving it, advising whatever skeptics would listen, "We're chilly. We're cool. Chamberlain won't give us any jitters." At some point, too (all accounts differ), McGuire told Kearns that if he was so cocky, he should go out and jump against Chamberlain at the start of the game. Kearns said sure.

The arena was thronged, almost all Kansas. But even this failed to undo the Tar Heels, who had played only eight home games all season. And they did have the governor, Luther Hodges, with them. He flew out after the Michigan State victory, possibly because the games were being specially televised back home, and the state was on its ear. Before this weekend, ACC basketball was popular as a sport; after this, it was woven into the fabric of North Carolina society. Governor Hodges looked around and then plunked himself down in the most visible place he could find, between McGuire and his team, on the bench.

The coach apologized and invited the governor to take a seat at the other end, and then, as the fans blinked and snickered, here came Kearns, 5'10" and change, elbowing his way into the center circle opposite Chamberlain. The big man glared down. Kearns played it for all it was worth, tensing, getting way down as if he could spring twenty feet into the air.

So began the most exciting game in NCAA tournament history.

Carolina immediately assumed control. The Tar Heels collapsed two or three men on Wilt and dared the other Jayhawks to stick the ball in from outside. Kansas played a box-and-one, with Maurice King shadowing Rosenbluth. It was a disastrous strategy; it didn't contain Rosenbluth, and it left the other Tar Heels free to shoot over the zone. Of the first seven shots they threw up, Brennan hit one, Rosenbluth, Kearns, and Quigg two apiece. Twenty-five years later, Wilt still has the vision of the Carolina center, Quigg, staying way out, chewing gum, throwing up the jumper. It was 17–7 before the Jayhawks went to man-to-man and still 29–22 for Carolina at the half.

Wilt led Kansas back, and before the second half was nine minutes gone, the Jayhawks were in front 36–35. Quigg and Rosenbluth were each to pick up his fourth foul along in here, too, but even when Chamberlain, then a fine free-throw shooter, made both shots of a one-and-one to put Kansas up by three, Harp kept Kansas in a deliberate offense. Ironically, Harp still maintains, "Had a shot clock been employed then, no one would've been able to come even close to beating Wilt." But still, he elected to hold the ball.

It almost worked, too. Say that. With 1:45 left, Chamberlain, moving up high, whipped a beautiful pass down into Gene Elstun, who not only made the shot but also drew Rosenbluth's fifth foul. As Elstun stood at the line, it was 44–41, and Chamberlain distinctly recalls glancing up into the stands at this moment, spotting a good friend and sighing at him, at last sure of victory.

But Elstun missed, the Tar Heels scratched back, and in the waning seconds Kearns tied it at 46 from the line.

In the first overtime, each team scored only one basket; in the second, none. Carolina was certainly tired by now, and both teams were tight. Kearns missed three straight foul shots, Quigg, the only one he tried. Chamberlain blew a free throw, too. Cunningham had fouled him and Brennan had grabbed him around the waist, angering Chamberlain. He had thrown the ball away and rapped Brennan on the head with an elbow; Brennan had stormed back at him, before others had rushed in to break it up. Then someone had torn over to the Carolina bench and tried to slug McGuire. Back in North Carolina, it was chiming midnight as the Tar Heels went into a third overtime for the second straight night.

Kearns made a basket first and all of a one-and-one to put Carolina up four. But Wilt came back with a three-pointer, and when King and Elstun sank free throws, Carolina had one shot, down 53–52. There were ten seconds left when Quigg ended up with the ball near the top of the key. "It's funny," he says, "I rarely wanted the ball. But this night I'd felt good, right from the start. Good players feel that way all the time, I guess, but it only occasionally happened to me. It just happened that one of those nights was the night of the championship game." He made a slight pump fake and drove against the invincible Wilt Chamberlain himself. King, coming across to help out, fouled Quigg just as he got the shot off.

There were six seconds left, and McGuire signaled time out. The universal sign. Right palm plane over tip of left middle finger. T: Time. You're not supposed to do that in these circumstances. That is canon. If anybody calls time, it's supposed to be the other coach, to get the shooter thinking, nervous. But Frank McGuire never called a bad time-out, and he knew his man, Joe Quigg.

Quigg had hit a solid 72 percent from the line on the year, but he'd missed the only free throw he'd taken in the game, under pressure in the first overtime. In this particular situation he wasn't a lock. So as soon as the Tar Heels huddled, the first thing McGuire said, calmly, was, "Now, Joe, as soon as you make 'em . . ." and then he went on to explain how they would work on defense.

Quigg sat on the bench and thought about his dream. He had often dreamed of just this situation. "Only in my dream, it was always a jump shot with no time left," he says. But this would have to do: down one, at the line for two, six seconds left for the NCAA championship.

As it turned out, there really was no time left for Quigg. He was a junior, and he had pro potential, but, as it was, these were the last two shots he would ever shoot.

Before he walked back to the free-throw line, he promised everybody that he would make them both.

And he did. *Swish. Swish.* 54–53.

Not only that, but Quigg was also the one who batted away the
last-ditch pass that was intended for Chamberlain in the low post.
Kearns retrieved the ball with a couple of seconds left, and after
dribbling once, he heaved it away, high up in the air. It's so strange
to see a game end that way, all the players looking straight up, half
of them helplessly, half in exultation. And then the clock runs out,
and all the Kansas players drop their eyes to the floor and walk off.
All the Carolina players suddenly lower their heads, too — but not
down, only around, finding one another, then running into each
other's arms. Thirty-two-and-oh, 33–0 if you count the McCrary
Eagles.

The Celebration

In those medieval times — there were, for example, only four
photographers at the game — the championship was played in an
arena lacking proper locker-room facilities, so the players dressed
in their hotels. Quigg remembers the odd sensation of winning the
national title and then "just running through the streets of Kansas
City, all by myself." The air was heavy with mist.

Back at their hotel, the Tar Heels sat around and sort of stared at
each other, goofy with delight, "a good tired." Their bodies were
only now beginning to comprehend what they had been asked to
do the past two nights. Brennan, Cunningham, and Kearns had
played all 110 minutes. What with the governor there, McGuire
quickly threw a victory party, and the tab for that affair came to
$1,500, which was so extravagant, the North Carolina athletic di-
rector thought, that he made McGuire spring for the Roquefort
dressing, which had been a $58 extra. McGuire has never gotten
over that.

But it was the only sour note. There was such a fuss made over
the Tar Heels that the plane that brought them home the next day
had to circle the Raleigh-Durham airport for some time until police
could clear the runway of well-wishers. The whole state adored the
team. On campus, fellow students would worshipfully ask the players for autographs. It was the spring of 1957, presumably a most
innocent time. It was the good old days. It was the absolute peak
year of the baby boom. "Young Love," by Sonny James, topped the
charts that month: "They say for every boy and girl/There's just

one love in this old world. . . ." It was that kind of time, crew cuts
and car coats, and, obviously, it would go on forever and a day.

The next weekend some of the players went home. Brennan, the
conquering hero, rushed over to Brooklyn from LaGuardia. His father was a subway motorman, and Pete was one of ten children.
The Brennans lived in a two-family house, with the Cocoas next
door. The hero dashed up the steps, just as Mrs. Cocoa was coming
out. "Hey, Petey," she said, "when did you get back from the soiv-
ice?"

The Thereafter

So it was, Brennan says, that his feet came back to earth. The
others would follow him down. They had caught lightning in a
bottle during that one season, but then the world became sane and
cruel again. Quigg got hit the hardest of all. The reason those free
throws were the last points he ever made was that the next fall he
fractured his right leg in a practice session, and he has never even
been able to straighten it properly since. And Rosenbluth. As great
a shooter as he was, at 6′5″, 170 pounds, he couldn't survive the
grind in the NBA. They beat him into the ground, and he quit after
two desultory seasons.

Cunningham, Brennan, and Kearns formed the heart of the
1957–58 Carolina team, and it was a good team, a nice team, and
Brennan made first-string All-America and Kearns third, but there
was no more magic. The Knicks drafted Brennan in the first round,
tried to convert him to guard, waived him to Cincinnati, and then
he got out. Kearns was drafted first by Syracuse, but he only played
seven minutes in one NBA game. He took one shot and made it: 2.0
ppg., 1.000 FG pct., for all time.

Kearns didn't make the Nats because in his stead they decided
to keep the unknown guard they had drafted on the second round.
His name was Hal Greer. And that proved more of an indication of
things to come than anything Carolina had done. The 1956–57 Tar
Heels, it turned out, were more of a transition, a bridge. Before
them, college basketball was a regional game, and after them, influenced by them, it went big-time, coast to coast. It was never the
same again, although it didn't go in the direction that appeared so
evident at the time. Soon there weren't that many guys crossing
themselves at the free-throw line.

The white people, the Catholics and the Jews, moved to the suburbs, and black people started moving onto the courts in increasing numbers. Softball can't take you anyplace. The only basketball player to come out of North Carolina at that time and become a pro star was a guy from North Carolina Central named Sam Jones, whom nobody at the NCAAs had ever even heard of.

Give-and-go.

Although this too: Maybe the Noo Yawk boys did make it easier for those who followed. Maybe if a bunch of Catholics and a Jew can play for your Dixie alma mater, maybe that makes it more palatable to accept blacks. Certainly, that's a possibility.

But once the Tar Heel players understood it was over, all of them went on about their lives. For athletes using sports to scratch their way up then, college was itself something to achieve; it was not, as it has become, merely basic training for the pros. Of the twelve guys on the championship team's roster, all graduated from Chapel Hill, and six earned advanced degrees. "That may be more of an accomplishment than the thirty-two-and-oh," Brennan says.

Of the starters, he and Quigg, the two Brooklyn boys, stayed in Carolina. Quigg is a dentist in Fayetteville, Brennan is the designer of his own men's fashion line, Pinehurst Clothing, in Charlotte. The other three all returned to work in Carolina for a while before moving on. Rosenbluth teaches American history at Coral Gables (Florida) High School, while coaching a basketball team at Deerborne, a nearby private school. Kearns and Cunningham both live in the Connecticut suburbs of New York, where Cunningham is president of a trucking firm, Advanced Delivery Systems, Inc., and Kearns is a partner with Bear Stearns, a Wall Street brokerage.

Kearns married his Duke sweetheart; the other four all married Chapel Hill coeds. None is divorced; you see, Sonny James was right. After Pat McGuire died of cancer, Frank married a Carolina belle, too, only Jane McGuire comes from across the line, in the Palmetto State. In 1961 McGuire was enticed to leave Chapel Hill to coach Philadelphia in the NBA. His star was Chamberlain; it was under McGuire that Wilt averaged 50 and went for 100 in one game. But then McGuire came back south, taking the coaching job at the University of South Carolina, where he had some right good teams. Retired, he and Jane still live in Columbia, very near to where Frankie, now 30, is institutionalized. It's important not to forget that all of this happened on account of Frankie.

The Loser

Wilt Chamberlain left the arena in Kansas City for the lonely walk back to his hotel, the old Muehlebach. Against what was now a light rain, he wore a little British driving cap. A small boy from Chapel Hill, who had flown out for the games, ran in circles around the big man, cruelly taunting him, chanting, "We wilted the Stilt, we wilted the Stilt," over and over. But Chamberlain didn't take the bait. He only looked ahead and kept on walking.

In another hour or two he was back on campus in Lawrence. Louis Armstrong was playing there that evening. It was envisioned as a victory ball. "Old Satchmo was playing 'When the Saints Go Marching In,' but we marched back losers instead," Chamberlain said ruefully a few weeks ago, smiling softly at a friend sitting next to him. The friend shrugged in sympathy.

It takes a lot of gumption for Wilt to talk like this, because as the years have passed he has come to understand how that one game in Kansas City changed the whole perception of him. He came in as the invincible giant, but when he went out, he carried with him some vague impression of defeat's being his destiny. It was with Bill Russell and the Celtics that this became a pox upon Chamberlain, but he knows only too well where the germ first alighted. He knows. "Of all the games in my career, and certainly so far as image is concerned, you understand, that goddamn one against Carolina was the biggest," he says.

It is ironic, too, that no one protests the unfairness of this stigma so much as McGuire and the champion Tar Heels do. Kearns, particularly Kearns, who was sent out to jump center, to somehow mock and rattle the giant, refutes the loser's tag that clings to Chamberlain.

That Kearns had jumped center might have disturbed Wilt more than he ever let on, too. McGuire recalls that four years later, when he first met Chamberlain at Philadelphia, Wilt was quick to ask McGuire why he had done that to him in Kansas City.

In fact, there's no consensus on exactly where the center-jump idea came from. In contrast, Kearns knows precisely why he had the presence of mind to hurl the ball up, free and clear, in the last seconds of the game. He remembered hearing that Hot Rod Hundley had pulled that stunt once at West Virginia, and "there were a couple guys around me, but Wilt was in the back of my mind. I just figured even he couldn't get the ball if it was four hundred feet up in the air."

Wilt did everything just right at the end, in the clutch. This is perfectly clear from the old films. When Quigg got the ball at the left of the top of the key, he gave a little fake as if to shoot, and Chamberlain came up on him some, as well he should have; he knew that the guy with the chewing gum could hit from outside. So then, when Quigg started to drive, he had a slight edge, maybe half a step, on Wilt. But Chamberlain angled back, so that he was comfortably between Quigg and the basket when Quigg shot. Wilt blocked the ball cleanly, and that would have been the end of that — except King had left his man and, helping out, had fouled Quigg. So that was how Chamberlain's man got the chance to sink the shots that put Carolina ahead.

Kansas called time, with five seconds to score. Everyone in the building knew the ball was going inside to Chamberlain, but still — although nobody seems to remember this except Wilt — Carolina botched it. Really. McGuire recalls telling Quigg to play in front of Chamberlain and Lotz *directly* behind. If Wilt got the ball, McGuire wanted Lotz to pin both Wilt's arms immediately. "At least make him beat us on the foul line," McGuire said. But if he gave those instructions, Lotz somehow failed to comprehend them, because when play resumed, Lotz was not only *not* behind Chamberlain, he was well in front, edging out to the foul line, where Ron Lopeski would receive the inbounds pass. Lotz laughs now at the part he played in the drama. "It wasn't very bright of me, was it?" he says.

Quigg did get in front of Chamberlain and then realized, to his horror, that he, at 6′7″, was all alone against Wilt. Brennan, the other forecourtman, was several steps to the side, ready to guard Elstun should he get the ball in the right corner. Quigg even remembers screaming in panic to Brennan, "Come back! Come back!" Brennan did, but it was too late. Brennan was never more than parallel to Chamberlain's right side, where he was defenseless to ward off a pass coming in from the left. If the pass had only been lofted a few inches higher, neither Carolina nor, for that matter, all the angels in heaven could have stopped Chamberlain from stuffing the winning basket through the hoop.

So the Tar Heels didn't execute that play well. Kansas didn't execute that play well. And for it, Chamberlain was the one who forever became a loser. That's all she wrote.

It's merely an added curiosity that Chamberlain retains a more vivid picture of the final seconds than do any of the winners. "The best teams I ever played against were the smartest," he says. "Bos-

ton, then New York in the pros. And Carolina this time. But you
know what's so funny? Carolina didn't do one dumb thing that
whole damn game until the worst possible time, the last five seconds. Then there just wasn't anybody behind me, you understand?"
He shook his head. "We should've won that game, Tommy."

The reason Chamberlain said Tommy was that he was having a
late dinner with Kearns at the Stage Deli, on New York's Seventh
Avenue. Somewhere along the way they had met again, far from a
center circle, and they have been fast friends for years. Kearns
handles Chamberlain's stock portfolio. "To tell you the truth, I've
never heard of any friendship like ours," Wilt says. "I mean, starting
off meeting in that game, like *that,* you understand, and then ending up friends, which is much more important than any game, ever."

This evening Chamberlain would be staying at Kearns's Manhattan apartment. They had gone to the Millrose Games together, and
of course everybody in Madison Square Garden recognized Wilt.
Many adults sent their children over for autographs. "I should have
worn my sunglasses," Wilt said, "so nobody could recognize me."

And some of Kearns's Noo Yawk pals saw their buddy there with
Chamberlain, and they walked by and in stage whispers said such
things as, "Hey, isn't that Tommy Kearns, who beat Wilt the Stilt
twenty-five years ago?"

Stuff like that.

Chamberlain wouldn't rise to the bait this time either. In reply,
he would say, loudly, things like: "Watch your wallets" or "Imagine
there being people still interested in some stupid game that happened twenty-five years ago."

Stuff like that.

Chamberlain provided the Millrose expertise. He's a notable
track aficionado, a member of the U.S. Olympic Committee. He
wears a fancy stopwatch around his neck and speaks in the arcane
language of splits. Track is his sport now. He even has his own team,
Wilt's Athletic Club, and this evening many of his runners and
jumpers were competing. Chamberlain obviously takes delight in
supporting his club — just this day he had bought a van for its
members — in being a patron of the athletic arts, someone who at
last can merely enjoy sports without being superhuman, without
being Wilt the Stilt, without always being expected to win.

At this time, in February, Chamberlain was still mulling over an
incredible offer of almost $1 million for him, at the age of 45, to

finish out the NBA season with the Philadelphia 76ers. He was obviously flattered by the proposal, but just as obviously he didn't
need the aggravation of returning to basketball. The older Chamberlain got, the better he could see that he would never really be
permitted to enjoy victory as other athletes do. If he won, so
what? — he should have. If he lost, he was a loser. It was his function to be played *against.*

But he seems at peace now. "I think I've always understood the
phenomenon pretty well," he says, eating his way through the Stage
Deli menu. "I was never all that surprised that people responded
to me so strongly, that a lot of them had strange thoughts about
Wilt. I mean, how would you expect most people to react to a
black seven-footer, especially if they'd never seen one before? That
didn't upset me. I could understand that. And my publicity always
preceded me. I could never be given any credit for what I accomplished. The media decided that I was a villain.

"But that's all behind me now. I'm very lucky. You're formed by
the people you know well, and I've always been fortunate, you
understand, to have good people close to me. Even Kearns," he said,
laughing, and he finished off this stage of his meal, washing it down
with cream soda. Then he began again. "But about that game
now — "

"Hey, Wilt," Kearns said in protest. "That's enough nostalgia. I
don't want to live back there twenty-five years ago, and we won."

"No," Chamberlain said, "maybe losing that one, and some of the
others, maybe that was to my advantage. I think, in the long run, it
gave me more insight. If you're a winner all the time, you'll never
see the other side of the coin, you'll never understand other
people's troubles."

He paused at that, and he examined Kearns for a moment. "Still,
still," he said, and then, for some reason, Chamberlain momentarily
lapsed into a Southern accent: "Still, Tommy, y'all were blessed."

And nobody on the team, nobody anywhere ever summed it up
quite so well.

The Friends

Chamberlain took a corned beef on rye and half a cheesecake to
go, as a postmeal snack. That is, not a half-piece of cheesecake, but
half a cheesecake. Then he and Kearns went outside to their limousine, and the little white guy and the huge black man who had

jumped center twenty-five years ago in as big a college game as there ever was got in the back, and the driver closed the door.

You couldn't see them because of the tinted glass; at last, Wilt had found a pair of sunglasses capable of concealing him. But the two old players were in there together, and not that far, either, from the playgrounds and kitchens of Tommy Kearns's youth. The limo turned the corner, and it was warming to think that after all these years, after a quarter of a century, Chamberlain and Kearns were riding along together. It wasn't a simple matter of nostalgia. No, at least for a moment it restored some faith in the fool system, in the games.

And then the limousine passed out of sight, carrying with it 1957, and 1982 as well.